# Liebman's
# NEUROANATOMY
# Made Easy
## and
# Understandable

## Fifth Edition

### S. David Gertz, MD, PhD
Associate Professor
Department of Anatomy and Embryology
The Hebrew University–Hadassah Medical School
Jerusalem, Israel
and
Visiting Associate Professor
Department of Medicine
Mount Sinai School of Medicine
New York, New York

with a contribution by

### Rina Tadmor, MD
Neuroradiology Section
Sheba Medical Center—Tel Hashomer
Tel-Aviv University–Sachler School of Medicine
Tel-Aviv, Israel

AN ASPEN PUBLICATION®
Aspen Publishers, Inc.
Gaithersburg, Maryland
1996

Library of Congress Cataloging-in-Publication Data

Gertz, S. David.
Liebman's neuroanatomy made easy and understandable.—5th ed./
S. David Gertz; with a contribution by Rina Tadmor.
p.    cm.
Rev. ed. of: Neuroanatomy made easy and understandable/
by Michael Liebman;
with a contribution by Rina Tadmor. 4th ed. 1991.
Includes bibliographical references and index.
ISBN 0-8342-0730-3
1. Neuroanatomy.  I. Tadmor, Rina.  II. Liebman, Michael.
Neuroanatomy made easy and understandable.  III. Title.
[DNLM: 1. Nervous System—anatomy & histology.
WL 101 G384L 1996]
QM451.L53 1996
611.8—dc20
DNLM/DLC
for Library of Congress
95-23488
CIP

Copyright © 1991 by Michael Liebman.
New material only, copyright © 1996 by Aspen Publishers, Inc.
All rights reserved.

Aspen Publishers, Inc., grants permission for photocopying for limited personal or
internal use. This consent does not extend to other kinds of copying, such as copying for
general distribution, for advertising or promotional purposes, for creating new collective
works, or for resale. For information, address Aspen Publishers, Inc., Permissions
Department, 200 Orchard Ridge Drive, Suite 200, Gaithersburg, Maryland 20878.

The authors have made every effort to ensure the accuracy of the information
herein, particularly with regard to technique and procedure. However, appropriate
information sources should be consulted, especially for new or unfamiliar procedures. It is the responsibility of every practitioner to evaluate the appropriateness of
a particular opinion in the context of actual clinical situations and with due consider-
ation to new developments. The author, editors, and the publisher cannot be held
responsible for any typographical or other errors found in this book.

Editorial Resources: Jane Colilla
Library of Congress Catalog Card Number: 95-23488
ISBN: 0-8342-0730-3

*Printed in the United States of America*

1  2  3  4  5

This book is dedicated to the memory of
its original author—our teacher, colleague, and good friend

## Michael Liebman, PhD

Department of Anatomy and Embryology
The Hebrew University–Hadassah Medical School
Jerusalem, Israel

# Table of Contents

# Don't Skip This Introduction

Today you are faced with the problem of having to know more and more material in a shorter and shorter period of time. With neuroanatomy this problem is compounded because it is one of the most difficult subjects to grasp. Most "neuro" texts are broad in scope and crammed with seemingly endless detail. At this stage, however, you're unable to separate the wheat from the chaff; that is, to distinguish what is important for you from what is not. Consequently, you usually try to learn it all because you are afraid something will appear on the exam that you missed. Under conditions of high pressure and little time, this usually results in a monumental effort of memory, accompanied by little understanding and retention.

In this book, the fat of extraneous details, theories, and the like has been cut out, leaving the essentials that form the basis of neuroanatomy, neurophysiology, neuropharmacology, physical diagnosis, and neurology and for passing exams. Although the subject is presented in a deceptively simple, breezy, and personal style, you must not assume that this was done by sacrificing material. The main reason for this approach was to make the subject easier to read, understand, and retain. Therefore, once you know the material in this book, you will be able to read, and quickly understand, more detailed neuroanatomy texts and reference books, should the need arise.

The terminology can throw you for three reasons. First, it is often redundant. For example, a group of nerve fibers may be called a tract, fasciculus, column, lemniscus, funiculus, or bundle—all terms accepted and used by the medical and scientific community. Second, the terminology is full of weird-sounding names of Greek and Latin origins. As for the first problem, the author obviously cannot at his whim cut out recognized terms, but he can point out those that are synonymous. As for the second, a special glossary has been prepared that not only explains the meaning and origin of the names but also lists a common everyday word derived from them. For example, *fornix* is a Latin word meaning "arch" and is applied to a curved bundle of nerve fibers. The related everyday word is *fornication*, and the reason for this is that in ancient Rome the prostitutes used to hang around the arches of the aqueducts! Third is the matter of eponyms, that is, structures named after their discoverers. Most of them have been removed; only those few that are widely used in the medical profession are retained. Consequently, you won't be assaulted by the bands of Von Bunger, the spirals of Perroncito, the comma tract of Schultze, the stria of Lancisi, etc, etc, etc.

It is strongly recommended that you read each chapter before going to each lecture; then, instead of furiously trying to write down every word, you'll be able to sit back, absorb, and understand the material and leisurely jot down additional notes and drawings. Good luck!

*Mike Liebman*

---

Mike unfortunately passed away nearly 3 years ago. He left us, his dear friends in the Department of Anatomy and Embryology, Hadassah Medical School, with many cherished memories and a wealth of lessons in focused pedagogy. I find it to be a great honor to have been given the task of producing a fifth edition of *Neuroanatomy Made Easy and Understandable*. During this process, I have been made aware of the great dedication and sincerity of Mike's efforts, which are reflected in the elegant simplicity of this book.

The fifth edition has been revised and updated with several new features. These include a group of 18 selected self-examination drawing pages; more sample examination questions; a section giving the essentials of the neurological examination; a new summary table of all cranial nerves, their innervation, and their principal associated clinical sign; and a new table of functions of principal structures of the telencephalon and diencephalon. Chapters with major revisions include "The Microscopic Basis of Neuroanatomy," which has considerably more updated information about the glial cells and recently discovered structure–function relationships. The chapter "Cranial Nerves" is reorganized for additional clarity and with greater attention to functional fiber types as well as additional tabular material. The chapter "Pathologic Conditions of the Central Nervous System" has been extensively revised and updated with new material and reorganized according to disease categories. It is our hope that Mike's memory will be perpetuated as students continue to benefit from "the one book that has it all," *Liebman's Neuroanatomy Made Easy and Understandable*.

Finally, I would like to thank my loving wife Adina for her constant encouragement during the easy (as well as the unexpectedly difficult) times, and my dear children Yonatan (Yoni), Yoseph (Seffi), Eliana, and Dov-Aryeh (Dovey), who I hope will be blessed with happy, healthy, long, and fulfilling lives.

*S. David Gertz*

# Chapter 1

# The Microscopic Basis of Neuroanatomy

The basic unit of the nervous system, as in all other systems of the body, is the cell, which here is called the *neuron*. The main properties that distinguish neurons from other types of cells are their specialization for conduction of impulses, their great sensitivity to oxygen deprivation, their importance for many vital functions, and the fact that they don't multiply. (It is this last fact that is responsible for so many of the incurable conditions that you will see—paralysis, chronic vegetative states, palsy, blindness, etc.) This text discusses many types of neurons, and they all have the above-mentioned characteristics.

A typical neuron (Figure 1–1) consists of a cell body with a large *nucleus* that has a dark central *nucleolus*. Fine particles, known as *Nissl granules*, are scattered throughout most of the cytoplasm. Projecting from the cell body are many short processes—the *dendrites*—which receive impulses from other neurons and conduct them to the cell body. From the cell body a single long process—the *axon*—conducts the nerve impulse away and out to the dendrites of other neurons and to muscles and glands. This impulse is an ionic current that is measurable with fine instruments.

The site of contact between the axon of one neuron and the dendrites of another is the *synapse*, and the site of contact between an axon and a muscle fiber is the *motor end plate*. In general, the impulse does not pass directly from neuron to neuron or from neuron to muscle. Rather, it is transmitted by chemical mediators called *neurotransmitters*, which may be excitatory or inhibitory. The most widespread of these is *acetylcholine*; others include epinephrine, norepinephrine, serotonin, dopamine, gammaaminobutyric acid (GABA), glutamate, aspartate, and, more recently, nitric oxide. The basic mechanism is as follows: The nervous impulse travels down the axon until it reaches the synapse. Here it causes the release of neurotransmitter from synaptic vesicles at the end of the axon. The transmitter then passes through the ultramicroscopic synaptic gap to the adjacent neuron, most frequently the dendrites, where it triggers a new impulse that is then propagated in the second neuron (Figure 1–1). A single axon may synapse with the

dendrites of several or even hundreds of neurons, and the dendrites of one nerve cell can receive impulses from the axons of many neurons. Finally, there can be a combination of these two situations (Figure 1–2). Recent studies have suggested that transmitter-mediated nerve impulse conduction may, in some cases, also occur by *dynamic signaling* along fiber tracts at sites that lack obvious vesicular means of transmitter transport.

The axons of nearly all neurons are covered with a fatty white substance called *myelin*; for most impulses to be propagated, myelin must be present. In infants, myelin has not yet been laid down completely, and the completion of this process is one of the factors in the development of walking. In certain diseases, such as multiple sclerosis, the myelin degenerates, and the patient experiences a loss of various sensations and/or a diminution of movements. The process of *myelinization* (laying down of myelin) is performed by special cells that form an outer, enveloping layer around the axon. This layer is known as the *sheath of Schwann (neurolemma)*. Myelin is not a continuous layer but has gaps—*the nodes of Ranvier*—and here the overlying sheath of Schwann dips down and comes in contact with the axon (Figure 1–1).

Functionally and structurally there are many kinds of neurons; several of the most common are shown in Figure 1–3. A *motor* or *efferent neuron* is one that transmits impulses to muscles and/or glands, whereas a *sensory* or *afferent neuron* propagates impulses from peripheral tissues toward the central nervous system (CNS). The nervous tissue of the brain and spinal cord is divided into *gray matter*, which is composed mostly of nerve cell bodies, and *white matter*, which consists primarily of the white axon fibers.

The supporting tissue of neurons within the CNS is the *glia*, which consists of three principal types: *astrocytes*, *oligodendroglia*, and *microglia*. The microglia have been shown to be derived from blood monocytes/macrophages that migrate into the CNS tissue during development. The microglia may become *ramified*, remaining stable, or *activated* in response to mechanical, chemical, or immunologic injury, resulting in enhanced phagocytic activity

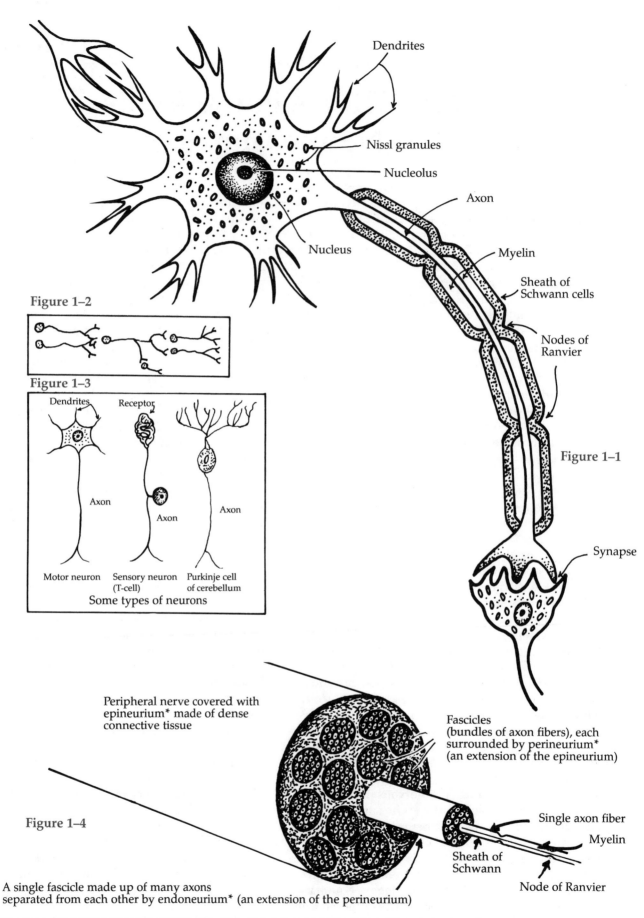

Dendrites

Nissl granules

Nucleolus

Axon

Myelin

Sheath of
Schwann cells

Nodes of
Ranvier

Nucleus

**Figure 1–2**

**Figure 1–3**

Dendrites   Receptor

Axon

Axon        Axon

Motor neuron   Sensory neuron   Purkinje cell
                (T-cell)        of cerebellum

Some types of neurons

**Figure 1–1**

Synapse

Peripheral nerve covered with
epineurium* made of dense
connective tissue

Fascicles
(bundles of axon fibers), each
surrounded by perineurium*
(an extension of the epineurium)

Single axon fiber

Myelin

**Figure 1–4**

Sheath of
Schwann

Node of Ranvier

A single fascicle made up of many axons
separated from each other by endoneurium* (an extension of the perineurium)

*The mnemonic "epe" helps in remembering the order: epineurium, then comes perineurium, and innermost endoneurium.

with production and release of a variety of vasoactive and neuroactive cytokines. As such, microglia have been shown to be involved with a variety of immune responses, including Alzheimer's disease and the HIV-related AIDS dementia complex.

Whereas Schwann cells form the myelin sheaths of the peripheral nervous system, the *oligodendroglia* are cells that form the myelin sheaths surrounding the axons within the CNS. The formation of myelin by the oligodendroglia involves the recruitment of two principal proteins—myelin basic protein and proteolipid protein—to select regions of the plasma membrane. The precise mechanism responsible for this recruitment remains unclear. Loss of oligodendroglia frequently accompanies the demyelination diseases, such as in the later stages of multiple sclerosis, and argyrophilic cytoplasmic inclusions have been described in the oligodendroglia of patients with multiple system atrophy (eg, olivopontocerebellar atrophy and Shy-Drager syndrome).

The third type of glial cells, the *astrocytes*, are now thought to be a more heterogeneous family of cells that function as the supportive scaffolding for the neurons. The astrocytes are actively involved in neuronal metabolism, especially carbohydrate metabolism; participate in uptake of released neurotransmitters; contribute to the formation, functional regulation, and repair of the blood–brain barrier; and may be involved in the modulation of a variety of local immune reactions. Recent studies have suggested the presence of an extensive, although still not well understood, receptor-mediated neuron-to-glia communication. This has opened a new door to studies focused on the intimate reciprocal structural and functional relationship between these two interdependent cell types. Tumors of astrocytes, the *astrocytomas* (all subtypes included), are the most common primary tumor of the CNS, being responsible for approximately 5000 deaths in the United States each year.

It is known that most substances that leave the capillaries to enter the surrounding tissues are unable to penetrate the capillaries of the CNS. This unique barrier is known as the *blood–brain barrier*. Oxygen, carbon dioxide, amino acids, a few sugars, and many lipid-soluble substances, such as general anesthetics, can pass the barrier, but most high–molecular weight substances, most sugars, and most protein-bound substances can't penetrate the CNS capillaries. It is generally accepted that this barrier is caused by two factors. First, the endothelial cells lining the capillaries of the CNS, unlike those of most other capillaries in the body, form tight junctions with each other. This endothelium also has a low rate of transcellular vesicular transport and contains a variety of carrier proteins and specific molecules not found in endothelial cells elsewhere. Second, the astrocytes have pseudopodialike extensions that surround and envelop the outer wall of the capillaries, contributing to the maintenance, regulation, and repair of the barrier.

In addition to neurons and glia, the *ependymal cells* line the central canal of the spinal cord as well as the ventricles of the brain and are the first cells to differentiate during the embryonic development of the nervous system. It has been suggested that, early in development, the ependymal cells are involved in the guidance of neuronal differentiation and axonal growth and in the maintenance of the developing glial cells. This should be considered within the context of the rapidly emerging concepts related to the intimate functional connections between neurons and glia via an elaborate network of trophic factors and cytokines, transmitters, and adhesion molecules, the complexity of which is only beginning to be appreciated.

Although the nerve pathways in the figures in other chapters are represented by a single axon, this is artistic license for the sake of clarity. In reality, every nerve and pathway is made up of many bundles, called *fascicles*, which in turn are made up of hundreds and hundreds of axons (Figure 1–4).

## CLINICAL NOTES

The great majority of *neoplasms* (tumors) of the nervous system arise from glial cells (eg, *astrocytoma* or *ependymoma*) or from the proliferation of other tissue cells found in conjunction with the brain, such as connective tissue cells (eg, *meningioma*) or the epithelial cells of the pituitary gland (*pituitary adenoma*). Rarely, neurons still in an immature state give rise to tumors known as *neuroblastomas*.

When a nerve is cut, a series of characteristic reactions takes place. That part of the axon distal to the injury quickly breaks down in a process known as *wallerian degeneration*. The section of axon still attached to the cell body initially undergoes some degeneration. During this process, the nucleus becomes eccentric, the cytoplasm swells, and chromatolysis occurs with paling of the Nissl bodies. If the damage isn't too extensive, the nerve will start growing. However, its growth is inhibited by the rapid proliferation of Schwann cells, which form a dense, scarlike mass. In cases where the epineural layer of the severed ends of a peripheral nerve is sewn back together, growth will occur, and there may be some renewal of normal function. The amount of renewal depends on such factors as the extent and location of injury, the quickness and skill of repair, the amount of glial cell proliferation at the repaired site, and the age of the patient.

*Multiple sclerosis* is a fairly common neurologic disease that primarily attacks young adults in the 20- to 40-year age group but almost never children younger than 10 years or adults older than 60 years. The myelin (but not the axons or cell bodies) in the CNS breaks down in multiple different areas, producing a variety of symptoms (multifocal presentation) such as a reduction in or loss of sensation, muscle weakness or fatigue, numbness or tingling in the extremities (paresthesia), vertigo, or diplopia (double vision). Indeed, the variety, mixture, and seeming unrelatedness of the symptoms are among the most important clues in diagnosing the illness. The cause of the disease is unknown, and at present there is no known cure or means of prevention. There is some evidence suggesting an early-life viral infection as the initial pathogenetic event, but no infective agent or specific antibodies have been demonstrated. Hereditary factors have been thought to play a part. In identical twins, if one of the twins has the disease, then there is a 25% chance that the second twin will develop it (ie, the concordance rate is 25%). Moreover, certain histocompatability antigens (eg, HLA-B7, HLA-A3, HLA-DR2, and HLA-DR3) have been reported to be more frequent in this population.

Strangely, the myelin often forms again because the oligodendroglia is are usually not destroyed in the initial phase of the disease, and the symptoms disappear until the myelin degenerates once again. This gives rise to three forms of the disease. First, a patient may have a few such episodes and then recover completely; second, in most individuals the attacks and remissions last for many years; and third, in some persons the attacks progress and spread rapidly, ending in death.

One of the most puzzling things about multiple sclerosis is that in tropical areas the incidence of the illness has been reported as 1 per 100,000, whereas in colder areas, such as Canada and northern Europe, the incidence soars to 30 to 80 per 100,000. Epidemiologic studies in Israel, a subtropical country that has received waves of immigrants from around the world, have been revealing. Those individuals who came from cold countries and had already passed puberty had the same incidence of multiple sclerosis as persons in their country of origin; whereas those from cold countries who came before puberty, while their thymuses were still large and active, had the low rate of incidence characteristic of inhabitants of warm climates. The explanation for this fact may hold important information concerning the pathogenesis of this disease. Of interest, individuals who have the disease do not benefit by moving to a warm or tropical climate. Also, it is curious that in Korea the disease is virtually unknown, with an incidence of 0.05 per 100,000.

Until recently it was difficult to make a final diagnosis of multiple sclerosis because laboratory examinations for it (eg, electrophoretic demonstration of oligoclonal IgG bands from the cerebrospinal fluid) were extremely nonspecific. Magnetic resonance imaging (MRI) has contributed considerably to the diagnosis of multiple sclerosis, permitting relatively easy demonstration of the degenerating plaques of myelin (Appendix IX, Figure 8). Attempts at treatment have included administration of corticotropin or prednisone to hasten resolution of some lesions, but this has not reduced the frequency of recurrences nor prevented the onset of later degenerative stages. A variety of other immunosuppressive regimens have been attempted with only partial success.

# Chapter 2

# The Macroscopic Basis of Neuroanatomy

This chapter deals with a topic that can be very boring. However, it is necessary because one can't proceed with the study of the nervous pathways without knowing where they start, through what structures they pass, and where they end.

The nervous system is divided arbitrarily into a central and a peripheral part. The *central nervous system* (CNS) consists of the brain and the spinal cord. The *peripheral nervous system* is made up of the 12 pairs of cranial nerves and all the remaining nerves of the body and their associated collections of cell bodies, the *ganglia*.

## FIVE PARTS OF THE BRAIN

The brain is divided on an embryologic basis into five parts: *telencephalon, diencephalon, mesencephalon, pons and cerebellum (metencephalon),* and the *medulla oblongata (mylencephalon).* In this chapter we consider these five parts one by one.

### Telencephalon

The telencephalon is the center for the highest functions and is therefore the most developed in humans. It is composed of two major structures: the *cerebral hemispheres* and the *basal ganglia.* The latter, which are the areas for crude motor activity, are buried deep in the cerebral hemispheres and can only be seen when the brain is cut. The cerebral hemispheres, on the other hand, are two large structures divided from each other by the *median longitudinal fissure* and represent most of the brain matter that is seen (Figure 2–1).* Their convex surface is made up of convolutions called *gyri,* which are separated from each other by shallow grooves, the *sulci* (a deep sulcus is called a fissure). Although certain gyri and sulci are present in almost every human brain, *no two brains (or even hemispheres of the same brain) have exactly the same pattern of gyri and sulci.* Two grooves, the *lateral fissure* and the *central sulcus,* help divide each hemisphere into four main areas, or *lobes* (Figure 2–2). The *frontal lobe* is anterior to the central sulcus, and the *parietal lobe* is posterior to it (Figure 2–2). Lying below the lateral fissure is the *temporal lobe,* and an imaginary line drawn down from the *parietooccipital fissure* separates the parietal lobe from the *occipital lobe* (Figure 2–2). As if there weren't enough divisions already, each lobe has its specific areas and gyri. For example, in the frontal lobe the *precentral gyrus,* lying just anterior to the central sulcus, is the motor center that initiates impulses to the voluntary muscles. The most anterior area, the *frontal pole,* is the seat of personality (Figure 2–3). Injuries here often result in alterations of personality. These and other areas are discussed later in greater detail. The telencephalon also occupies much of the base of the brain. Here are situated the *orbital gyri,* and resting on them are the *olfactory nerves,* which are the nerves of smell, and the *optic nerves,* which transmit visual impulses from the eye to the brain (Figure 2–4). The optic nerves converge on each other, cross at the *chiasm,* and then proceed posteriorly as the *optic tracts* (Figure 2–4). This view of the telencephalon also reveals the parahippocampal gyrus of the temporal lobe with its characteristic bulge, the *uncus.*

When the brain is cut in a horizontal plane, one sees that the cerebral hemispheres have an outer gray layer, the *cortex,* which is composed primarily of cell bodies, and an inner white mass made up of myelinated axons (Figure 2–5). Axons that pass from one hemisphere to the other are called *commissural fibers;* the best example is the large *corpus callosum* (Figures 2–5 and 2–6). Long and short *associative fibers* are those that pass from lobe to lobe or from gyrus to gyrus in the same hemisphere. Finally, those axons that ascend to, or descend from, the cerebral hemisphere to other areas of the CNS are called *projection fibers,* and most are situated in the *internal capsule.* This structure has an *anterior limb,* a *posterior limb,* and a section between the two called the *genu* (Figure 2–5). Just lateral to the genu are located some of the *basal ganglia,* for example the globus pallidus and the putamen (Figure 2–5).

---

*In addition to the drawings in this chapter and in Appendix II, the reader should refer to the computed tomography scans in Figures 1 through 5 in Appendix VIII and to the magnetic resonance imaging (MRI) scans in Appendix IX.

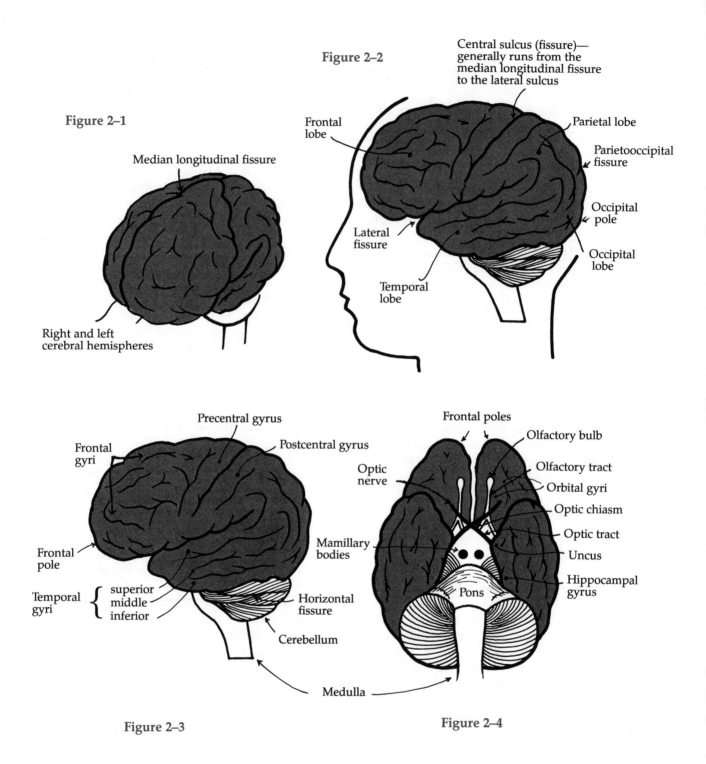

Figure 2–1

Median longitudinal fissure

Right and left cerebral hemispheres

Figure 2–2

Central sulcus (fissure)—generally runs from the median longitudinal fissure to the lateral sulcus

Frontal lobe

Parietal lobe

Parietooccipital fissure

Occipital pole

Occipital lobe

Lateral fissure

Temporal lobe

Precentral gyrus

Postcentral gyrus

Frontal gyri

Frontal pole

Temporal gyri { superior middle inferior

Horizontal fissure

Cerebellum

Medulla

Figure 2–3

Frontal poles

Olfactory bulb

Olfactory tract

Optic nerve

Orbital gyri

Optic chiasm

Optic tract

Mamillary bodies

Uncus

Pons

Hippocampal gyrus

Medulla

Figure 2–4

Some neuroanatomy texts maintain that there are five lobes of the brain, whereas others refer to six. If the lateral fissure is spread apart, one sees the *insula*. The insula is considered a fifth lobe, but its function in humans is not well understood. The cerebral cortex of the frontal, parietal, and temporal lobes surrounding the lateral fissure is known as the *operculum*. The *limbic*, or sixth, lobe is made up of the *cingulate*, *parahippocampal*, and *dentate gyri*.

## Diencephalon

The diencephalon is the second division of the brain. It is a small area situated between the cerebral hemispheres and is seen best on a midsagittal view (Figure 2–6). The diencephalon is divided into the *thalamus*, which is the main sensory relay center for the nervous system, and, below it, the *hypothalamus* (Figure 2–6). The hypothalamus is a vital area concerned with temperature control, emotional states, and control over the autonomic nervous system. In addition, the diencephalon contains the *medial* and *lateral geniculate bodies*, which constitute the *metathalamus*, and the *pineal body* and *habenula*, which make up the epithalamus. (See plates IV and IX in Appendix II, *Atlas of the Brain*.)

## Mesencephalon

The mesencephalon, the pons, and the medulla oblongata together form a wedge-shaped structure, the *brain stem*, which extends down from the base of the brain to the *foramen magnum* of the skull (Figure 2–6). The mesencephalon, or *midbrain*, is the smallest of the five divisions of the brain and is located between the diencephalon and the pons (Figure 2–6). The area above the *aqueduct of Sylvius* (cerebral aqueduct) is the *tectum*, which is made up of four rounded projections, the *corpora quadrigemina*. The upper two projections form the *superior colliculi* and the lower two the *inferior colliculi*. In the body or *tegmentum* of the midbrain pass various fiber tracts. Also situated there are the *red nucleus*, the *oculomotor nerve* and its nucleus, and the trochlear nerve and its nucleus. At the base of the midbrain there is a pair of huge fiber bundles, the *crus cerebri* (or *basis pedunculi cerebri*), which is a continuation of the descending projection fibers of the internal capsule (Figure 2–7). Finally, situated between the tegmentum and the crus cerebri is the *substantia nigra*. The latter plus the crus and tegmentum make up the *cerebral peduncle*. Although there isn't a specific center for consciousness, it is known clinically that damage or pressure on the brain stem, especially the midbrain, leads to unconsciousness, coma, and possibly death.

## Pons and Cerebellum

The pons and cerebellum together make up the fourth division of the brain (Figures 2–6, 2–8, and 2–9). The cerebellum is a many-folded structure located under the occipital lobe and is concerned with equilibrium, muscle tone, and the coordination of voluntary muscle activity (ie, synergy).

The names of the subdivisions and fissures of the cerebellum are numerous, but only the important ones are mentioned here and in the figures. The *archicerebellum* is the oldest part of the cerebellum and is made up of the central nodulus and the paired flocculus. Together they form the *flocculonodular lobe* (Figure 2–9), which is concerned with equilibrium. The *paleocerebellum* is an old part of the cerebellum composed of the anterior lobe and part of the vermis and is primarily concerned with muscle tone (Figure 2–9). The newest and largest part of the cerebellum is the *neocerebellum*, which is made up of the posterior lobe and most of the vermis (Figure 2–8) and deals with the coordination (synergy) of voluntary muscle activity. Four important nuclei, the dentate, emboliform, fastigial, and globose (DEFG), are also situated within the cerebellum.

Passing between the cerebellum and the underlying brain stem are three pairs of fiber bundles: the *superior*, *middle*, and *inferior cerebellar peduncles* (see Chapter 11). They are also known as the *brachium conjunctivum*, the *brachium pontis*, and the *restiform body*, respectively. The pons is located between the midbrain and the medulla and is separated from the overlying cerebellum by a cavity, the *fourth ventricle* (Figure 2–6). Through the pons pass various ascending and descending fiber tracts. Also in the pons are the nuclei of the fifth cranial nerve (*trigeminal nerve*), the sixth cranial nerve (*abducens nerve*), and the seventh cranial nerve (*facial nerve*).

## Medulla Oblongata

The medulla oblongata (mylencephalon) is the last division of the brain. It becomes continuous with the spinal cord at the foramen magnum (Figure 2–6). Like the pons and midbrain, it contains ascending and descending fiber tracts as well as the

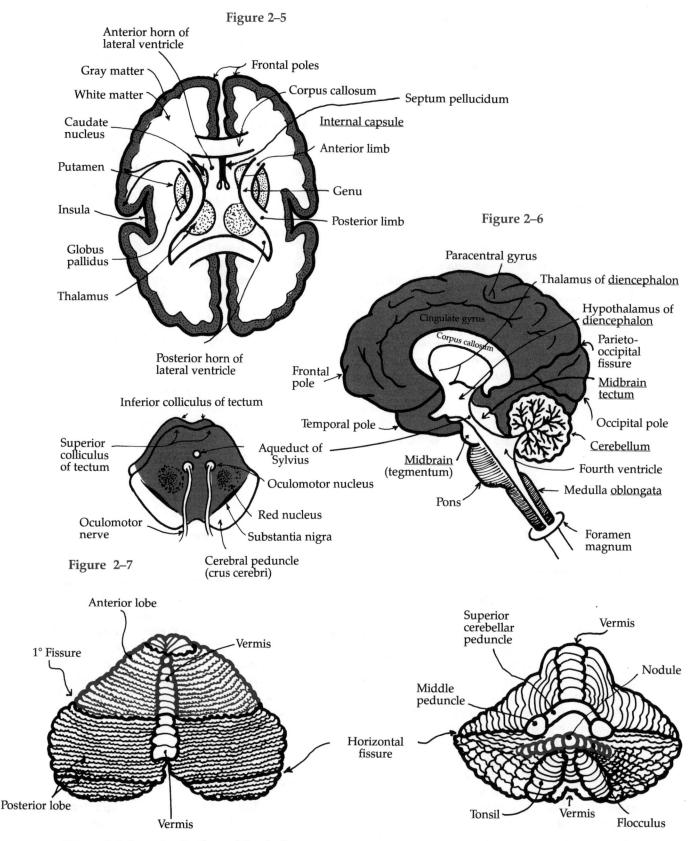

Figure 2–5

Anterior horn of lateral ventricle
Gray matter
White matter
Caudate nucleus
Putamen
Insula
Globus pallidus
Thalamus
Frontal poles
Corpus callosum
Septum pellucidum
Internal capsule
Anterior limb
Genu
Posterior limb
Posterior horn of lateral ventricle

Figure 2–6

Paracentral gyrus
Thalamus of diencephalon
Hypothalamus of diencephalon
Parieto-occipital fissure
Midbrain tectum
Occipital pole
Cerebellum
Fourth ventricle
Medulla oblongata
Foramen magnum
Cingulate gyrus
Corpus callosum
Frontal pole
Temporal pole
Midbrain (tegmentum)
Pons

Inferior colliculus of tectum
Superior colliculus of tectum
Aqueduct of Sylvius
Oculomotor nucleus
Red nucleus
Substantia nigra
Cerebral peduncle (crus cerebri)
Oculomotor nerve

Figure 2–7

Anterior lobe
1° Fissure
Vermis
Horizontal fissure
Posterior lobe
Vermis

**Figure 2–8** Superior Surface of Cerebellum

Superior cerebellar peduncle
Vermis
Nodule
Middle peduncle
Tonsil
Vermis
Flocculus

**Figure 2–9** Inferior Surface of Cerebellum

nuclei of cranial nerves VIII through XII. The respiratory and cardiac centers are also situated in the medulla, and pressure on them due to herniation, increased intracranial pressure, and the like can lead to coma and death.

## SPINAL CORD

The spinal cord is a long, cylindric structure beginning at the foramen magnum and descending in the vertebral canal to about the level of the second or third lumbar vertebra (L-2 to L-3). The cord serves as the main pathway (highway) for the ascending and descending fiber tracts that connect the peripheral and spinal nerves with the brain. The peripheral nerves are attached to the spinal cord by *31 pairs of spinal nerves.*

Each pair of spinal nerves (with one exception) exits between adjacent vertebrae. There are 8 pairs of cervical spinal nerves (C-1 to C-8), 12 pairs of thoracic nerves (T-1 to T-12), 5 pairs of lumbar nerves (L-1 to L-5), 5 pairs of sacral nerves (S-1 to S-5), and 1 coccygeal nerve pair. If you're wondering why there are 8 cervical spinal nerve pairs and only 7 cervical vertebrae, remember that the first pair, C-1, exits between the base of the skull and the first cervical vertebra (the atlas).

A cross-section of the spinal cord reveals gray matter in the form of an H or butterfly surrounded on all sides by white matter. As in the cerebral hemispheres, the gray matter is composed mostly of cell bodies, whereas the white is made up of myelinated axon fibers (Figure 2–10). The upper limbs of the gray matter are the *dorsal* or *posterior horns*, and the lower are the *ventral* or *anterior horns*. The white matter is grouped into dorsal, ventral, and lateral *columns* (Figure 2–10).

After reading this chapter, some individuals may prefer to skip to Chapters 20 to 22 on the meninges, blood supply, and ventricular system before proceeding to the chapters on the various pathways.

## CLINICAL NOTES

A question that's frequently asked is: Is there any relationship between brain size and intelligence? The answer is no. The normal human brain has a volume ranging between 1000 and 1400 cm³, and despite many studies no correlation has ever been found between great intelligence and a large brain. Individuals who have brains smaller than 1000 cm³ are most often mentally defective, although not all mental defectives have small brains.

In Alzheimer's disease, a chronic, progressive degenerative disease of the cerebral cortex that affects older people, there is frequently a widening of the sulci, which can be seen on a CT scan and used as a physical basis for supporting the diagnosis.

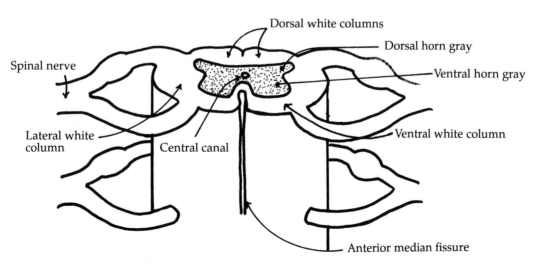

Figure 2–10

# Chapter 3

# Pain and Temperature Pathway from the Extremities and Trunk

Most people who consult a physician do so because they are in pain. Therefore, a fundamental understanding of the pain and temperature pathway is essential for quick and accurate diagnosis. Fortunately, this is a simple pathway, and a good grasp of it is easily obtained.

The receptors of pain and temperature are found in the dermis and epidermis of the skin. Nerve fibers pass from the dermis toward the spinal cord, with the cell bodies being situated in the *dorsal root ganglion* (Figure 3–1). These fibers then enter the cord through the dorsal root of the spinal nerve and end in the *dorsal horn of the gray matter*. Here the first neuron synapses with a second one that then crosses to the contralateral (opposite) side of the cord in the *ventral white commissure*, enters the lateral white column, and ascends to the ventral posterolateral (VPL) nucleus of the thalamus (Figure 3–1). This ascending bundle of crossed pain and temperature fibers is known as the *lateral spinothalamic tract*. In the VPL nucleus, the axons of the lateral spinothalamic tract synapse with tertiary neurons that leave the thalamus and ascend in the posterior limb of the internal capsule to reach the *postcentral gyrus* (Figure 3–1). The cortical gray matter of the postcentral gyrus (also known as area 3,1,2) is the primary somatic sensory area of the brain and is concerned with interpreting pain and temperature sensations as well as other cutaneous sensations, such as pressure and touch (see following chapters).

Pain pathways from the viscera are poorly understood, but it is generally accepted that these impulses travel via nerve fibers of the autonomic nervous system (see Chapter 12).

## ACCESSORY DETAILS

The primary pain and temperature axons have branches that synapse in the dorsal horn with short neurons that pass down to the ventral horn (Figure 3–1). Here these short *internuncial* (messenger) neurons synapse with motor neurons, the axons of which pass out through the ventral root and go out to voluntary muscles, causing movement. This involuntary motor response to a sensory

stimulus is called a *reflex*. It is a defense mechanism of the nervous system that permits quick, automatic responses to painful and potentially damaging situations. The internuncials may cross over to the other side of the cord and stimulate motor neurons there, or they may descend or ascend the cord and stimulate motor neurons at different levels of the cord. It all depends on which group of muscles needs to be "called into action."

One interesting reflex involves the pupils of the eye, which dilate during severe pain. Thus, even though the patient may deny or not express his or her pain, the pupils will reveal it to the astute observer.

The dorsal root of the spinal nerve is composed of sensory (afferent) axons whose cell bodies are situated in the dorsal root ganglion. The ventral root, on the other hand, is made up of motor or efferent axons, the cell bodies of which are located in the gray matter of the ventral horn. In some cases the ventral root also has autonomic motor fibers (see Chapter 12).

The fibers of each dorsal root come from a fairly circumscribed area of skin known as a *dermatome*.* There is, however, at each boundary of the dermatome an area that is supplied by the adjacent segmental nerves. This overlap acts as a kind of biologic "insurance." For example, if the second thoracic nerve (T-2) is severed, then many of the pain and temperature sensations from the skin area supplied by T-2 will be carried by the T-1 and T-3 sensory neurons (Figure 3–2). There is also an overlap pattern in the spinal cord. The entering axon, before it passes into the dorsal horn, sends branches that ascend and descend one spinal segment in the dorsolateral fasciculus (or column) of Lissauer and then enters the dorsal horn at that segment (Figure 3–2).

## CLINICAL NOTES

The suffix *-algia* means pain; hence neuralgia is pain in the nerves. An analgesic is some substance, such as morphine, aspirin, or alcohol, that deadens

---

*Dermatome maps can be found in Appendix IV.

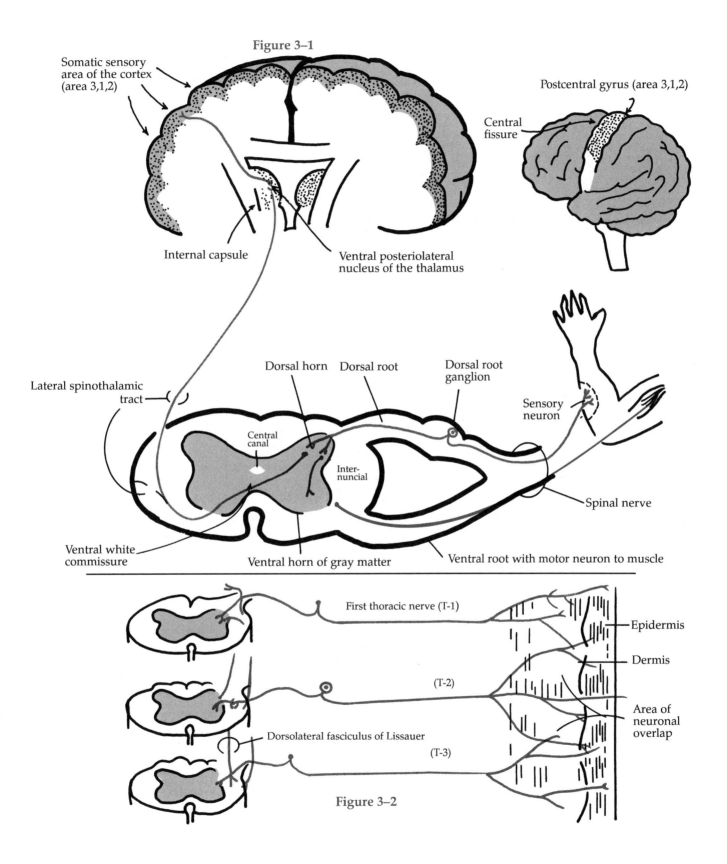

Figure 3–1

Somatic sensory area of the cortex (area 3,1,2)

Postcentral gyrus (area 3,1,2)

Central fissure

Internal capsule

Ventral posteriolateral nucleus of the thalamus

Dorsal horn    Dorsal root    Dorsal root ganglion

Sensory neuron

Lateral spinothalamic tract

Central canal

Inter-nuncial

Spinal nerve

Ventral white commissure

Ventral horn of gray matter

Ventral root with motor neuron to muscle

First thoracic nerve (T-1)

Epidermis

Dermis

(T-2)

Area of neuronal overlap

Dorsolateral fasciculus of Lissauer

(T-3)

Figure 3–2

11

or dulls pain. (In the "Special Neuroanatomic Glossary" in Appendix I you will find interesting facts about various pharmacologic agents.) The suffix *-esthesia*, on the other hand, means sensations. Thus an anesthetic is something that deadens or dulls all sensations.

A common cause of neuralgia is pressure from an intervertebral disc (a "slipped" disc in layperson's language) upon the spinal cord (Appendix IX, Figure 6) or a spinal nerve, which can produce great pain. If the condition occurs in the lumbar (lower back) area, the pain most often radiates down the length of one leg, producing a condition known as sciatica.

### Referred Pain

The pain pathway from the viscera (internal organs) is poorly understood. Visceral pain is not well localized; in certain cases it isn't felt at the organ site but is experienced at the surface of the body some distance from the affected organ. Such a reaction is known as referred pain, and in many instances it is quite specific and can serve as an excellent diagnostic aid. For example, a person experiencing a coronary attack often feels a sharp pain that radiates along the inner aspect of the left arm; pain originating from the ureters is felt in the inguinal area, and pain from the lungs and diaphragm is experienced at the shoulders near the root of the neck.

### Phantom Limb

In many cases after amputation, the patient complains of excruciating pain from the fingers or toes that no longer exist! The explanation for this strange phenomenon is as follows. A stimulus applied anywhere along the nerve fiber is experienced by the sensory cortex as coming not from the site of stimulation but rather from the skin area supplied by the nerves being stimulated. The nerve fibers at the stump are frequently squeezed by the scar tissue, and this pain stimulus passes to the sensory cortex, which interprets it as coming not from the stump area but from the skin areas of the fingers or toes of the missing limb.

### Syringomyelia

This is a rare degenerative disease of the spinal cord of unknown etiology that begins most frequently in the central canal area of the cervical cord (central cavitation of the cord). As the lesion expands, it first destroys the adjacent ventral white commissure, producing the classic symptoms of loss of pain and temperature sensations, but not touch, in both upper limbs. Thus it produces what is known as a dissociative anesthesia (ie, sparing some sensations while affecting others; Appendix IX, Figure 7).

### DIAGNOSTIC TESTS

### Pain

Have the patient close his or her eyes. With a pin, lightly prick the areas where pain sensations are thought to be absent. Ask when the patient feels the pin and when he or she does not.

### Temperature

Take two test tubes, one with warm water and the other with cold. Again ask the patient to close his or her eyes. Alternately touch the test tubes to the areas where the sensations are believed to be lost and inquire whether the patient can feel the hot or cold.

### HISTORICAL NOTES

General anesthesia wasn't discovered until the period 1842–1846 by four Americans—Drs Long, Jackson, Morton, and Wells—each working independent of the others. Before the use of ether, the patient would be given some alcohol to drink and then would be held on the table by strong men while the physician operated. Speed was essential, and some physicians were able to do a complete amputation of the leg above the knee in 90 seconds.

Acupuncture has been used in China for thousands of years, but the exact way it works is still unknown. It is now believed that insertion of the needles stimulates the body to release endorphins, which are morphinelike substances. In addition, there is a great deal of suggestibility and autosuggestibility involved in its use. It must be stressed that acupuncture isn't a cure for the underlying cause of pain but is an analgesic method that has best results with pain that involves the musculoskeletal system.

# Chapter 4

# Pathway for Pressure and Simple (Crude) Touch from the Extremities and Trunk

The receptors for pressure and crude touch are situated in the dermis of the skin, and the nerve fibers travel in the peripheral nerves toward the spinal cord. The cell bodies are aggregated in the dorsal root ganglion, and from here axons enter the cord through the dorsal root (Figure 4–1). Upon entering, the axons pass into the *ipsilateral* (ie, the same side) *dorsal white column* and bifurcate. One branch immediately enters the *dorsal horn gray matter* and synapses with a second (or secondary) neuron. The other branch ascends in the ipsilateral dorsal column for as many as 10 spinal segments and then enters the dorsal horn gray matter to synapse with a second neuron (Figure 4–1). In both cases, the secondary neurons *decussate*\* (ie, cross over to the other side) and enter the *ventral white column*, where they form the *ventral spinothalamic tract*. This tract ascends to the *ventral posterolateral nucleus of the thalamus*, where it synapses with third (or tertiary) neurons (Figure 4–1), which then relay the pressure and crude touch sensations to the *postcentral gyrus* of the cortex, which is concerned with interpreting sensations.

Many neuroanatomists claim, and some books state, that there is no basis for separating the lateral and ventral spinothalamic tracts, and that the two are really one large bundle—a spinothalamic tract that has intermingled in it both pain and temperature axons as well as those for pressure and simple touch. These tracts may form one bundle, but clinical data have shown that the pain and tem-

perature fibers are concentrated in its lateral portion (ie, in the lateral white columns), whereas the pressure and simple touch axons are situated in its ventral medial part (ie, in the ventral white columns). So you can say it's either one bundle with a lateral and ventral portion or two adjacent bundles, the lateral and ventral spinothalamic tracts (and such are the controversies that divide neuroanatomists!).

**CLINICAL NOTES**

Because one branch of the first neuron synapses immediately with a second neuron and the second branch ascends ipsilaterally for many segments, injuries to the spinal cord rarely result in complete loss of pressure and crude touch sensations. For example, if there is any injury to the spinal cord at point A in Figure 4–1 and the ventral spinothalamic tract is cut, one sees that the long ascending branch of the primary neuron bypasses the injury (on the uninjured side), and thus the sensations can still reach the postcentral gyrus. Naturally, if the sensory cortex, the internal capsule, or the thalamus is injured, then the pressure and crude touch sensations are lost on the contralateral side of the body.

**DIAGNOSTIC TEST FOR SIMPLE TOUCH**

Have the patient close his or her eyes. Then gently stroke the skin area with a wisp of cotton and ask whether the patient feels it.

---

\*See Appendix I for origin of terms.

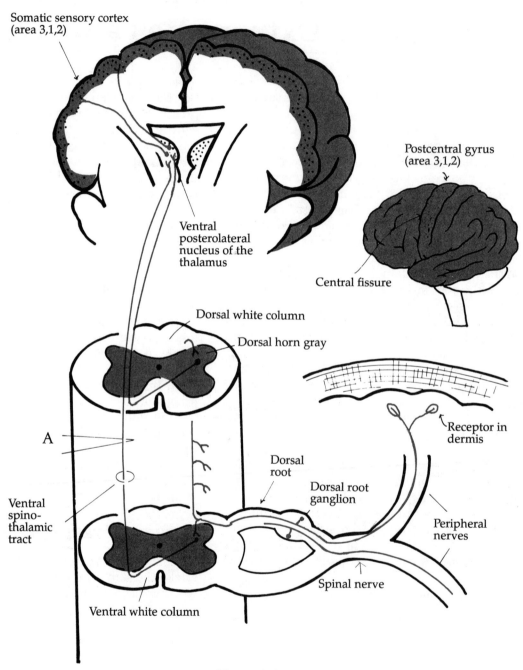

Somatic sensory cortex (area 3,1,2)

Postcentral gyrus (area 3,1,2)

Central fissure

Ventral posterolateral nucleus of the thalamus

Dorsal white column

Dorsal horn gray

Receptor in dermis

A

Dorsal root

Dorsal root ganglion

Peripheral nerves

Ventral spino-thalamic tract

Spinal nerve

Ventral white column

Figure 4–1

# Pathway for Proprioception, Fine (Discriminatory) Touch, and Vibratory Sense from the Extremities and Trunk

Three different sensations—proprioception, fine touch, and vibratory senses—all use the same pathway. Proprioception is the sense that enables one to know exactly and at all times where the parts of the body are in space and in relation to each other. Thus it enables a person, with the eyes closed, to bring up the hand and touch the tip of the nose with the index finger. Its receptors are located in muscles, tendons, and joints. Fine touch is the sense that enables a person, again with the eyes closed, to identify various objects, such as keys, velvet, coins, and ping-pong balls, by touch. This property is known in medicine as stereognosis. Fine touch also involves the facility to discriminate between two points when one is being touched by both points simultaneously, as with the two points of a drawing compass. These receptors are situated in the dermis of the skin, and they are most sensitive in the fingertips and lips and least sensitive on the back. Vibratory sense is, as its name implies, the sensation of vibrating objects.

The fibers of all three sensations conveyed by different neurons pass toward the spinal cord in the peripheral nerves, and the cell bodies are aggregated in the *dorsal root ganglion*. From here, axons enter the spinal cord and immediately pass into the ipsilateral dorsal white columns, where they ascend all the way up to the medulla (Figure 5–1). Axons that enter the cord at the sacral and lumbar levels are situated in the medial part of the dorsal column, which is called the *fasciculus gracilis*, whereas those axons that enter at the thoracic and cervical levels form the more lateral *fasciculus cuneatus* (Figure 5–1). The axons of each fasciculus terminate in their respective nucleus in the medulla. The second-order neurons leave the *nucleus gracilis* and the *nucleus cuneatus* and cross over to the other side of the medulla, where they form a bundle known as the *medial lemniscus*, which ascends to the *ventral posterolateral nucleus of the thalamus* (Figure

5–1). Here, the second-order neurons synapse with third-order neurons that pass up through the *internal capsule* to reach the *postcentral gyrus* (area 3,1,2), which is the primary cerebral somesthetic (somatic sensory) region (Figure 5–2).

## CLINICAL NOTES

The pathway for the neurons of each of the three sections discussed here is the same. Thus, damage to the postcentral gyrus, the medial lemniscus, the dorsal column, or the cell bodies in the dorsal root ganglion can result in several distinct clinical symptoms:

- astereognosis, or loss of the ability to distinguish between objects through touch and manipulation
- loss of the vibratory sense
- loss of two-point tactile discrimination (ie, when touched simultaneously with two points of a drawing compass, the patient reports feeling only one point)
- loss of proprioception, so that there is an inability to know where the limbs are (therefore, such a patient looks down at the feet when walking and in the dark would stagger or fall; when asked to stand erect with both feet together and the eyes closed, the patient sways—a positive *Romberg sign*)

If the injury is bilateral, then of course symptoms will be on both sides of the body. If, however, the lesion is on one side, then the symptoms will appear on one side only, depending on where the damage is. If the damage is before the decussation—that is, in the dorsal root ganglion, the posterior column, or the medullary nuclei—then the signs will be on the same side; if it is after the decussa-

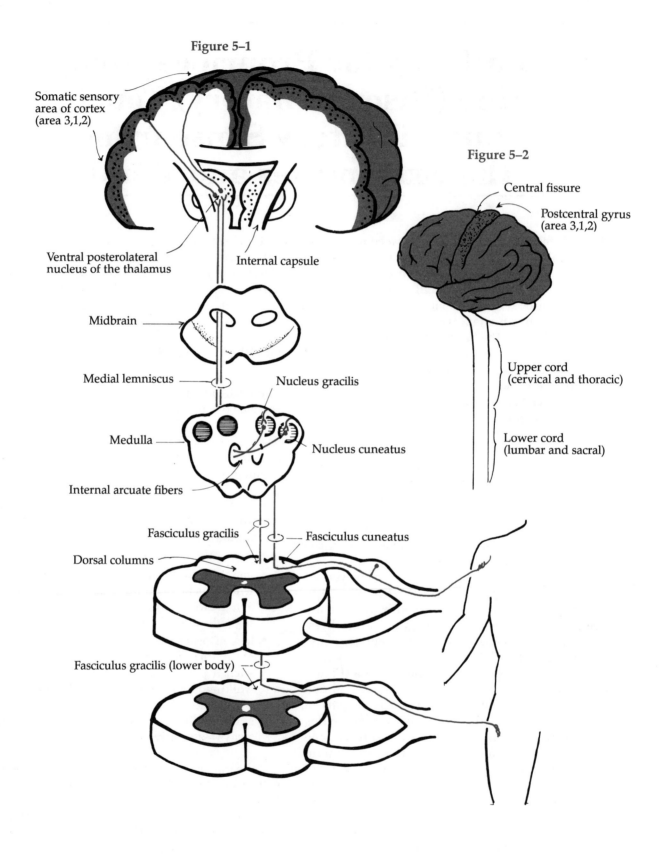

Figure 5–1

Somatic sensory area of cortex (area 3,1,2)

Ventral posterolateral nucleus of the thalamus

Internal capsule

Midbrain

Medial lemniscus

Nucleus gracilis

Medulla

Nucleus cuneatus

Internal arcuate fibers

Fasciculus gracilis

Fasciculus cuneatus

Dorsal columns

Fasciculus gracilis (lower body)

Figure 5–2

Central fissure

Postcentral gyrus (area 3,1,2)

Upper cord (cervical and thoracic)

Lower cord (lumbar and sacral)

tion—in the medial lemniscus, the thalamus, or the cerebral cortex—then the signs will be on the side opposite the lesion.

Damage to the dorsal root ganglion frequently occurs in the third stage of *syphilis*, when the bacterial organisms selectively attack and destroy the proprioceptive cell bodies but initially spare those of pain, temperature, crude touch, and pressure. Tabetics (those who have the third stage of the disease) therefore exhibit ataxia, a characteristic staggering gait and lack of coordination.

## DIAGNOSTIC TESTS

Have the patient close his or her eyes. Then place in succession different objects (eg, a key, a coin, and a matchbox) in the patient's hand and have the patient describe the shape, size, and consistency of the object and identify it. Inability to do so is astereognosis and indicates loss of fine touch.

With the patient's eyes still closed, ask him or her to touch the tip of the nose with the index finger, or have the patient stand erect and observe whether the patient sways when the eyes are closed. Failure to perform the first task or swaying in the second indicates proprioceptive impairment.

## HISTORICAL NOTES

Syphilis has been present in the New World for thousands of years, but it only appeared in Europe in 1495 at the siege of Naples. From there it spread rapidly throughout the Continent and became one of the most feared and prevalent diseases. The French called it the Italian disease, the Italians in turn called it the Spanish disease, the Spaniards called it the English disease, and so on. Therapy then consisted of spreading a cream containing mercury over the affected area for a period of several months. This gave rise to the joke "You spend one night with Venus and 6 months with Mercury."* This scourge was finally cured with the discovery of salvarsan by Paul Ehrlich. Salvarsan was also known as "606" because 606 experiments were done until he discovered it. Today penicillin is the drug of choice in the treatment of this illness, which is caused by the spirochete *Treponema pallidum.*

---

*Mercury in those days was called *quacksalver*, which later became *quicksilver*, a word that is still used today. From quacksalver came the word *quack*, or one who prescribes quacksalver (the treatment really didn't help very much).

# Chapter 6

# Sensory Pathways from the Face and Related Areas

Our discussions of somatic sensory pathways have so far not included descriptions of nerves from the face and related areas because these areas do not "use" the spinal nerves. Sensations for these areas pass in the fifth cranial nerve, the trigeminal, which has three main branches, the ophthalmic (V₁), the maxillary (V₂), and the mandibular (V₃); these innervate the respective named areas. The basic ground plan is pretty much the same, and an understanding of it is important, especially for those studying dentistry or who have chosen a specialty involving the cranial region.

The trigeminal nerve is the major somatic sensory nerve for the face, the anterior half of the scalp, the mouth cavity, the meninges, the sinuses, the teeth, the tongue, the cornea and the rest of the eyeball, and the outer surface of the eardrum. It transmits the sensations of pain and temperature and all kinds of touch, pressure, and proprioception, but not those of the special senses, such as hearing, taste, smell, vision, and equilibrium, which are carried by other cranial nerves.

## PAIN AND TEMPERATURE PATHWAY

The pain and temperature pathway for the face and its adjacent regions is shown by the red lines in Figure 6–1. From receptors situated in the above-mentioned areas, fibers pass in the peripheral branches of the trigeminal nerve toward the brain. Their cell bodies are located in the *semilunar (trigeminal) ganglion* (Figure 6–1), which is the analogue of the dorsal root ganglion. From here the axons enter the pons and are immediately concentrated in a bundle, the *descending* or *spinal tract of cranial nerve V*, which swings down and in many cases reaches the upper cervical region of the cord. Along this course the primary neurons peel off and enter the adjacent *nucleus of the descending tract of cranial nerve V*, where they synapse with secondary neurons. These leave the nucleus, cross over to the contralateral side, and ascend to terminate in the *ventral posteromedial nucleus of the thalamus* (Figure 6–1). This crossed pain and temperature bundle is called the ventral secondary ascending tract of cranial nerve V (or the *ventral trigeminal tract*) and is analogous to the lateral spinothalamic

tract. From the thalamus, tertiary neurons pass into the internal capsule, ascend in it, and end in the postcentral gyrus (area 3,1,2), the primary or main somesthetic region of the cortex.

## PRESSURE AND TOUCH PATHWAY

These neurons (represented by the dashed lines in Figure 6–1) also have their cell bodies in the semilunar ganglion, but their axons terminate immediately in the *main sensory nucleus of cranial nerve V*, situated in the pons (Figure 6–1). The secondary neurons reach the ventral posteromedial nucleus of the thalamus via the dorsal secondary ascending tract of cranial nerve V (or the *dorsal trigeminal tract*), which is a crossed and uncrossed tract. That is, some axons travel ipsilaterally and some contralaterally. Tertiary neurons are relayed from the thalamus to the postcentral gyrus (Figure 6–1). Thus we see that, whereas pain and temperature are projected on the contralateral cerebral cortex, pressure and touch are *bilaterally projected*. Therefore, if one side of the sensory cortex is damaged, the patient will experience no loss of pressure or touch from the face but will lose the pain and temperature feelings on the contralateral side.

## PROPRIOCEPTION PATHWAY

This pathway is composed of trigeminoproprioceptive fibers from the muscles of mastication, the temporomandibular joint (TMJ), and the peridontal ligament around the teeth. However, the trigeminoproprioceptive fibers are an exception in that their primary cell bodies aren't in a ganglion outside the central nervous system but are situated in the *mesencephalic nucleus in the midbrain* (Figure 6–2). The precise route of continuation of this pathway to the postcentral gyrus is not well known.

## ACCESSORY DETAILS

There are several reflexes involving the trigeminal nerve, of which the most important is the *corneal* or *"blink" reflex*. If an object touches the cornea of one eye, *both* eyes will blink immediately. The

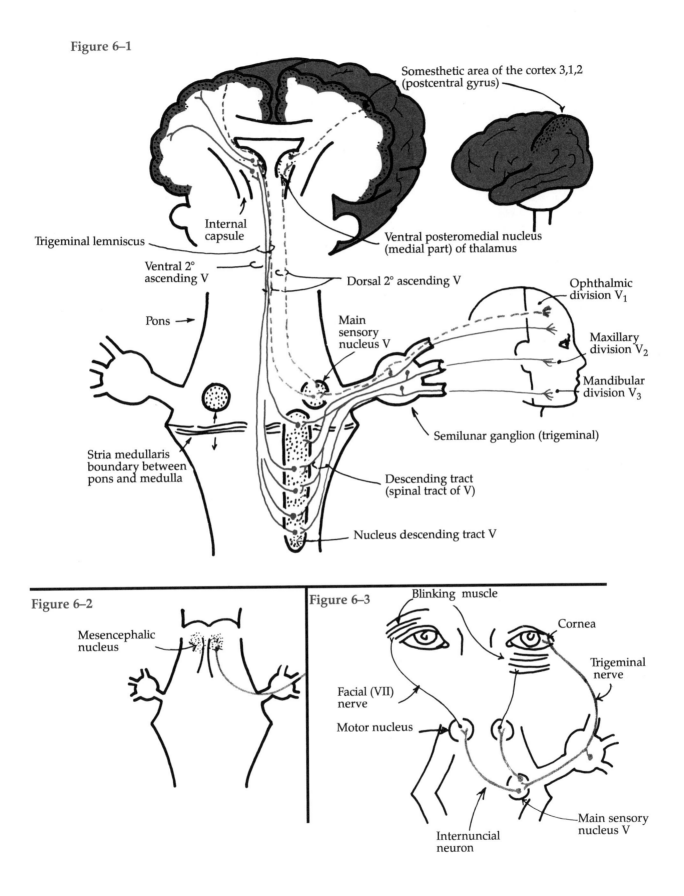

Figure 6–1

Somesthetic area of the cortex 3,1,2
(postcentral gyrus)

Trigeminal lemniscus

Internal
capsule

Ventral posteromedial nucleus
(medial part) of thalamus

Ventral 2°
ascending V

Dorsal 2° ascending V

Ophthalmic
division V₁

Pons →

Main
sensory
nucleus V

Maxillary
division V₂

Mandibular
division V₃

Semilunar ganglion (trigeminal)

Stria medullaris
boundary between
pons and medulla

Descending tract
(spinal tract of V)

Nucleus descending tract V

Figure 6–2

Mesencephalic
nucleus

Figure 6–3

Blinking muscle

Cornea

Trigeminal
nerve

Facial (VII)
nerve

Motor nucleus

Internuncial
neuron

Main sensory
nucleus V

19

pathway is as follows: The touch stimulus from the cornea reaches the ipsilateral main sensory nucleus of cranial nerve V. This sends out internuncial neurons that pass to the right and left *motor nuclei of the facial nerve.* From here motor neurons pass out and stimulate the muscles that cause blinking (Figure 6–3).

## CLINICAL NOTES

Reflexes are not only a defense mechanism but also are useful diagnostically, enabling the physician to test the integrity of nerve pathways. If, upon testing, a reflex is not elicited, the physician then has to find out where the interruption in the pathway is: in the sensory pathway, the internuncial connections, or the motor pathway. In addition, there are reflexes that appear only in pathologic conditions, informing the physician that something is wrong (eg, the Babinski reflex; see Chapter 7).

When a person is anesthetized in surgery, specific reflexes disappear as deeper and deeper levels of unconsciousness are reached. Thus the anesthetist is able to gauge accurately the level or depth of unconsciousness by means of the presence or absence of these reflexes.

If the trigeminal nerve is transected or the semilunar ganglion is damaged, then the individual will experience loss of all facial sensations on the same side as the injury. As mentioned previously, injury to one side of the sensory cortex, internal capsule, or other area results in loss of facial pain and temperature sensation contralaterally, but pressure and touch remain.

*Trigeminal neuralgia (tic douloureux)* is a condition of unknown etiology in which the patient, usually of middle age or older, experiences paroxysms of excruciating pain on one side of the face, almost always along $V_2$ and $V_3$. Carbamazepine (Tegretol) controls pain in 90% of cases, and in the remaining 10% surgical treatment is used (eg, cutting the superficial descending tract of cranial nerve V or injecting alcohol into the trigeminal ganglion).

Brain tissue itself has no sensations whatsoever, and therefore operations on it can be done using only local anesthetics. Headaches are usually the result of pressure or pain in nonnervous structures on or within the brain or skull, such as the arteries or the meninges (the coverings of the brain). They can be caused by many factors, and there are many types of headaches. Among the most common are migraine, cluster, and tension headaches.

The exact cause of *migraine* is unknown, but it tends to run in families and affects women three times as often as men; its attacks are often triggered by stress, certain foods, or increased levels of hormones, as in menstruation or the taking of birth control pills. The individual generally has one or two attacks per month that each last from several hours to a couple of days. The attack is generally preceded by a visual aura, such as "stars before the eyes," and then there is a severe throbbing pain on one side of the head that is often accompanied by nausea and vomiting. The pain is due to severe dilation of cerebral arteries, generally on one side of the head.* Migraine headaches have been treated by drugs of the ergotamine family that produce vasoconstriction, thereby reducing the dilation and pain. Propranolol, a beta-blocker, is also used for reducing the frequency and intensity of attacks. During an attack, migraine patients characteristically get relief by lying down in a dark, quiet room.

*Cluster headaches* are sudden, severe, retrobulbar headaches behind one eyeball that occur once a day over a period of a week to 2 to 3 months. The cause is unknown, but they are 10 times more frequent in men than women, occur most often at night, and are frequently triggered by drinking alcoholic drinks. In contradistinction to migraine, the excruciating pain of cluster headaches is of such a nature that it causes the individual to be restless, sweat, pace up and down, slam his or her fist into things, and in some cases rip down doors. Prednisone is widely used in the treatment of cluster headaches.

In *tension headache*, which is probably the most common and widespread type, there is a dull, steady ache, often encircling the head like a hat band. It's believed that the many and varied stresses of modern life, along with fatigue and bottled-up anger, cause the muscles of the head and neck to tense up, which constricts nerves and arteries and in turn produces the headaches. These can be relieved by ingesting aspirin, paracetamol, or similar drugs; taking hot baths to relax the muscles and mind; and by massaging the scalp, neck, and shoulders to reduce muscular tension.

Tumors can also produce headaches as a result of increased intracranial pressure, but here the headaches are often accompanied by a projectile type of vomiting.

---

*See Appendix XIII, "Odds and Ends," for the interesting derivation of the word *migraine.*

# Chapter 7

# Pathway for
# Voluntary Muscle Activity

Everyone has undoubtedly seen at one time or another individuals who can't walk and are confined to wheelchairs, those who walk slowly and drag one leg, or those whose arm lies helplessly flexed on one side; in short, persons who have some form of paralysis. In most of these conditions, the muscles are fundamentally intact, and the condition is due to some kind of injury to the nerves. Because damage to this pathway is responsible for so much suffering and sorrow, a first-class understanding of it is mandatory.

The *corticospinal tract* is the main tract for nearly all voluntary muscle activity. It originates in the precentral gyrus (area 4, the motor cortex) of the frontal lobe. Here its large cell bodies are located. Because many of these have a pyramidal shape, the corticospinal tract is also called the *pyramidal tract*.* (How a conscious wish is "translated" into cortical nerve impulses is an age-old question involving the mind–matter problem and probably will never be answered satisfactorily.) From the cell bodies, axons leave the cortex and pass down through the internal capsule, which is not a capsule but rather the main passageway for ascending and descending fiber tracts (Figure 7–1). Leaving the internal capsule, the axon fibers pass down into the basis pedunculi cerebri of the midbrain and continue down the brain stem to reach the medulla oblongata. Here, about 80% to 90% of the axons decussate to the opposite or contralateral side of the medulla and, having crossed over, descend in the spinal cord (Figure 7–1). Because these descending fibers are situated in the lateral white columns of the cord, they are called the *lateral corticospinal tract*. Those axons that do not cross over in the medulla continue down on the same side to enter the ventral white columns of the spinal cord and are therefore known as the *ventral corticospinal tract*.

At each level of the cord, axons from the lateral corticospinal tract peel off and enter the gray matter of the ventral horn, where they terminate by synapsing with second-order neurons. At each corresponding level of the cord, axons of the ventral corticospinal tract peel off and cross over to the other side of the cord (Figure 7–1). Here they also enter and terminate upon second-order neurons in the ventral horn. It must be emphasized that, in their entire course from the precentral gyrus to the ventral horn, both the lateral and ventral corticospinal tracts consist primarily of *single uninterrupted neurons*; that is, the tracts are a single neuron pathway. These neurons are called *upper motor neurons*. The second-order neurons on which the upper motor neurons synapse send their axons out of the spinal cord via the ventral roots. They then branch out in the peripheral nerves and supply the voluntary muscles. These second-order neurons are *lower motor neurons*, and this differentiation between them and the upper motor neurons is important clinically, as we shall soon see. In a person who is 6 ft tall, the axons that supply the toe muscles are nearly 1 yd long. The upper motor neurons begin in the precentral gyrus and end in the lower part of the cord, whereas the lower motor neuron begins in the lower cord, and its axon passes down to supply the muscle situated on the sole of the foot.

## DETAILS

### Cerebral Localization

The nerve cell bodies of the upper motor neurons are arranged in a specific pattern in the gray matter of the precentral gyrus, so that neurons supplying the foot and leg muscles are located dorsomedially in the gyrus. As one passes inferolaterally, one finds the areas for the abdomen, chest, arm, hand, and face. One can describe this more colorfully by saying that the pattern is that of a person hanging upside down, with the feet in the longitudinal fissure and the head at the edge of the lateral fissure (Figure 7–1). The area of neurons that supplies the muscles of the hand is disproportionately large, reflecting the great number of neurons needed to carry out such fine and complicated movements as violin playing, surgery, and writing. This localization is also seen in the internal capsule, the main cerebral passageway for ascending and descending fiber tracts. In a horizontal section of the cerebral hemisphere (Figure 7–2), one sees

---

*Others say that it is called the pyramidal tract because it decussates in the pyramids of the medulla.

Figure 7–1

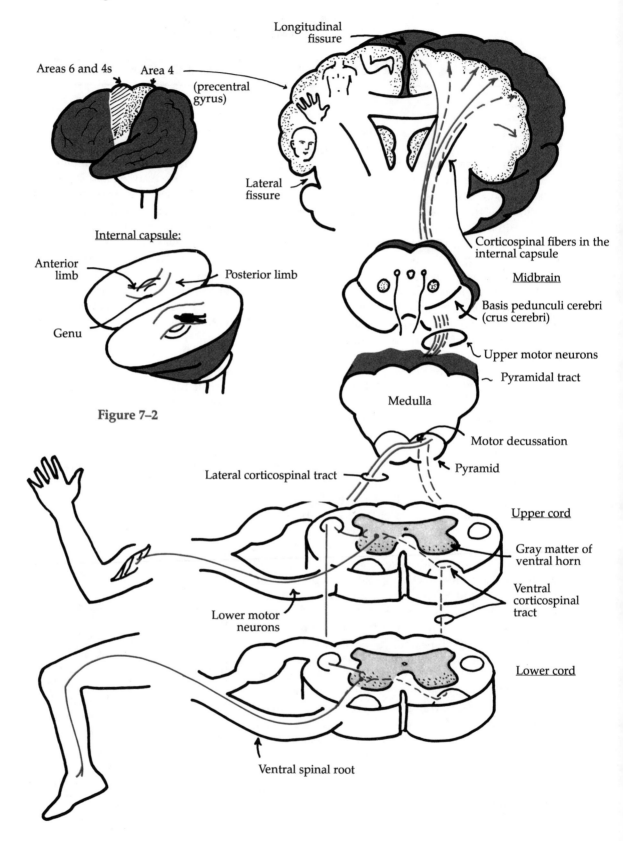

Longitudinal fissure

Areas 6 and 4s    Area 4

(precentral gyrus)

Lateral fissure

Corticospinal fibers in the internal capsule

Internal capsule:

Anterior limb          Posterior limb

Genu

Midbrain

Basis pedunculi cerebri (crus cerebri)

Upper motor neurons

Pyramidal tract

Medulla

Figure 7–2

Motor decussation

Pyramid

Lateral corticospinal tract

Upper cord

Gray matter of ventral horn

Ventral corticospinal tract

Lower motor neurons

Lower cord

Ventral spinal root

that the internal capsule consists of an *anterior limb*, a *posterior limb*, and a connecting area between them called the *genu*. The fibers that supply the face are situated in the genu, and those supplying the rest of the body are found in the anterior two thirds of the posterior limb. If the genu is damaged, then the muscles of the face are affected, but if the middle part of the posterior limb is injured, then the leg muscles will not receive nervous supply.

## Suppressor Part of the Pyramidal Tract

Not all the neurons of the pyramidal tract have their origins in the precentral gyrus. Many of them originate in areas 4s and 6, which lie just anterior to the precentral gyrus (Figure 7–1). Pyramidal tract fibers originating here do not initiate impulses to voluntary muscles but act as inhibitors, suppressors, or "brakes" on the lower motor neurons and prevent them from overdischarging when responding reflexively to sensory stimuli. If for some reason the suppressor fibers are damaged, then the lower motor neurons are freed from their control and fire excessively in response to reflex stimuli or discharge spontaneously. These conditions are known as *hyperflexion* and *spasticity*, respectively, and are discussed in the next section.

## CLINICAL NOTES

### Lower Motor Neuron Paralysis

The best examples of lower motor neuron paralysis are when a nerve to a muscle is cut and when the cell bodies of the ventral horn are destroyed by poliomyelitis, which selectively attacks them. In both cases, the muscles are deprived of their immediate nerve supply; they are unable to contract and become soft, flabby, and atrophic—characteristics of a *flaccid paralysis*. Naturally, because the motor limb of the reflex arc is damaged, the muscles can't respond reflexively to sensory stimuli.

If the cell bodies are destroyed, as in polio, then the axons cannot regenerate, and the paralysis is permanent. If, however, a nerve is cut, then the part of the axon attached to the cell body can regenerate, and some of the functions can be restored (see Chapter 1).

### Upper Motor Neuron Paralysis

Upper motor neuron paralysis occurs when there is damage to the corticospinal tract anywhere along its path: the cell bodies in the precentral gyrus or their descending axons in the internal capsule, brain stem, or spinal cord. The most common site of injury is the cerebral hemisphere before the decussation. Injury results most often when an artery becomes occluded and the neurons, deprived of their oxygen supply, die, producing what is known as a cerebrovascular accident (CVA) or, in popular language, a *stroke*. Strokes are also due to an artery rupturing (ie, a cerebral hemorrhage). If the site affected is above the motor decussation, then the signs and symptoms will be seen in the muscles on the opposite side of the body. If the injury is below the decussation—say, a cut in the left half of the spinal cord—then the ensuing paralysis will be on the same side as the damage. This type of paralysis is different from a lower motor neuron paralysis in a number of essential ways. First of all, the lower motor neurons are not affected, and the reflex arc is complete; thus reflexes can be elicited. Second, the suppressor fibers originating in areas 4s and 6 are knocked out, and their braking effect on the lower motor neurons is no longer effective. The lower motor neurons now overdischarge to stimuli or even fire spontaneously. Clinically, this hyperreflexia manifests itself as follows: When the wrist of a paralyzed arm is grasped firmly, there will be a series of rapid, strong muscular contractions known as *clonus*. When the lower motor neurons discharge spontaneously without upper motor neuron modulation, the muscles contract strongly, a condition known as *spasticity*. This upper motor neuron paralysis is spastic, unlike lower motor neuron paralysis, which is flaccid. In upper motor neuron paralysis a characteristic and specific type of reflex, the *Babinski reflex*, can be elicited. When the sole of the foot of a healthy person is stroked in a heel-to-toe direction, the toes will curl. However, in a patient who has an upper motor neuron lesion, the toes will fan apart, and the big toe will flex dorsally. The exact route and mechanism of the Babinski reflex are still not fully understood. (In a normal infant up to the age of 6 months or so, in whom the myelinization of the axons is not complete, a Babinski response can be elicited routinely.) Also, certain superficial reflexes, such as the abdominal and cremasteric, which are elicited when the skin is stroked, are lost. Once again, the exact reason and mechanism are not clear.

A person who is paralyzed on one side of the body can frequently make crude movements of the trunk musculature on the affected side. The explanation for this is as follows: It is known that some of the lateral corticospinal fibers do not cross over at all, and it is believed that these uncrossed fibers, along with some of the crossed ones, supply the muscles of the trunk. Thus the trunk muscles of each side receive axons from both the right and left cerebral cortex. This arrangement is known as *bilateral innervation*.

Because a CVA may not destroy all the upper motor neuron axons to a group of muscles, those remaining intact can be utilized to regain some of the lost functions. This requires rehabilitation and involves such personnel as physiotherapists and occupational therapists as well as emotional support from family and friends.

Paralytic conditions may be defined according to the part(s) of the body affected. *Monoplegia* is paralysis of either an upper or a lower limb; *hemiplegia* is paralysis of an upper and a lower limb on the same side; *paraplegia* is paralysis of both lower limbs; and *quadriplegia* is paralysis of all four limbs.

### Cerebral Palsy

*Cerebral palsy* (CP) is the name given to a large group of motor disorders of infants and children in which there is paralysis or disturbed motion (eg, spasticity, tremors, athetosis, etc) caused by brain damage. There may also be disturbed posture and muscle tone. In addition, mental retardation and other neurologic symptoms are often present. Damage to the brain may occur in utero, during delivery, or postpartum and may be due to infection or difficulties during delivery, such as trauma or decreased oxygen supply. Other cases are idiopathic, that is, from unknown causes. Generally, one sees gross or microscopic lesions in the precentral gyrus, the pyramidal tract, or the extrapyramidal system, but in some cases there is no demonstrable brain pathology. The early detection of CP is difficult because the corticospinal tracts aren't completely myelinated until the child is 1 to 1.5 years of age.

### Amyotrophic Lateral Sclerosis (Lou Gehrig's Disease*)

Amyotrophic lateral sclerosis (ALS) is a chronic, progressive, degenerative disease that selectively attacks the corticospinal tracts in the lateral white columns as well as the lower motor neuron cell bodies in the ventral gray horn (ie, it hits *both upper and lower motor neurons*). It usually starts in middle age (40 to 50 years) and affects men three times as often as women.

The disease most often begins at the midcord level, and as a result one sees the characteristic triad of muscle weakness, muscle atrophy, and hyperreflexia in the hand, forearm, and, later, the shoulder girdle *without pain or any other sensory disturbances*. In addition, one sees fasciculation (fine contractions or twitches of individual muscle fibers) in the muscles of the arm, forearm, and hand, which is a sign of slow degeneration of lower motor neuron cell bodies situated in the ventral horn gray. With time, the disease progresses upward and involves the brain stem but spares intellect and sensations. Like so many other neurologic diseases, there is no known cause, cure, or means of prevention for ALS, and it ends fatally within 3 to 5 years.

ALS is a relatively rare disease, hitting about 1 person in 50,000, yet there have been reports of "groupings" of the disease. For example, on the 44-man roster of the 1964 San Francisco Forty-Niners football team, 3 men came down with the disease, and there have been other such cases. On the island of Guam and on Kii Peninsula in Japan, ALS is 50 times more common than in the United States, but in these latter cases it is probably based on genetic factors.

## HISTORICAL NOTES

Hippocrates, one of the greatest physicians in history, noted more than 2000 years ago that injuries to one side of the head often produce paralysis on the contralateral (opposite) side of the body. Later, Aretaeus of Cappadocia (circa 120–200 AD) said that this fact must be due to the nerves crossing somewhere in their pathway.

---

*Lou Gehrig was one of baseball's greatest players. Between 1925 and 1938 he played 2310 consecutive games for the New York Yankees and was the Most Valuable Player in 1927, 1931, 1934, and 1936. He had a lifetime batting average of .350 and also batted in more than 100 runs per year in 13 years. In 1927, he hit .376 and, along with Babe Ruth (.356), Early Combs (.356), and Tony Lazzer (.309), formed the batting sequence known as "Murderer's Row"; one can imagine the nervous condition of the pitchers who had to face them. Lou Gehrig died of ALS in 1941 at the age of 38.

# Chapter 8

# Pathway to Voluntary Muscles of the Head

Our discussion of the pyramidal tract centered on those fibers that descend into the spinal cord and synapse there with lower motor neurons that go out and innervate voluntary muscles of the body. It did not include fibers to the voluntary muscles of the head because the lower motor neurons supplying them are not situated in the spinal nerves but are associated with cranial nerves originating in the brain stem. The basic framework, however, is the same as for the corticospinal tracts. It is a two-neuron pathway consisting of an upper motor neuron originating in the cerebral cortex, the axon of which descends and synapses with a lower motor neuron, which in turn goes out and stimulates voluntary muscles.

The cell bodies of the upper motor neurons are located in the lowest part of the precentral gyrus (motor cortex, area 4) adjacent to the lateral fissure (Figure 8–1). There is, in addition, another motor area for eyeball movements, which is situated in the middle frontal gyri (Figure 8–2). Axons from here join descending fibers from the face area, and together they pass through the genu of the internal capsule. Because the fibers then enter the brain stem, or bulb, and terminate there on lower motor neurons, they are called the *corticobulbar tract*, in contradistinction to the corticospinal tract. The cell bodies of the lower motor neurons are concentrated in specific areas of the brain stem called *nuclei*, and their axons form many of the cranial nerves. These nerves differ from spinal nerves in that the sensory and motor fibers do not separate into dorsal and ventral roots. Furthermore, some cranial nerves have no sensory axons; all their fibers are lower motor neurons. To complicate the matter even further, there are cranial nerves that are entirely sensory in their make-up. Be that as it may, the cranial nerves that interest us here are those whose axons supply voluntary muscles. These are the oculomotor (III) and the trochlear (IV) nerves, whose nuclei are situated in the midbrain, and the trigeminal (V), the abducens (VI), and the facial (VII) nerves, which originate in the pons. The oculomotor, trochlear, and abducens innervate the extrinsic muscles of the eyeball. The trigeminal nerve innervates the muscles of mastication as well as the an-

terior belly of the digastric, mylohyoid, tensor tympani, and tensor veli palatini muscles. The facial nerve, as its name implies, supplies all the muscles of facial expression. Finally, in the medulla are situated the nucleus of the glossopharyngeal nerve (IX), which innervates a single muscle in the pharynx (throat); the nucleus of the vagus nerve (X), which supplies muscles in the throat concerned with talking and swallowing (the nucleus of IX and X is really a single common nucleus called the nucleus ambiguus); the nucleus of the hypoglossal nerve (XII), which supplies all the muscles of the tongue except for one; and the accessory nerve (XI), which is an exception in that it doesn't supply muscles in the head but rather two important ones in the neck, the sternomastoid and the trapezius.*

No mention has yet been made of the crossing over of the corticobulbar tract because it isn't the same for all the cranial nerves just mentioned. The motor nuclei of all the cranial nerves mentioned, except VII and XII, receive innervation from both the right and left corticobulbar tracts; that is, each corticobulbar tract supplies both the right and left cranial nuclei (Figure 8–1). This bilateral innervation is a kind of biologic insurance. If the right tract is damaged, for example, the nuclei will still receive the upper motor neuron impulses from the intact left corticobulbar tract, and there will be no impairment of muscle function. The nuclei of cranial nerve XII, the hypoglossal nerve, receive only contralateral innervation; that is, the nucleus of the right side is supplied by axons from the left corticobulbar tract, and vice versa. The clinical implication is fairly obvious: A lesion to the left corticobulbar tract would result in loss of nerve supply to the right nucleus, and the muscles of the right side of the tongue would be paralyzed.

The nucleus of the facial nerve, cranial nerve VII, combines features of both types of nuclei discussed so far. Its nucleus is divided into an upper part, which supplies the muscles of the upper half of the

---

*The cranial nerves are discussed in greater detail in Chapter 13. See also Appendix VI, "Summary of Cranial Nerves."

Figure 8–1

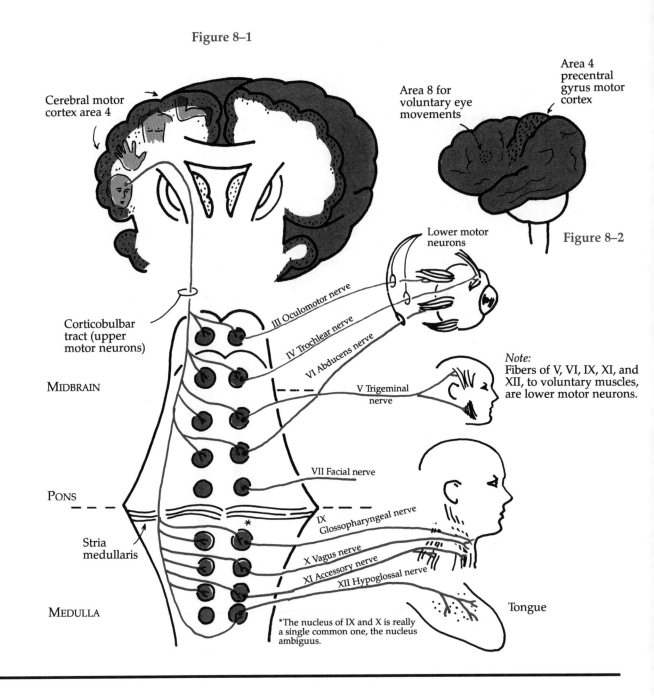

Cerebral motor cortex area 4

Area 8 for voluntary eye movements

Area 4 precentral gyrus motor cortex

Figure 8–2

Lower motor neurons

Corticobulbar tract (upper motor neurons)

III Oculomotor nerve

IV Trochlear nerve

VI Abducens nerve

MIDBRAIN

V Trigeminal nerve

*Note:*
Fibers of V, VI, IX, XI, and XII, to voluntary muscles, are lower motor neurons.

VII Facial nerve

PONS

IX Glossopharyngeal nerve

Stria medullaris

X Vagus nerve

XI Accessory nerve

XII Hypoglossal nerve

MEDULLA

Tongue

*The nucleus of IX and X is really a single common one, the nucleus ambiguus.

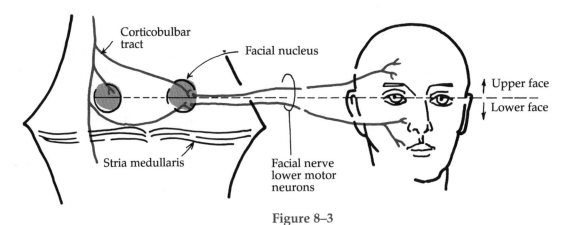

Corticobulbar tract

Facial nucleus

Upper face

Lower face

Stria medullaris

Facial nerve lower motor neurons

Figure 8–3

face, and a lower part, which supplies muscles in the lower half of the face. The upper part of the nucleus receives bilateral innervation from the corticobulbar tract, whereas the lower part receives its supply only from the contralateral tract (Figure 8–3).

## CLINICAL NOTES

### Upper Motor Neuron Lesions

As we have just seen, all the cranial motor nuclei (except the lower part of the facial and hypoglossal nerves) receive bilateral innervation. Therefore, if there is a lesion in one of the corticobulbar tracts, none of the nuclei or the muscles they supply would be affected. However, an upper motor neuron lesion (also known as a supranuclear lesion) could affect cranial nerve XII and/or the lower part of VII. If corticobulbar fibers to the facial nucleus are damaged, there is paralysis of the lower part of the facial muscles on the side opposite the lesion (Figure 8–3). The paralysis is spastic, and reflexes are present. Because the upper part of the facial muscles receives bilateral innervation, the patient can still move the brow on the paralyzed side of the face (Figure 8–3). If corticobulbar neurons to the hypoglossal nucleus are destroyed, the tongue muscles on the contralateral side will be paralyzed but will not atrophy (Figure 8–1). When the patient is asked to protrude the tongue, the muscles on the unaffected side will cause it to deviate to the side on which the muscles are paralyzed.

### Lower Motor Neuron Lesions

Lower motor neuron lesions of the head are discussed in Chapter 13.

# Chapter 9

# Subcortical Motor Areas

In lower forms of animals, such as sharks and birds, that do not have a cerebral motor cortex, movement is initiated by a group of nuclei, the basal ganglia, together with other subcortical areas. Such movement is highly coordinated and often quick, but it is instinctive and crude. In humans, there has been added to this old motor system a new, "higher" one, the cerebral motor cortex, which enables us to perform exceptionally skilled and purposeful movements, especially with the hands. This new system is called the pyramidal system. The older, cruder one is the extrapyramidal system. For a while it was thought that the two were independent of each other, but now it is known that they are very much interconnected. Our knowledge of the old system is incomplete, and a lot of what we think today may have to be modified by new discoveries tomorrow. With respect to terminology, there has been a tendency recently to use terms other than *pyramidal* and *extrapyramidal*, but this change in semantics hasn't been accompanied by any great increase in understanding. Also, many of the nuclei are grouped together and are given special names (eg, *corpus striatum*, *lentiform nucleus*, etc). Because terminology differs sometimes among authors, in this book we will name the various nuclei and areas individually.

Deep in the cerebral hemispheres are three well-defined nuclei: the *caudate nucleus*, which lies medial to the anterior limb of the internal capsule, and the *globus pallidus* and *putamen*, which lie lateral to the genu (Figure 9–1). These three constitute the basal ganglia. In the diencephalon is the subthalamic nucleus of Luys, and in the midbrain are the red nucleus, the substantia nigra, and the reticular formation (Figures 9–2 and 9–3). All the above-mentioned structures are parts of the subcortical or primitive motor areas.

Various areas of the cerebral motor cortex, including areas 4, 4s, and 6, send fibers to the caudate nucleus, putamen, and globus pallidus (Figure 9–3). The globus pallidus, which also receives fibers from the caudate nucleus and putamen, is the main discharge center and is therefore connected with the subthalamic nucleus, substantia nigra, reticular formation, and red nucleus (Figure 9–3). In addition, the subthalamic nucleus and substantia nigra are connected to the reticular formation and red nucleus, which discharge to the lower motor neu-

rons at all levels of the cord via the reticulospinal and rubrospinal tracts (Figure 9–3). Thus there is, as was so aptly described by the neuroanatomist Elliot, a "cascading effect" with respect to nuclei and their discharges. Finally, the globus pallidus is connected to the thalamus by two tracts, the *ansa lenticularis* and the *lenticular fasciculus*. As they enter the thalamus, these two tracts merge to form the *thalamic fasciculus*. The thalamus in turn is connected back to the caudate nucleus and areas 4, 4s, and 6, thus establishing a feedback mechanism. If our knowledge of the interconnections among different subcortical nuclei and their relationship to areas 4, 4s, and 6 is poor, then our understanding of how they operate and regulate motor activity is almost nil.

## CLINICAL NOTES

Lesions in the primitive subcortical nuclei produce several diseases characterized by disturbances of muscle tone and various abnormal involuntary movements (dyskinesias). The most common and best known of these is *Parkinson's disease (paralysis agitans)*, a slow, progressive, degenerative disease of older people (50 to 70 years) first described by James Parkinson, a 19th century English physician. This disease affects more than 0.5 million people in the United States, with more than 50,000 new cases occurring each year. Clinically, one sees a great increase in muscle tonus, leading to *rigidity* and slowness of movement (*bradykinesia*). The face often loses all signs of expression and becomes masklike as a result of this hypertonicity, and blinking is greatly reduced, producing a characteristic stare. Combined with this is tremor, seen especially in the arms and hands, where it manifests itself in a characteristic pill-rolling motion. This tremor is most evident when the patient is not using his or her hands (*resting tremor*), and it often disappears during purposeful movements. During walking, the head and shoulders are stooped, the gait is short and shuffling, and there is a loss of automatic movements such as swinging of the arms. In the end, patients may lose their ability to move and may be unable to swallow.

The disease affects every ethnic, socioeconomic, and national group, but twin and family studies

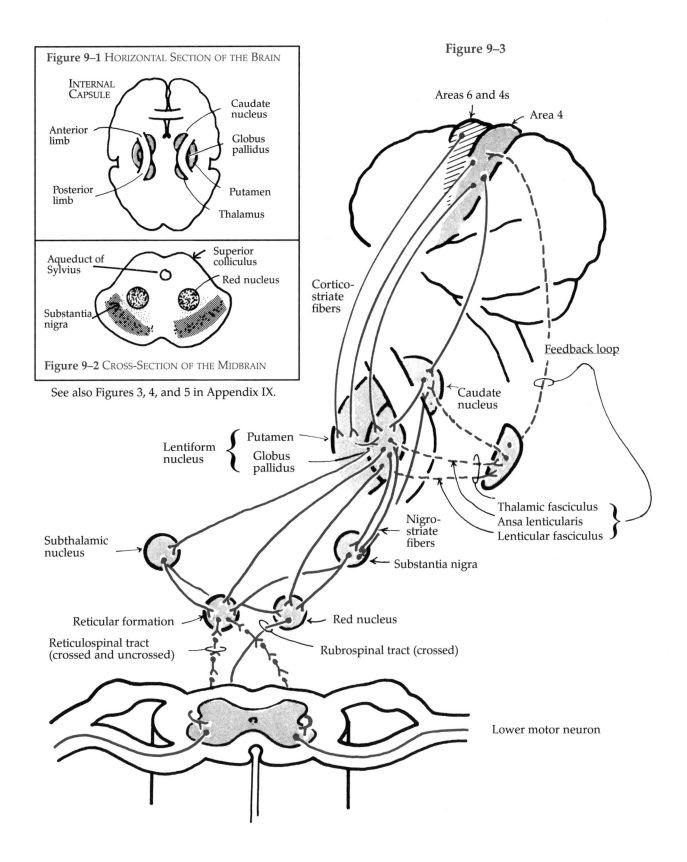

**Figure 9–1** HORIZONTAL SECTION OF THE BRAIN

INTERNAL CAPSULE

Caudate nucleus

Anterior limb

Globus pallidus

Posterior limb

Putamen

Thalamus

Aqueduct of Sylvius

Superior colliculus

Red nucleus

Substantia nigra

**Figure 9–2** CROSS-SECTION OF THE MIDBRAIN

See also Figures 3, 4, and 5 in Appendix IX.

**Figure 9–3**

Areas 6 and 4s

Area 4

Corticostriate fibers

Feedback loop

Caudate nucleus

Lentiform nucleus { Putamen / Globus pallidus

Thalamic fasciculus
Ansa lenticularis
Lenticular fasciculus

Nigro-striate fibers

Subthalamic nucleus

Substantia nigra

Reticular formation

Red nucleus

Reticulospinal tract (crossed and uncrossed)

Rubrospinal tract (crossed)

Lower motor neuron

have shown that Parkinson's disease is neither genetic nor familial. In one study of 43 pairs of identical (monozygotic) twins where one of the twins had the disease, there were only two cases where the other twin had it also, resulting in a low concordance rate of 5% (in multiple sclerosis the concordance rate for identical twins is 25%, while in schizophrenia it is greater than 60%). Parkinson's disease affects about 1% of the population older than age 50 years in every country of the world.

At autopsy, one sees depigmentation associated with degeneration of the substantia nigra with evidence of degeneration within the caudate nucleus and globus pallidus as well. Microscopically, in the substantia nigra one sees small, characteristic inclusions known as Lewy bodies. It has been shown that dopamine is an essential neurotransmitter in the basal ganglia. It is produced in the neurons of the substantia nigra and passes up fibers by axonal transport to be used in the caudate nucleus and putamen (ie, the striatum; Figure 9–3). In most cases of Parkinson's disease the substantia nigra is destroyed, and as a result there is a decrease in the amount of dopamine reaching the basal ganglia, which produces the signs and symptoms of the illness. On the basis of this theory rests one of the current methods of treatment: supplying the basal ganglia with the missing dopamine. Dopamine cannot be given directly, however, because it does not pass the blood–brain barrier (see Chapter 1). Therefore, L-dopa, a necessary precursor of dopamine, is given because it can pass the blood–brain barrier and is then synthesized into dopamine. One often sees great improvement in patients after the administration of L-dopa, but as the disease progresses (it may last 10 to 15 years) it has less of a beneficial effect, and symptoms reappear along with the appearance of serious L-dopa side effects. These side effects can include uncontrolled, involuntary jerky movements and hallucinations.

In recent years there has been a revival of an old surgical procedure that was used in the 1940s but was abandoned when L-dopa was introduced. This procedure, known as *pallidotomy*, is based on the concept that loss of dopamine-secreting neurons in the substantia nigra results in loss of inhibitory inputs to the globus pallidus, which in turn puts out uncontrolled impulses, resulting in the abnormal movements characteristic of parkinsonism. Through recently perfected stereotactic microsurgical techniques, areas of the globus pallidus are destroyed, usually on one side. This technique, however, has met with mixed successes, with some patients being reported to have developed serious side effects. Nonetheless, this procedure has brought new hope for many intractable cases.

Several years ago it was reported[1–3] that a group of young drug addicts rapidly developed a parkinsonian-like disease; in one of these patients, autopsy revealed destruction of the substantia nigra. Investigating further, researchers found that the addicts had used synthetic narcotics that had become contaminated with $N$-methyl-4 phenyl-1,2,5,6-tetrahydropyridine (MPTP), which virtually overnight brought on the parkinsonian-like condition. MPTP can also cause irreversible parkinsonism in monkeys by destroying their substantia nigra. So at last, this condition can be reproduced experimentally in animals, but the question still remains: What causes parkinsonism in older people? Parkinsonian-like symptoms may be seen in other conditions, such as Wilson's disease, in which there is abnormal copper metabolism that results in copper deposition in the globus pallidus, putamen, and liver, causing their degeneration. In psychiatric patients high doses of chlorpromazine often produce signs of parkinsonism as temporary and unpleasant side effects.

Transplantation of fetal substantia nigra into the brain of parkinsonian patients has also been attempted in a few centers, but in addition to the complicated ethical and legal issues involved, as of yet there has been insufficient evidence to evaluate the promise of this treatment.

*Huntington's chorea* is a much less common condition characterized by rapid, jerky, nonrhythmic, involuntary movements of the extremities, trunk, and/or face and by dementia. It has been demonstrated that this is a hereditary, *autosomal dominant* illness involving a disorder on the short arm of chromosome 4. The disease generally manifests itself after the age of 40 and is usually fatal within 15 years.

In reality, patients with Huntington's chorea may have a variety of types of movement disorders, including athetotic and dystonic symptoms in addition to the chorea. Athetosis may also occur alone, as in other degenerative diseases of the basal ganglia, or in association with drug intoxication (eg, phenothiazines or haloperidol). It is characterized by slow, bizarre, twisting movements, especially in the arms and fingers. Although Huntington's chorea may involve loss of neurons throughout the striated body, the principal pathologic feature is loss of neurons in the caudate nucleus with glial scarring, identifiable by computed tomography and magnetic resonance imaging as a change of contour of the medial surface of the caudate.

*Hemiballismus* is caused by a lesion in the subthalamic nucleus. In this disease there is a violent swinging motion of the arm or leg. There is as yet no cure or relief for most of these patients, and the movements cease only in sleep.

The causes of all three of these diseases are still unknown.

## ACCESSORY DETAILS

- Corpus striatum = putamen, globus pallidus, and caudate nucleus
- Paleostriatum = globus pallidus
- Neostriatum = putamen and caudate nucleus
- Lenticular nucleus = putamen and globus pallidus

### REFERENCES

1. Langston JW. The case of the tainted heroin. *Science.* 1985;25:34–40.
2. Langston JW, Ballard P. Chronic parkinsonism in humans due to product of meperidine analog synthesis. *Science.* 1983;219:979–980.
3. Gusella JF, Wexler NS, Conneally PM, Naylor SL, Anderson MA, Tanzi RE, et al. A polymorphic DNA marker genetically linked to Huntington's disease. *Nature (London).* 1983; 306:234–238.

# Chapter 10

# The Vestibular System

It happens to all of us: Suddenly, for one reason or another, one loses one's balance and starts to fall, and immediately a reflex reaction known as the *righting mechanism* comes into play in an attempt to regain equilibrium. This sense of loss of equilibrium and the reflex mechanisms to regain and maintain it are the function of the vestibular division of the eighth cranial nerve, the acoustovestibular nerve. The vestibular system is considered part of the extrapyramidal network because it does not involve the cerebral motor cortex and because its actions are reflexive.

The receptor organ is located in the inner ear and consists of two fluid-filled sacs, the utricle and the saccule, and three fluid-filled semicircular canals (see Appendix IX, Figure 5) lying perpendicular to each other, which represent the three spatial planes (Figure 10–1). The fluid is *endolymph*, and suspended in it are specialized receptor cells, the *hair cells*, which are sensitive to fluid currents. When there is a shift or change of position of the head, the endolymph is set in motion. It stimulates the receptors, which transmit this information to the brain, which in turn sets off the appropriate reflex responses.

From the inner ear, primary neurons pass to the brain; their cell bodies are aggregated in the vestibular ganglion. Axons leave this ganglion and enter the brain stem, where they terminate in four vestibular nuclei situated in the area acoustica of the floor of the fourth ventricle (Figure 10–1). These nuclei have five major connections, which are discussed below one by one.

## VESTIBULOCEREBELLAR CONNECTIONS

The cerebellum is the coordination center for motor activity and equilibrium. Therefore, from the superior and lateral vestibular nuclei, second-order (secondary) neurons pass up into the cerebellum via its inferior peduncle and terminate in the flocculonodular lobe (Figure 10–1). In addition, there are a few first-order axons that do not end in the vestibular nuclei but pass directly to the floccular nodulus (Figure 10–1). This then discharges back to the vestibular nuclei of both sides via the fastigial nucleus and the inferior peduncle. Thus a cerebellar–vestibular feedback mechanism is established (Figure 10–1).

## VESTIBULOSPINAL TRACTS

From the lateral vestibular nucleus, secondary neurons descend in the ipsilateral ventral white column and end by synapsing on lower motor neurons. These second-order neurons, which discharge reflexively to maintain equilibrium, form the lateral vestibulospinal tract (Figure 10–2). (*Lateral* here refers not to the fact that it originates in the lateral nucleus but to the fact that it lies medial to the vestibulospinal tract, which is discussed next.)

From the medial, superior, and inferior vestibular nuclei, second-order crossed and uncrossed neurons descend in the ventral white columns and terminate on lower motor neurons. These secondary neurons, which form the medial vestibulospinal tract, also discharge reflexively to maintain body equilibrium (Figure 10–2).

## VESTIBULOOCULAR CONNECTIONS

Besides helping maintain body equilibrium, the vestibular system also has the function of regulating eyeball movements in certain cases. For example, if one looks straight ahead and fixes one's eyes on an object and then turns one's head to the side, the appropriate eyeball muscles must contract for the eyes to remain "locked in" on the object. The regulation or control of this contraction is a function of the vestibular system. It works as follows: When one turns one's head, the endolymph in the semicircular canals, sacculus, and utricle is set in motion and stimulates the hair cells. This stimulus passes via the nerve and vestibular ganglion to the vestibular nuclei. We just mentioned that, from the medial, superior, and inferior vestibular nuclei, crossed and uncrossed neurons descend as the medial vestibulospinal tract. Just before descending, these neurons branch and give off axons that ascend in the pons and midbrain, where they synapse in the sixth (abducens), fourth (trochlear), and third (oculomotor) nuclei, which are all concerned with eyeball muscle movement. These ascending axons regulate the amount of eyeball muscle contraction and form the medial longitudinal fasciculus (MLF, Figure 10–2); some neuroanatomy books refer to the lateral vestibulospinal tract as the vestibulospinal tract, whereas the medial vestibulospinal tract is called the MLF.

**Figure 10–1**

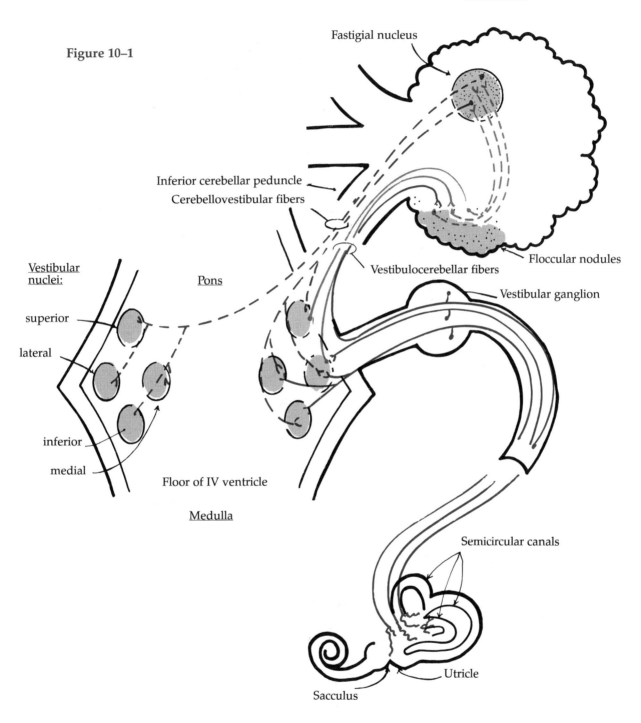

Cerebellum

Fastigial nucleus

Inferior cerebellar peduncle

Cerebellovestibular fibers

Vestibulocerebellar fibers

Floccular nodules

Vestibular ganglion

Vestibular nuclei:

superior

lateral

inferior

medial

Pons

Floor of IV ventricle

Medulla

Semicircular canals

Utricle

Sacculus

Figure 10–2

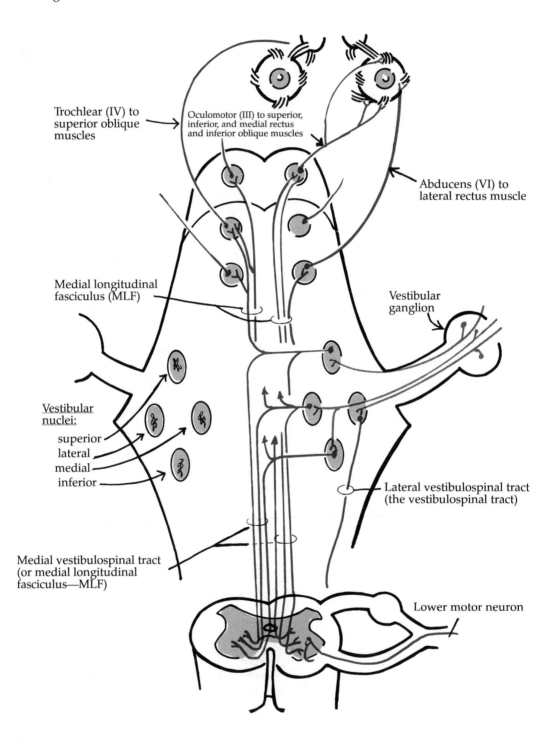

Trochlear (IV) to superior oblique muscles

Oculomotor (III) to superior, inferior, and medial rectus and inferior oblique muscles

Abducens (VI) to lateral rectus muscle

Medial longitudinal fasciculus (MLF)

Vestibular ganglion

Vestibular nuclei:

superior
lateral
medial
inferior

Lateral vestibulospinal tract (the vestibulospinal tract)

Medial vestibulospinal tract (or medial longitudinal fasciculus—MLF)

Lower motor neuron

## VESTIBULOCORTICAL CONNECTIONS

We can all sense a loss of equilibrium, or dizziness, if we are spun around quickly. This sensation implies vestibular connections to the thalamus, cerebral cortex, and consciousness. Until now, however, no such connections have been demonstrated morphologically. Some evidence has been obtained from electrophysiologic studies, but the problem remains unsolved.

## ACCESSORY PATHWAY

We mentioned above that the fastigial nucleus of the cerebellum is part of the feedback mechanism to the vestibular nuclei, which then discharge to the lower motor neurons via the lateral and medial vestibulospinal tracts. There is, in addition, another pathway to maintain equilibrium. The fastigial nucleus is connected to the descending reticular areas and nuclei of the brain stem, which then discharge to the lower motor neurons via the multisynaptic reticulospinal tract (see Figure 11–3 and also Chapter 17, on the reticular systems).

## CLINICAL NOTES

Lesions of the vestibular system often produce disturbances in equilibrium and walking straight. Because this system is connected with eyeball movements, lesions in it may also produce abnormal to-and-fro movements of the eyes, known as nystagmus. In nystagmus the eyes are constantly moving. First they move slowly to one side as far as they can go, then they snap back quickly, then again they move slowly, and so on. There is thus a slow movement to one side and a quick one to the other; the nystagmus is called left or right nystagmus according to the direction of the quick movement. Most nystagmi are horizontal in direction, but there can also be vertical nystagmus. Nystagmus is often seen in albinos. Normal nystagmus can be seen in persons riding on trains. While they are looking out the window, their eyes will automatically focus on an object, follow it slowly until it is out of sight, and then snap back quickly and focus on another object. This slow–fast pattern of movement is repeated.

Another common symptom of vestibular injury is dizziness, although other conditions can also produce it. *Meniere's disease* is a disease of uncertain etiology in which the patient experiences attacks of dizziness, ringing in the ears (tinnitus), and progressive hearing loss. The patients are usually middle-aged, although young adults as well as older individuals may have it.

Dizziness may also be caused by an acoustic neuroma (tumor) of the eighth cranial nerve. (See Figures 11 and 14 in Appendix IX.)

# Chapter 11

# The Cerebellum and Its Pathways

The cerebellum (see Appendix II, Plates I, II, and III; and Appendix VIII, Figure 4) is the control center for the coordination of voluntary muscle activity, equilibrium, and muscle tonus. It does not initiate movement, and therefore a person who has cerebellar injury does not become paralyzed. Rather, his or her movements are slow, clumsy, tremulous, and uncoordinated. The muscles may be hypotonic, and the person is unable to walk steadily and tends to sway, stagger, and fall. To carry out its three important functions, the cerebellum needs to receive a steady stream of information concerning:

1. the position and state of the muscles and joints and the amount of tonus present
2. the equilibrium state of the body
3. what "orders" are being sent from the cerebral motor cortex

Receiving these three information "inputs," the cerebellum is then able to integrate them and, by means of "feedback" pathways, regulate and control motor activity, equilibrium, and muscle tonus automatically and at an unconscious level. The discussion in this chapter considers each of the information inputs separately and then presents the feedback pathways.

## THE SPINOCEREBELLAR PATHWAYS

Information concerning the condition of the muscles, the amount of tonus, and the position of the body is supplied by unconscious proprioceptive fibers, whose receptors are found in joints, tendons, and muscles. The cell bodies of these neurons are situated in the dorsal root ganglion, and the axons pass into the cord, from which they can reach the cerebellum by either one of two tracts. Most of those from the lower part of the body enter the dorsal horn, where they synapse with second-order neurons (Figure 11–1). Some of these secondary neurons ascend on the same side, in the ventral spinocerebellar tract of the lateral columns, and enter the cerebellum through its *superior peduncle*. The remaining secondary axons cross over to the contralateral side, enter the ventral spinocerebellar tract there, and ascend to the cerebellum.

However, before passing into the superior cerebellar peduncle they cross back to the side from which they started (Figure 11–1).

Proprioceptive fibers from the upper part of the body mainly use the dorsal spinocerebellar tract. Here primary neurons synapse with secondary ones in Clarke's nucleus (Figure 11–1), which is found only in the upper part of the spinal cord (C-8 to L-2). Secondary axons pass into the lateral columns on the same side to form the dorsal spinocerebellar tract, which enters the cerebellum through the inferior cerebellar peduncle. The important thing to remember is that *all spinocerebellar fibers enter the cerebellum on the same side on which they entered the cord.*

The dorsal and ventral spinocerebellar tracts are the main bundles supplying proprioceptive impulses to the cerebellum. There are, however, a number of others, such as the trigeminocerebellar tract from the muscles of mastication and the mandibular joint, the olivocerebellar tract, and the reticulocerebellar and arcuocerebellar tracts.

## VESTIBULOCEREBELLAR TRACT

From the superior and lateral vestibular nuclei arise the fibers that supply information concerning the equilibrium state of the body. They enter through the ipsilateral (homolateral) inferior peduncle and pass to the cerebellar cortex, especially that of the *flocculus* (Figure 11–2). Phylogenetically, the flocculus is the oldest part of the cerebellum and a center for equilibrium.

## CORTICOPONTOCEREBELLAR TRACTS

When the cerebral motor cortex discharges to the lower motor neurons, the cerebellum must receive information about the nature of the discharge: to what muscles it is going, how strong it is, and so on. It gets this information through the corticopontocerebellar tracts. The fibers originate in the cerebral cortex, descend through the internal capsule, and, at the level of the pons, synapse with second-order neurons in the pontine nuclei (Figure 11–2). The secondary axons now *cross over* to the other

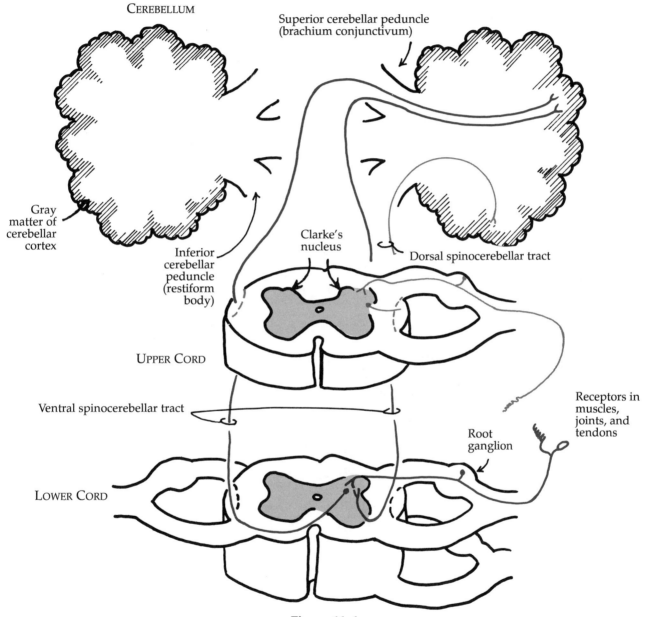

CEREBELLUM

Superior cerebellar peduncle
(brachium conjunctivum)

Gray
matter of
cerebellar
cortex

Inferior
cerebellar
peduncle
(restiform
body)

Clarke's
nucleus

Dorsal spinocerebellar tract

UPPER CORD

Ventral spinocerebellar tract

Receptors in
muscles,
joints, and
tendons

Root
ganglion

LOWER CORD

Figure 11–1

37

Figure 11–2

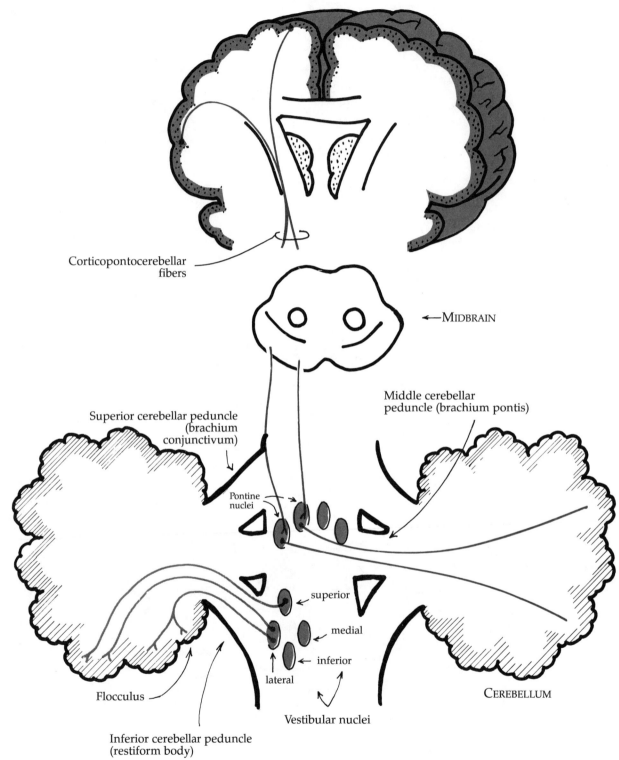

Corticopontocerebellar fibers

← MIDBRAIN

Superior cerebellar peduncle (brachium conjunctivum)

Middle cerebellar peduncle (brachium pontis)

Pontine nuclei

superior

medial

← inferior

lateral

Flocculus

CEREBELLUM

Vestibular nuclei

Inferior cerebellar peduncle (restiform body)

side and enter the cerebellum through its *middle peduncle*.

## FEEDBACK PATHWAYS

The cerebellum, having received information concerning muscle states, tonus, and equilibrium as well as the nature of the motor discharge to the muscles, integrates all this input and exerts its control via a feedback mechanism back to areas 4, 4s, and 6 and by pathways to lower motor neurons.

From the cerebellar cortex, short neurons pass to several cerebellar nuclei: the *emboliform*, *fastigial*, *globose*, and *dentate nuclei*. The last-named nucleus is the most important; it sends out fibers through the superior peduncle that decussate and then enter the red nucleus of the midbrain (Figure 11–3). Not surprising, they are called the *dentorubro fibers*, or the dentorubrothalamic tract, because some of them bypass the red nucleus and go up to the thalamus. The red nucleus can discharge up to the thalamus, which relays the information to the cerebral motor cortex; thus the feedback circuit is completed (Figure 11–3). The red nucleus can also discharge down to the lower motor neurons by means of the rubrospinal tract (Figure 11–3) and thus can influence the corticospinal impulses at the spinal level.

The cerebellum also discharges back, directly or through the fastigial nucleus, to the vestibular nuclei. These in turn relay the stimuli to the lower motor neurons by means of the vestibulospinal tract (Figure 11–3).

Finally, the cerebellum can influence the lower motor neurons by discharging to the reticular area and nuclei of the pons, midbrain, and medulla, which relay the discharge by the lateral and medial reticulospinal tracts (Figure 11–3).

## CLINICAL NOTES

Lesions of the cerebellum or its afferent and efferent tracts produce several characteristic signs, usually on the same side of the body as the injury:

- *Asynergia* is the loss of coordination in performing motor acts. One sees decomposition of movement; that is, it is done in jerky stages instead of smoothly.
- *Dysmetria* is the inability to judge distance and to stop movement at a chosen spot. Thus, in reaching for an object, a patient's hand will overreach or underreach it. When asked to touch the tip of the nose, the patient's finger will hit the cheek, a pass-pointing phenomenon.
- *Adiadochokinesia* is the inability to perform rapidly alternating movements, such as pronation and supination of the hands.
- *Intention tremor* occurs during a movement and not at rest. In Parkinson's disease one sees just the opposite, a resting tremor.
- *Abnormal gait (ataxia)* may be present, and to compensate, the patient walks with the feet spread apart.
- *Falling* may occur, especially to the injured side.
- *Hypotonia* may be seen. The muscles are floppy and weak but may be hypertonic in some cases.
- *Dysphonia* is a slurred, explosive speech.
- *Nystagmus* may be present.

Not all these signs or symptoms are present in every case of cerebellar damage. To test, ask the patient to perform the various movements described above, and check for their presence or absence.

Medulloblastoma (Appendix VIII, Figure 16) is the most common central nervous system tumor in children and is found mostly in the 4- to 8-year age group. It is situated in the vermis or roof of the fourth ventricle, and the first characteristic signs are ataxia (ie, stumbling gait) and frequent unexplained falls. This tumor is sensitive to radiation, and with correct therapy there is a 60% 5-year survival time.

**Figure 11–3**

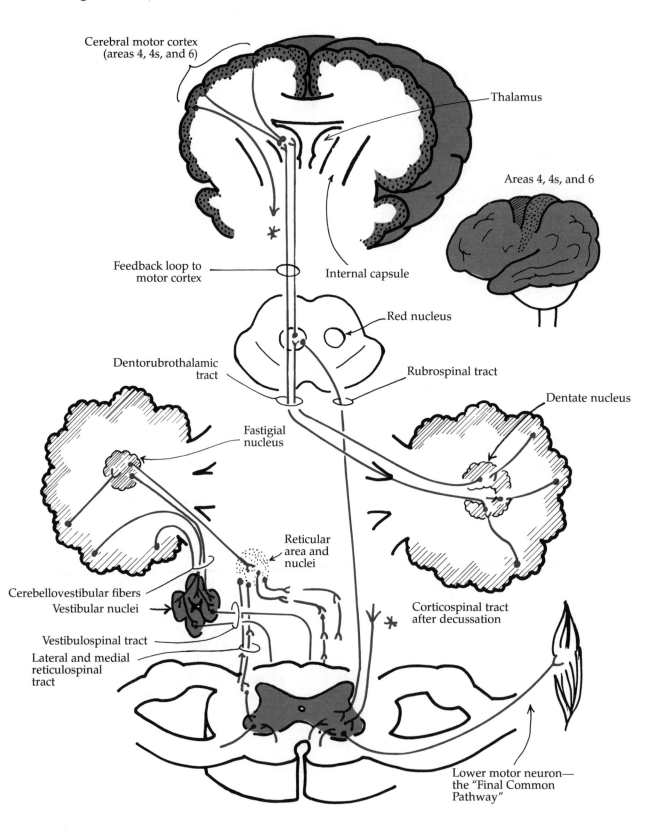

Cerebral motor cortex
(areas 4, 4s, and 6)

Thalamus

Areas 4, 4s, and 6

Feedback loop to
motor cortex

Internal capsule

Red nucleus

Dentorubrothalamic
tract

Rubrospinal tract

Dentate nucleus

Fastigial
nucleus

Reticular
area and
nuclei

Cerebellovestibular fibers
Vestibular nuclei

Corticospinal tract
after decussation

Vestibulospinal tract

Lateral and medial
reticulospinal
tract

Lower motor neuron—
the "Final Common
Pathway"

# Chapter 12

# The Autonomic Nervous System

The autonomic nervous system, which is also known as the visceral or vegetative nervous system, stimulates and controls structures not under conscious control. If, for example, you are suddenly told that you're getting a surprise exam, your heart rate will probably increase, your mouth will go dry, you'll get "butterflies" in your stomach, and you'll start sweating—all automatic reactions to a stress situation. The autonomic nervous system stimulates three types of tissues: *cardiac muscle*, *most glands*, and *all smooth muscle* (found in many organs and structures). The autonomic system is divided into two parts: the *sympathetic nervous system* and the *parasympathetic nervous system*, both of which supply (with two or three exceptions) the same organs and structures. However, the two systems are antagonistic to each other. For example, sympathetic stimulation of the heart results in an increased pulse rate, whereas parasympathetic stimulation slows it down. Sympathetic discharge results in dilation of the pupils, whereas parasympathetic stimulation produces constriction. The two systems are constantly discharging to the structures they supply, but there is a balance between them (Figure 12–1a). *This balance can be changed in two ways: by increasing the amount of stimulus in one part of the system* (Figure 12–1b) *or by decreasing the amount of discharge in the other* (Figure 12–1c). This important principle forms the basis of much of neuropharmacology and is discussed later in greater detail. It can be remembered easily as the "water tap" principle. If you have the hot (sympathetic) and cold (parasympathetic) taps open equally, then lukewarm water flows. If you want the water warmer, you can either open the hot water tap more or close the cold one.

## THE SYMPATHETIC NERVOUS SYSTEM

The sympathetic nervous system is the one that dominates when a person is in a stress situation, be it physical or psychologic. In both instances one feels threatened, and the body automatically reacts by preparing for "fight or flight." In these conditions the muscles will work harder, will need more oxygen, and will use more energy (a catabolic process). Therefore, one breathes faster, and the bronchioles open up for quicker and greater passage of air; the heart beats stronger and faster, to increase cardiac output, and blood pressure rises. The arteries to the heart and voluntary muscles dilate, thereby bringing more blood to them; the arteries to the skin and peripheral areas of the body constrict, thereby shunting more blood to the active muscles (as a result, the skin feels cold). The liver secretes glycogen for quick supply of energy, peristalsis slows down because the body has no energy or time for digestion, the pupils dilate to get a better view of the surroundings, one sweats to reduce elevated body temperature, and the hair "stands on end." The last has been referred to as an evolutionary carryover of more primitive defense reactions. If a cat is threatened by a dog, its hairs stand up so that if the dog attempts to bite the body it gets a mouthful of hair instead.

The sympathetic nervous system, like the parasympathetic system, is based on a two-neuron motor pathway. The cell bodies of the first neurons are located in the lateral (intermediolateral) gray horn of the spinal cord between the first thoracic and the third lumbar (T-1 to L-3) segments (Figure 12–2; the system is therefore also called the thoracolumbar outflow). The axons leave the cord via the ventral roots and enter the sympathetic trunk, which is made up of a series of ganglia and axon fibers on each side of the vertebral column that extends from the neck to the sacrum. (It is also referred to as the paravertebral chain ganglia or the *sympathetic chain*.) Now the question is: How do the primary axons that exit at T-1 reach the glands and smooth-muscle structures up in the head? After entering the sympathetic trunk, the axons ascend until they reach the *superior cervical ganglion* in the upper region of the neck (Figure 12–2). Here they synapse with secondary neurons, which go out and innervate the glands and other structures. The first neuron is called the *preganglionic neuron*, and its axon is myelinated; the second is the *postganglionic neuron*, and its axon is unmyelinated (actually lightly myelinated). This postganglionic axon reaches its destination by leaving the superior cervical ganglion and wrapping itself around the arteries that supply the innervated structures. It thus "hitches a ride" on the arteries until it comes to the glands and smooth-muscle structures, where it then peels off to innervate them (Figure 12–2).

Cell bodies of sympathetics destined to supply the heart and lungs are situated in the lateral gray horn of segments T-1 to T-5. The axons leave the cord and enter the chain ganglia, where they synapse with

**Figure 12–2**

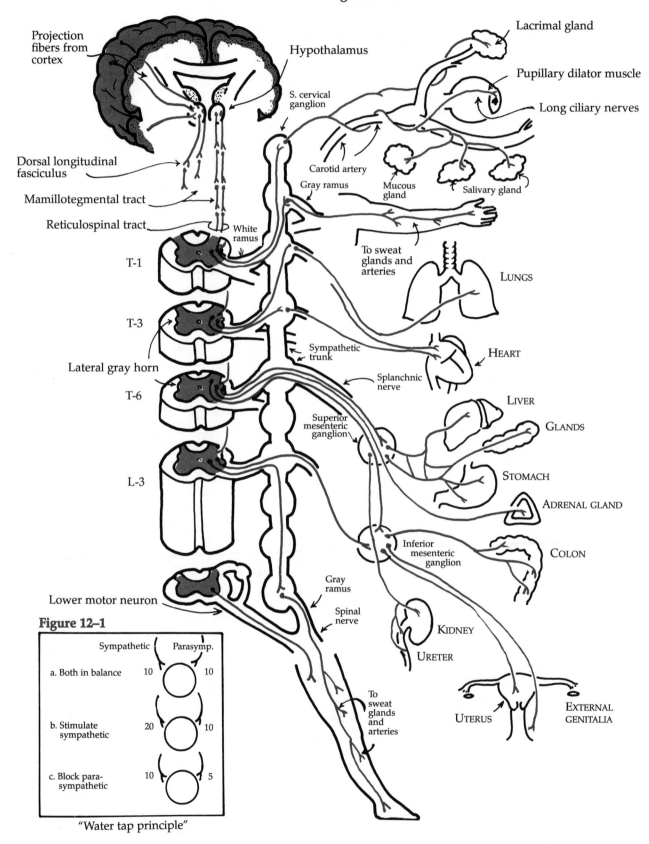

Projection fibers from cortex

Hypothalamus

Lacrimal gland

Pupillary dilator muscle

Long ciliary nerves

S. cervical ganglion

Dorsal longitudinal fasciculus

Carotid artery

Gray ramus

Mucous gland

Salivary gland

Mamillotegmental tract

Reticulospinal tract

White ramus

To sweat glands and arteries

LUNGS

T-1

T-3

Sympathetic trunk

HEART

Splanchnic nerve

Lateral gray horn

T-6

Superior mesenteric ganglion

LIVER

GLANDS

STOMACH

ADRENAL GLAND

COLON

L-3

Inferior mesenteric ganglion

Gray ramus

Lower motor neuron

Spinal nerve

KIDNEY

URETER

**Figure 12–1**

To sweat glands and arteries

UTERUS

EXTERNAL GENITALIA

| | Sympathetic | Parasymp. |
|---|---|---|
| a. Both in balance | 10 | 10 |
| b. Stimulate sympathetic | 20 | 10 |
| c. Block para-sympathetic | 10 | 5 |

"Water tap principle"

postganglionic neurons. The axons of the latter leave the chain ganglia and form specific nerves that reach the heart and lungs (Figure 12–2).

Those sympathetics that supply the abdominal viscera are found in the lateral horn of T-5 to T-12. Their axons enter the chain ganglia but do not synapse there. Rather, they pass through it and leave to form distinct nerves, the greater and lesser splanchnics, which terminate in the superior and inferior mesenteric ganglions of the abdomen. The postganglionic axons leave and form a netlike plexus that spreads out over the arteries to reach the various organs. Some of the preganglionic axons pass to the adrenal gland, the medullary cells of which are the postganglionic neurons that are specialized to secrete the hormone adrenaline (Figure 12–2).

Most of the preganglionic sympathetic nerve cell bodies to the pelvic organs are located in the lateral horn of spinal segments L-1 to L-3 (Figure 12–2). Their axons enter the sympathetic chain, pass through it without synapsing, and descend to end in the inferior mesenteric ganglion. From here, the postganglionics fan out to supply the urinary and genital organs as well as the descending and sigmoid colon and the rectum.

## ACCESSORY DETAILS

The preganglionic sympathetic axons are myelinated and therefore are white. They leave the cord and peel off from the spinal nerve to form the *white rami communicantes*, which connect the spinal nerves with the sympathetic ganglia (Figure 12–2). The postganglionic axons are unmyelinated and therefore appear gray. Many rejoin the spinal nerves through the *gray rami communicantes* and pass out to supply the sweat glands and peripheral arteries of the head, upper extremities, trunk, and lower limbs (Figure 12–2).

The chemical transmitter between the postganglionic sympathetic axons and the structures they innervate is not acetylcholine but rather primarily *noradrenaline* and a small amount of *adrenaline*. If a patient is given a shot of adrenaline, the reaction is the same as if the sympathetic nervous system had discharged. Consequently, this system is also called the *adrenergic nervous system*. There are drugs that block the parasympathetic system, resulting in an imbalance between the two parts of the autonomic nervous system, and what one sees is similar in many ways to what happens when the sympathetics discharge (Figure 12–1c).

## THE PARASYMPATHETIC NERVOUS SYSTEM

This system is also based on a two-neuron motor pathway consisting of preganglionic and postganglionic neurons. However, there are great physiologic, anatomic, and pharmacologic differences between the two systems. Whereas the sympathetic nervous system is dominant in stress situations and its activities are largely catabolic, the parasympathetic is most active when a person is relaxed and resting; the heart beat slows down, peristalsis and other digestive functions are active, pupils constrict, respiratory rate is reduced, and the person feels relaxed—an anabolic process.

The chemical transmitter between the postganglionic parasympathetic axons and the structures they innervate is acetylcholine, and if one gives a patient such a drug the reaction resembles parasympathetic discharge.

As for the anatomy, the preganglionic cell bodies are located in the brain stem and in the gray matter of the cord in the sacral region, and so another name for this system is the cranial–sacral outflow. In the brain stem the cell bodies are aggregated in four specific nuclei (see below), and the axons join cranial nerves III, VII, IX, and X. Being components of these nerves, the preganglionic parasympathetic fibers exit with them, pass out to the different regions, and, near their destinations, enter specific named ganglia (eg, otic, ciliary, etc). Here the preganglionic axons synapse with short postganglionic fibers that innervate glands, the heart, and structures having smooth muscle. In many cases the ganglia are situated near, on, or within the structures innervated, and the postganglionic fibers are microscopic.

At the level of the superior colliculus of the midbrain, preganglionic cell bodies are located in the *Edinger-Westphal nucleus* (Figure 12–3). The axons join the lower motor fibers of the oculomotor nerve (cranial nerve III), and together they leave the midbrain and course out to the eyeball (Figure 12–3). Near it, the preganglionic axons peel off and enter the ciliary ganglion, where they synapse with postganglionic neurons. These send out short axons, the short ciliary nerves, to the pupillary constrictor muscle.

The preganglionic cell bodies associated with the facial nerve (cranial nerve VII) are situated in the *superior salivatory nucleus*, and their axons pass out to the sphenopalatine (pterygopalatine) and submandibular (submaxillary) ganglia (Figure

**Figure 12–3**

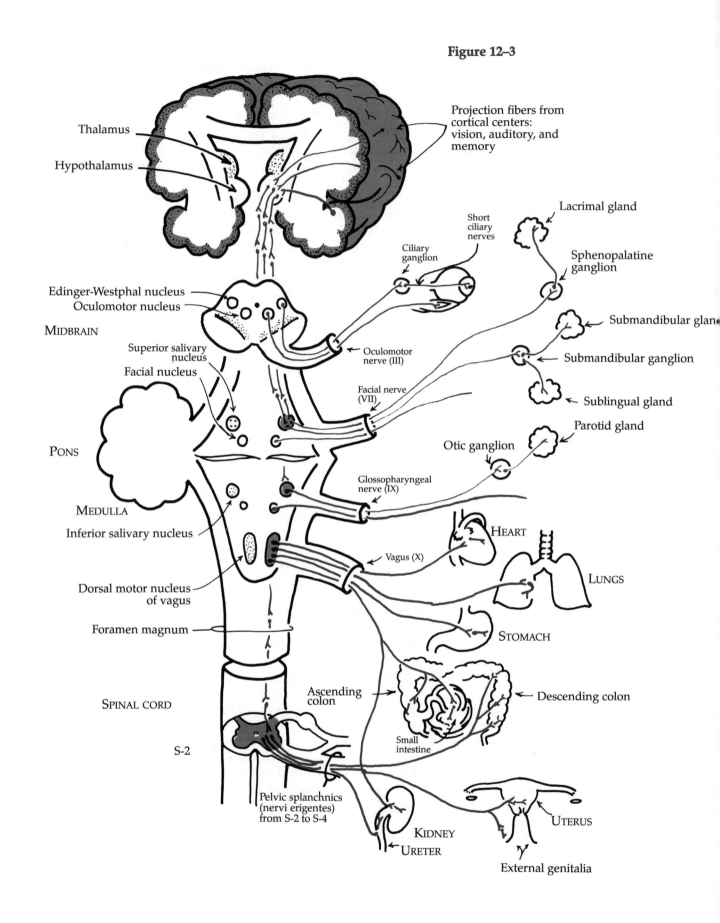

Thalamus

Hypothalamus

Projection fibers from cortical centers: vision, auditory, and memory

Lacrimal gland

Short ciliary nerves

Sphenopalatine ganglion

Ciliary ganglion

Submandibular gland

Edinger-Westphal nucleus
Oculomotor nucleus

MIDBRAIN

Oculomotor nerve (III)

Submandibular ganglion

Superior salivary nucleus
Facial nucleus

Facial nerve (VII)

Sublingual gland

Parotid gland

PONS

Otic ganglion

Glossopharyngeal nerve (IX)

MEDULLA

Inferior salivary nucleus

HEART

Vagus (X)

LUNGS

Dorsal motor nucleus of vagus

STOMACH

Foramen magnum

SPINAL CORD

Ascending colon

Descending colon

S-2

Small intestine

Pelvic splanchnics (nervi erigentes) from S-2 to S-4

KIDNEY
URETER

UTERUS

External genitalia

12–3). From here the postganglionic axons course out to the lacrimal gland as well as to the sublingual and submandibular glands.

As for cranial nerve IX, the glossopharyngeal, its preganglionic cell bodies are in the *inferior salivatory nucleus*, and the axons go out to the otic ganglion, which sends out postganglionic fibers to the parotid gland (Figure 12–3).

The vagus nerve (cranial nerve X) is the most important cranial nerve because most of its fibers are parasympathetic neurons that innervate the heart, lungs, and all the abdominal viscera up to the left colic flexure (through the proximal two thirds of the transverse colon). The preganglionic cell bodies are aggregated in the *dorsal motor nucleus of the vagus*, and the axons pass out and terminate in ganglia situated near or in the walls of the above-mentioned organs (Figure 12–3). From these ganglia, postganglionic neurons innervate the structures.

The distal one third of the transverse colon, the descending colon, and the genital and urinary systems are supplied by the sacral outflow. Here the preganglionic cell bodies are situated in the lateral (intermediolateral) area of the gray matter of spinal segments S-2 to S-4. The axons leave through the ventral roots and soon separate from the spinal nerve to form the pelvic splanchnic nerves or nervi erigentes, which reach the mural ganglia of the descending colon, ureter, and genital organs (Figure 12–3).

## ACCESSORY DETAILS

The hypothalamus is the control and integrative center for the autonomic nervous system, and its actions are automatic and not regularly subject to conscious control. (The hypothalamus is part of the diencephalon and lies below the thalamus on either side of the third ventricle; see Figure 12–3.) It receives fiber bundles mainly from higher cortical centers, such as vision, auditory, personality, and the like, and then discharges the appropriate impulses down the cord to the sympathetic or parasympathetic preganglionic neurons. It does this by means of the dorsal longitudinal fasciculus, the mamillotegmental tract, and the multisynaptic reticulospinal tract (see Chapters 17 and 18 on the reticular formation and the hypothalamus).

Pain and other sensory pathways from the viscera are still poorly understood, but it is generally accepted that the impulses travel via the autonomic nerves. Thus the system really is afferent (sensory) as well as efferent (motor).

## CLINICAL NOTES

The action of adrenergic drugs (eg, adrenaline [epinephrine], noradrenaline [norepinephrine], and dopamine) mimics sympathetic activity. They are also known as sympathomimetics and are used primarily in hospitals to deal with cases of falling blood pressure and cardiac arrest. They are also used to dilate the bronchioles in asthma and in cases of anaphylactic shock. Adrenergic drugs are also injected at sites of local anesthesia to constrict blood vessels, thereby slowing the rate of anesthetic absorption and increasing the duration of its effect. Sympathetic antagonists (eg, alpha- and beta-receptor blockers) are those drugs that block sympathetic activity. In recent years they have become among the most important and widely used drugs, primarily in the treatment of hypertension and heart problems.

The action of cholinergic (or parasympathomimetic) drugs duplicates parasympathetic activity, being employed in limited cases where smooth muscle activation is needed (eg, to stimulate an incontinent bladder or bowel after surgery). The parasympathetic blocking agents have a wider use; among the most common are atropine (belladonna*) and its derivatives, which cause marked pupillary dilation and are therefore used by ophthalmologists when they want to take a good look at the retina. However, before administering atropine one must make sure that the patient doesn't have glaucoma because dilating the pupil in such a patient can precipitate an oculogyric attack with a great increase in ocular pressure and subsequent damage to the retina.

Damage to the sympathetic system centrally, or to the sympathetic chain or superior cervical ganglion, may result in a constellation of signs on one side of the face known as *Horner's syndrome*. This consists of no sweating (anhydrosis), a fixed small pupil (miosis), flushing of the face on the affected side, and some drooping of the eyelid (ptosis). The levator palpebrae superior muscle, which lifts the upper eyelid, is innervated primarily by fibers of the oculomotor nerve (cranial nerve III; see next chapter), but some smooth muscle fibers intermingled within it (the orbital muscle of Muller) are stimulated by sympathetic nerves, and so, if these are injured, ptosis may result.

---

*This drug got its name from the fact that, during the Renaissance, women used it to dilate their pupils in an attempt to make their eyes more beautiful (*bella donna* is Italian for "beautiful lady"), even though it seriously blurred their vision.

Chapter **13**

# Cranial Nerves

The 12 pairs of cranial nerves, which we have already discussed in passing in previous chapters, are considered in detail here. These nerves can be grouped in several ways—the first according to their central location (see figures in this chapter and also Appendix II). Cranial nerves I and II, the olfactory and optic nerves, are connected to the telencephalon and diencephalon, respectively. Nerves III and IV, the oculomotor and trochlear nerves, are connected with the midbrain. The trigeminal (V), the abducens (VI), and the facial (VII) nerves are located in the pons. The remaining nerves (VIII, IX, X, XI, and XII) are associated with the medulla. It is important to know this location plan because, if a patient exhibits signs of a specific cranial nerve injury, then the site of the lesion can be pinpointed.

Another way to group cranial nerves is according to their functional neuronal components. Some have *only sensory neurons;* these are (Figure 13–1):

- I, the *olfactory* nerve, concerned with smell (see Chapter 16)
- II, the *optic* nerve, which deals with vision (see Chapter 15)
- VIII, the *vestibulocochlear* nerve, concerned with hearing and equilibrium (see Chapters 10 and 14)

Other cranial nerves are composed *only of motor neurons* to voluntary muscles; these are (Figure 13–2):

- IV, the *trochlear* nerve, which innervates the superior oblique muscle of the eyeball. If the nerve or its nucleus is damaged, the muscle will be paralyzed, and there will be difficulty in turning the affected eye downward and laterally.
- VI, the *abducens* nerve, which innervates the lateral rectus muscle of the eyeball. If this nerve or its nucleus is injured, the muscle becomes paralyzed, and the patient can't turn the eye laterally. In time, the unopposed medial rectus causes the eye to be pulled medially, thus producing a medial strabismus (squint).
- XI, the *accessory* nerve, which innervates two important muscles outside the head—the trapezius and the sternocleidomastoid muscles. These two neck muscles are also supplied by spinal nerves; thus, if the accessory nerve or its nucleus is damaged, the muscle will still function partially. However, the patient will have difficulty shrugging the shoulder on the affected side and turning the head to the opposite side.

- XII, the *hypoglossal* nerve, which supplies all the muscles of the tongue except the palatoglossus. Again, if this nerve or its nucleus is damaged, then the muscles on the affected side become paralyzed, and the tongue, when protruded, will deviate to the paralyzed side. The reason for this is that tongue muscles are so arranged that, if one side is paralyzed, then, upon protrusion, the muscles on the unparalyzed side push the tongue over to the paralyzed side.

The remaining cranial nerves (III, V, VII, IX, and X) have mixed functional neuronal components (Figure 13–3). Each of these mixed cranial nerves is discussed below in detail.

## THE OCULOMOTOR NERVE (III)

The oculomotor nerve has two principal components:

1. voluntary motor fibers to extrinsic ocular muscles
2. parasympathetic fibers to the sphincter pupillae and ciliary muscle

The motor nucleus of the oculomotor nerve is located in the midbrain, below the aqueduct of Sylvius at the level of the superior colliculus (Figure 13–4 and Appendix II, Plate X). From it emerge voluntary motor fibers (lower motor neurons), which leave the brain stem at the interpeduncular fossa and pass into the orbit through the superior orbital fissure. Here they supply the following four eyeball muscles: the superior rectus, inferior rectus, and medial rectus muscles and the inferior oblique muscle. In addition, they innervate the levator palpebrae superioris, which is responsible for lifting the upper eyelid.

46

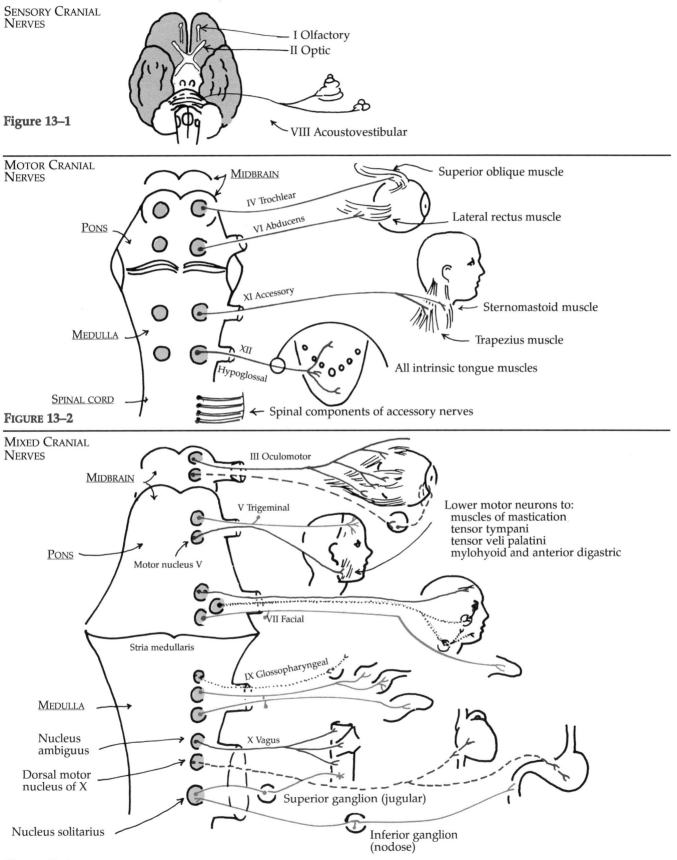

SENSORY CRANIAL NERVES

— I Olfactory
— II Optic
— VIII Acoustovestibular

**Figure 13–1**

MOTOR CRANIAL NERVES

MIDBRAIN
IV Trochlear
VI Abducens
PONS
XI Accessory
MEDULLA
XII
Hypoglossal
SPINAL CORD

Superior oblique muscle
Lateral rectus muscle
Sternomastoid muscle
Trapezius muscle
All intrinsic tongue muscles
← Spinal components of accessory nerves

**FIGURE 13–2**

MIXED CRANIAL NERVES

MIDBRAIN
III Oculomotor
V Trigeminal
PONS
Motor nucleus V
Stria medullaris
VII Facial
IX Glossopharyngeal
MEDULLA
Nucleus ambiguus
X Vagus
Dorsal motor nucleus of X
Superior ganglion (jugular)
Nucleus solitarius
Inferior ganglion (nodose)

Lower motor neurons to:
muscles of mastication
tensor tympani
tensor veli palatini
mylohyoid and anterior digastric

**Figure 13–3**

**Figure 13–4 Oculomotor or Cranial Nerve III**

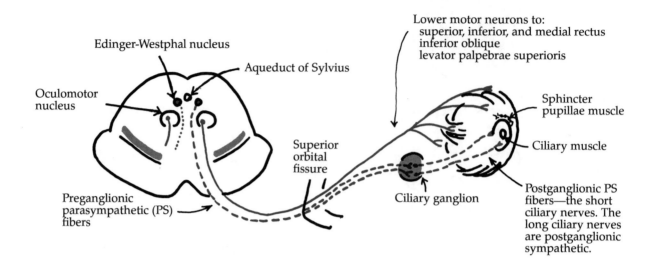

The *Edinger-Westphal nucleus* is the parasympathetic nucleus of the oculomotor nerve and is situated just dorsal to the motor nucleus (Figure 13–4). Preganglionic fibers leave it, join the voluntary motor fibers, and pass out to the orbit. There the parasympathetic fibers separate, and most of them terminate in the ciliary ganglion (Figure 13–4). Here they synapse with postganglionic fibers—the short ciliary nerve—that stimulate the sphincter pupillae muscle, causing the pupil to constrict. Other postganglionic fibers from the ciliary ganglion pass to the ciliary muscle, which is concerned with lens accommodation for near vision.

## CLINICAL NOTES

Because the oculomotor nucleus receives a bilateral upper motor neuron supply via the corticobulbar tract (Chapter 8), one rarely sees an upper motor (supranuclear) lesion that affects this nerve. However, if the oculomotor nerve is damaged, there is a lower motor neuron paralysis of the muscles it supplies, and the *eyeball is pulled laterally and downward* by the unopposed lateral rectus muscle (supplied by the abducens nerve) and the superior oblique muscle (supplied by the trochlear). Because the levator palpebrae is paralyzed, the upper eyelid droops (*ptosis*). In addition, the parasympathetic fibers will be damaged, and as a result the sphincter pupillae will be paralyzed. The dilator pupillae, supplied by the sympathetics, is now unopposed, and consequently the *pupil is widely dilated* and cannot constrict (in other words, there is a "fixed pupil"). Also, oculomotor nerve damage causes *difficulty in visual accommodation* because the ciliary muscle is paralyzed.

*Note:* A very old mnemonic device for use in naming the 12 cranial nerves is
"*O*n *O*ld *O*lympus' *T*owering *T*op, *A F*inn *A*nd *G*erman *V*iewed *A H*ouse"

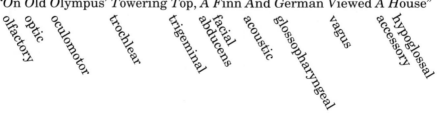

Modesty prevents presentation of the racier versions—ask the upperclassmen.

Damage to a basis pedunculi cerebri (crus cerebri) along with the exiting cranial nerve III will produce *Weber's syndrome*. This consists of an ipsilateral paralysis of the nerve and a contralateral hemiplegia due to damage of the pyramidal tract (corticospinal and upper motor neurons) before the decussation in the medulla.

## THE TRIGEMINAL NERVE (V)

The trigeminal nerve has two principal components:

1. general sensory fibers from the skin of the face
2. voluntary motor fibers to the muscles of mastication

The sensory fibers (Chapter 6) convey general sensations of pain, temperature, touch, pressure, and proprioception from the face, cornea, mouth, nose sinuses, tongue, teeth, meninges, outer surface of the eardrum, and temporomandibular joint. The motor component consists of voluntary or lower motor neurons that supply the four muscles of mastication: the temporalis, the masseter, and the lateral and medial pterygoids (Figure 13–3). In addition, the trigeminal motor fibers innervate the anterior belly of the digastric, the mylohyoid, and the tensor tympani and tensor veli palatini muscles. The motor nucleus of the trigeminal nerve is located in the pons near the main sensory nucleus.

## CLINICAL NOTES

If the entire nerve is cut or damaged, there will be a complete loss of sensation in the facial area on the same side as well as a lower motor neuron lesion that produces difficulty in chewing and speaking. Because this nerve receives a bilateral innervation from the cerebral cortex, one rarely sees cases of upper motor neuron lesions (see also "Clinical Notes" in Chapter 6).

## THE FACIAL NERVE (VII)

The facial nerve is a more complex nerve that has four major components:

1. general sensory fibers from the skin of the external ear
2. visceral sensory fibers for taste from the anterior two thirds of the tongue and the hard and soft palates
3. voluntary motor fibers to all the muscles of facial expression
4. parasympathetic fibers to the submandibular (submaxillary), sublingual, and lacrimal glands

The taste receptors are located on the anterior two thirds of the tongue, and their fibers pass back to the brain stem (Figure 13–5). In their course, they merge with the lingual branch of the trigeminal nerve but then separate from it to form the nerve known as the *chorda tympani*. This nerve enters the skull through a small fissure (the petrotympanic fissure) and passes into the temporal bone, in which is situated the geniculate ganglion. Here are located the cell bodies of the taste neurons as well as the general sensory neurons. *The axons of the taste fibers pass into the pons and end in the nucleus solitarius, but the axons of the general sensory fibers end, like those of most other general sensory fibers associated with cranial nerves, in the spinal nucleus of the trigeminal nerve* (Figures 13–5 and 13–6). From the nucleus solitarius, second-order ascending gustatory tracts arise that reach conscious levels; however, their exact course is still uncertain. In addition, there are reflex pathways for taste sensations. For example, when one tastes something pleasant there is a reflex salivation, and this pathway involves the parasympathetic component of both the seventh and ninth cranial nerves. From the nucleus solitarius, internuncials pass down to the superior salivatory nucleus and synapse with preganglionic neurons (Figure 13–5). Their axons leave the pons, enter the internal auditory meatus, and travel through the geniculate ganglion. They then separate from the rest of the facial nerve's fibers to form the chorda tympani, which merges with the lingual nerve. After "hitching a ride" with the lingual nerve, the preganglionic parasympathetics again separate and terminate in the submandibular (submaxillary) ganglion. Here they synapse with the postganglionic neurons that stimulate the submandibular and sublingual salivary glands. From the superior salivatory nucleus, other preganglionic parasympathetic neurons follow a different course and reach the sphenopalatine (pterygopalatine) ganglion, where they synapse with postganglionic neurons (Figure 13–5). These postganglionic neurons follow a complicated pathway to reach the lacrimal gland within the orbit and the mucus-secreting cells of the nasal and oral cavities (Figure 13–5).

**Figure 13–5  The Facial or VII Cranial Nerve**

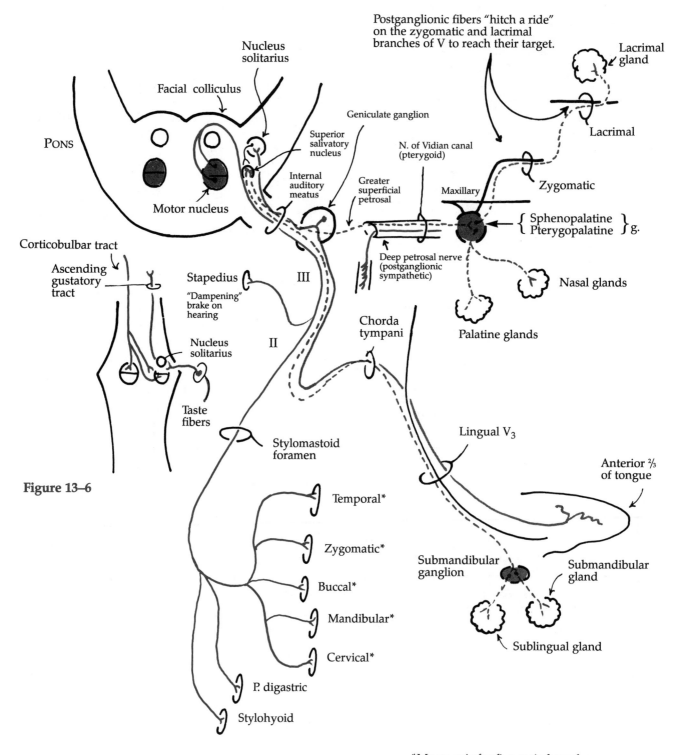

Postganglionic fibers "hitch a ride" on the zygomatic and lacrimal branches of V to reach their target.

Lacrimal gland

Nucleus solitarius

Facial colliculus

Geniculate ganglion

Lacrimal

PONS

Superior salivatory nucleus

N. of Vidian canal (pterygoid)

Zygomatic

Internal auditory meatus

Greater superficial petrosal

Maxillary

{ Sphenopalatine Pterygopalatine } g.

Motor nucleus

Corticobulbar tract

Deep petrosal nerve (postganglionic sympathetic)

Nasal glands

Ascending gustatory tract

Stapedius

III

"Dampening" brake on hearing

Chorda tympani

Palatine glands

Nucleus solitarius

II

Taste fibers

Lingual V₃

Anterior ⅔ of tongue

Figure 13–6

Stylomastoid foramen

Temporal*

Zygomatic*

Submandibular ganglion

Submandibular gland

Buccal*

Mandibular*

Cervical*

Sublingual gland

P. digastric

Stylohyoid

*Mnemonic for five main branches: **T**welve **Z**ulus **B**ecame **M**y **C**lients

50

The facial nerve has voluntary motor fibers to all the muscles of facial expression. Their nucleus is found in the tegmentum of the pons below the nucleus of cranial nerve VI (Figure 13–5). The emerging motor fibers pass up and loop around the abducens nucleus, causing a bulge on the floor of the fourth ventricle known as the *facial colliculus*. These motor fibers then join the rest of the components and enter the internal auditory meatus. After the taste and parasympathetic neurons have separated from the main bundle, the remaining voluntary motor fibers leave the skull via the stylomastoid foramen and separate into five main branches that supply all the muscles of facial expression as well as the posterior belly of the digastric muscle and the stylohyoid. Within the temporal bone some motor fibers supply the stapedius muscle of the middle ear, which acts as a "brake" on the hearing apparatus and prevents hyperacusis (ie, normal sounds heard abnormally loud on the affected side.)

## CLINICAL NOTES

The most common pathologic condition involving the seventh cranial nerve is *Bell's palsy*. In this condition, nerve damage of uncertain etiology quickly results in a characteristic lower motor neuron paralysis consisting of varying degrees of involvement of the muscles of facial expression on one side of the face. The person is unable to close the affected eye because the orbicularis oculi muscle is paralyzed. The unopposed muscles on the unaffected side contract and pull the mouth up in a characteristic grotesque grin. The lesions may affect the stapedius muscle, and the patient will have hyperacusis. In addition, there may be a partial loss of taste and salivation and a total loss of lacrimation on the affected side. From a treatment point of view, there is no cure. There is evidence suggesting that a viral infection (eg, herpes simplex) might be responsible for the associated inflammation (neuritis), and the associated edema may result in compression of the nerve during its course through the temporal bone. In most cases the condition disappears slowly over a period of time ranging from weeks to months. Steroids are usually suggested to reduce the associated inflammation and possibly to shorten its course. Of prime importance is psychologic support of the patient throughout the episode.

Because the lower part of the motor nucleus receives its upper motor neuron supply only from the contralateral corticobulbar tract (Chapter 8), an upper motor or supranuclear lesion will produce a contralateral spastic paralysis of the muscles of the lower half of the face. Because the muscles of the upper half of the face have a bilateral nerve supply, the patient with such a lesion can still close the eyes and wrinkle the brow. These two actions help differentiate Bell's palsy, which is a lower motor neuron paralysis, from an upper motor neuron lesion. Bilateral Bell's palsy is often seen and is characteristic of Lyme disease, which is a spirochete infection transmitted by the bite of the deer tick (see more in Chapter 23).

## THE GLOSSOPHARYNGEAL NERVE (IX)

The glossopharyngeal nerve also has four major components:

1. general sensory fibers from the skin of the external ear and meatus
2. visceral sensory fibers, including taste neurons from the posterior third of the tongue; pain, temperature, and touch from the posterior third of the tongue; the eustachian tube and the inner surface of the tympanic membrane; posterior nasopharynx and oropharynx; and inputs from the carotid sinus
3. voluntary motor fibers to the stylopharyngeus muscle
4. parasympathetic fibers to the parotid gland

The cell bodies of the general sensory fibers of the glossopharyngeal nerve from the external auditory meatus are located primarily in the superior glossopharyngeal ganglion. Centrally, these fibers end, like all general sensory fibers associated with cranial nerves, in the spinal nucleus of the trigeminal nerve (V).

The cell bodies of the neurons of all visceral afferent modalities listed above are located in the inferior glossopharyngeal (petrosal) ganglion (Figure 13–7). Their axons, like those of *all visceral afferent fibers associated with cranial nerves*, end in the *nucleus solitarius*, which extends down from the pons into the medulla. Here they synapse with cell bodies, whose central connections may, as in the case of the ascending gustatory fibers associated with taste, eventually reach conscious levels. The precise pathway and final cortical localization of many of these fibers remain unclear. Other connections from the nucleus solitarius involve important reflexes, such as the gag reflex (see "Clinical Notes"). Another example involves the carotid sinus, which is sensitive to blood pressure changes. A

**Figure 13–7 Glossopharyngeal or Cranial Nerve IX**

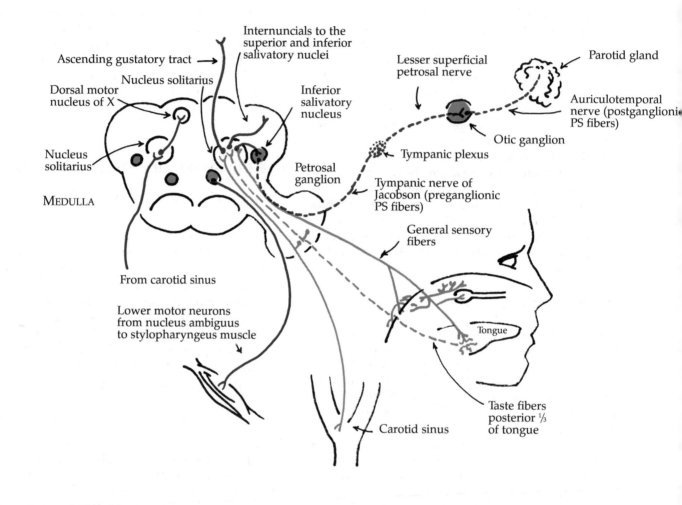

change in blood pressure stimulates this receptor, which initiates a compensatory reflex involving, for example, internuncial neurons that pass to the dorsal motor nucleus of the vagus nerve (cranial nerve X) and synapse with a parasympathetic neuron associated with, for example, the vagus nerve, which might lower the heart rate.

As with the seventh nerve, there are also reflex arcs involving taste. From the nucleus solitarius, short internuncials pass to the inferior salivatory nucleus and synapse with preganglionic parasympathetic neurons. The axons of the latter leave the medulla along with the other glossopharyngeal fibers, but then they separate and follow a long course (Figure 13–5) to reach the otic ganglion. Here they synapse with postganglionic parasympathetic neurons that stimulate the parotid salivary gland. Other internuncials from the nucleus

solitarius pass up and synapse in the superior salivatory nucleus, the fibers of which reach the sublingual and submandibular glands (see the discussion of the facial nerve above).

The motor components of the glossopharyngeal nerve are its parasympathetic innervation of the *parotid gland* and the voluntary motor innervation of the *stylopharyngeus muscle* (Figure 13–7). This is the only muscle innervated by the glossopharyngeal nerve. *The cell bodies of the voluntary motor fibers of the glossopharyngeal (IX), vagus (X), and accessory (XI) nerves are found in the nucleus ambiguus.*

## CLINICAL NOTES

If the uvula or oral pharynx is touched, a gag or swallowing reflex (Figure 13–8) is set off, and the

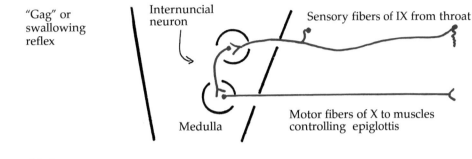

"Gag" or swallowing reflex

Internuncial neuron

Sensory fibers of IX from throat

Medulla

Motor fibers of X to muscles controlling epiglottis

**Figure 13–8**

trachea is closed by the epiglottis. However, when a patient is under general gas anesthesia, this reflex does not work. Furthermore, the unconscious patient often vomits. It is therefore absolutely imperative that, before general surgery, no food or liquid be given to the patient for 8 to 12 hours before the procedure; otherwise the patient may vomit while unconscious, and the acid contents from the stomach may enter the now wide-open trachea and lungs with the potential for aspiration pneumonia or death.

## THE VAGUS NERVE (X)

The vagus nerve (Figure 13–3) also has four major components:

1. general sensory fibers from the external auditory meatus
2. visceral sensory fibers from the lower pharynx (including taste from the area of the epiglottis), larynx, carotid body (chemoreceptor), viscera, and dura
3. voluntary motor fibers to all the muscles of the larynx and pharynx (except the stylopharyngeus)
4. parasympathetic fibers to all the autonomic structures of the chest and abdomen up to the left colic flexure (ie, heart, coronary arteries, bronchioles, stomach, small and large intestine arterioles, and glands; see Figure 12–3)

The cell bodies of the general sensory fibers of the vagus nerve from the external ear are situated in the *superior (jugular) vagal sensory ganglion*, and, like all general sensory fibers of all cranial nerves, their central processes end within the *spinal nucleus of the trigeminal nerve (V)*.

On the other hand, the cell bodies of visceral sensory fibers from the pharynx, larynx, carotid body, and viscera as well as taste fibers from the epiglottis and aryepiglottic folds are located in the *inferior (nodose) vagal ganglion*. Their central processes terminate, like all visceral sensory fibers, in the *nucleus solitarius*.

The parasympathetic motor fibers of the vagus arise from the *dorsal motor nucleus of the vagus nerve*, which is found in the floor of the fourth ventricle of the medulla, just lateral to the hypoglossal nucleus (Appendix II, Plate XIII). The preganglionic fibers leave and descend into the chest and abdomen, where they synapse in ganglia that are situated on or in the organs that are innervated (see Figures 13–3 and 12–3).

The cell bodies of voluntary motor fibers are found in the nucleus ambiguus of the medulla, like those of cranial nerves IX and XI (Figure 13–3 and Appendix II, Plate XIII), and leave the brain stem with the parasympathetic fibers. They soon branch away from the vagus and supply all the muscles of the larynx and pharynx except for the stylopharyngeus. Damage to these motor fibers or their nuclei results in a lower motor neuron paralysis, with difficulty in talking (dysphonia) or swallowing (dysphagia).

# Ganglia Associated with Cranial Nerves

*Sensory Ganglia*                                                     *Parasympathetic Ganglia*

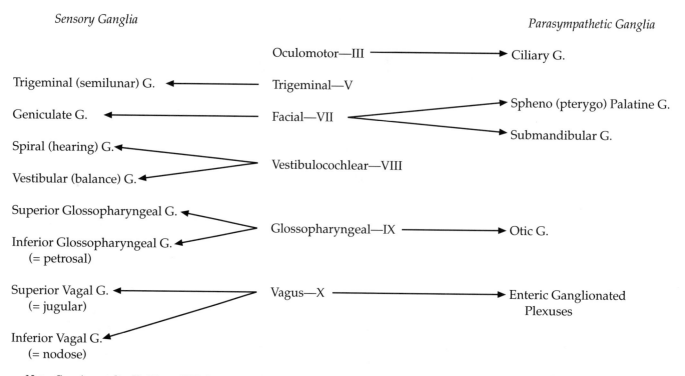

Oculomotor—III ⟶ Ciliary G.

Trigeminal (semilunar) G. ⟵ Trigeminal—V

Geniculate G. ⟵ Facial—VII ⟶ Spheno (pterygo) Palatine G.

Facial—VII ⟶ Submandibular G.

Spiral (hearing) G. ⟵ Vestibulocochlear—VIII

Vestibular (balance) G. ⟵

Superior Glossopharyngeal G. ⟵ Glossopharyngeal—IX ⟶ Otic G.

Inferior Glossopharyngeal G. ⟵
(= petrosal)

Superior Vagal G. ⟵ Vagus—X ⟶ Enteric Ganglionated
(= jugular)                                            Plexuses

Inferior Vagal G. ⟵
(= nodose)

*Note:* See Appendix II, Plate XVI for exiting points of the cranial nerves. See also Appendix VI, "Summary of Cranial Nerves: Innervation and Principal Clinical Signs."

# Schematic of Sensory Innervation of Tongue

| | Posterior ⅓ | Anterior ⅔ |
|---|---|---|
| Pain, Temperature, and Touch | IX | V |
| Taste | IX | VII |

*Note:* Cranial nerves that convey taste:
VII—Anterior ⅔ of tongue and palate
IX—Posterior ⅓ of tongue
X—Epiglottis and aryepiglottic folds

# Chapter 14

# The Auditory Pathway

The eighth cranial nerve, the vestibulocochlear (acoustovestibular), is entirely sensory and has two important parts: the acoustic part, which transmits sound impulses from the ear to the brain, and the vestibular part, which is concerned with maintaining body equilibrium. This chapter deals with the acoustic division, which is basically very simple.

In the cochlear apparatus of the inner ear (see Appendix VIII, Figure 7 and Appendix IX, Figure 5) are situated specialized receptors, the *hair cells*, which are stimulated by auditory vibrations from the external and middle ear. In the cochlea these hair cells synapse with primary neurons, the cell bodies of which are localized in the spiral ganglion, also situated in the cochlea (Figure 14–1). From here, axons pass to the brain stem, enter it at the pontomedullary junction, and immediately bifurcate, with one branch terminating in the *dorsal cochlear nucleus* and the other in the *ventral cochlear nucleus* (Figure 14–1). From the dorsal cochlear nucleus some secondary axons cross over to the other side and ascend to reach the *nucleus of the inferior colliculus*. Others do not cross but rather ascend ipsilaterally and also terminate in the nucleus of the inferior colliculus (Figure 14–1). These ascending crossed and uncrossed fibers make up the *lateral lemniscus*.

Most of the axons from the ventral cochlear nucleus decussate and pass up in the lateral lemniscus to end in the nucleus of the inferior colliculus. A few do not cross over but rather ascend in the ipsilateral lateral lemniscus (Figure 14–1). Thus, both the dorsal and the ventral cochlear nuclei send out *crossed and uncrossed fibers* to the nucleus of the inferior colliculus. From here, fibers are relayed out via the *brachium of the inferior colliculus* to the *medial geniculate body*, which lies adjacent to the superior colliculus. In this body they synapse with neurons, the axons of which form the *auditory radiations* that end in the *transverse gyri of Heschl* located on the dorsomedial surface of the superior temporal gyrus, known as areas 41 and 42—the primary hearing center.

## ACCESSORY DETAILS AND CLINICAL NOTES

The decussating axons from the dorsal and ventral cochlear nuclei form a large, distinct mass, the *trapezoid body* (Figure 14–1). The right and left nuclei of the inferior colliculus are connected to each other by commissural neurons (Figure 14–1). Some of the fibers in the lateral lemniscus don't end in the nucleus of the inferior colliculus but rather pass straight up to the medial geniculate body (Figure 14–1).

On the other hand, many axons from the dorsal and ventral cochlear nuclei do not ascend directly to the midbrain but rather make many synaptic stops along the way. For example, crossed fibers from both nuclei synapse in the superior olivary nucleus, which then relays up to the higher areas (Figure 14–1). This is not important clinically. What is important is the fact that *each auditory cortex receives fibers from the left and right cochlear nuclei;* put another way, the cochlear nuclei of the right side project onto the left and right auditory cortex, and left cochlear nuclei project to both hearing centers. The clinical significance of this bilateral representation is obvious. If, for example, the right auditory cortex is damaged, then the patient will still hear from both ears using the intact left auditory cortex. This holds true for damage at other sites along the central pathway, namely the right medial geniculate body, the right nucleus of the inferior colliculus, or the right lateral lemniscus. However, if the right auditory nerve is cut or damaged anywhere along its path, from the ear up to and including the cochlear nuclei, then the person will be deaf in the right ear, and what holds true for the right side is also true for the left. From the nucleus of the inferior colliculus, internuncial axons pass out to various motor centers to mediate auditory reflexes. For example, when one hears a sudden loud noise, the eyes close and the body "jumps," both of which are reactions of the startle reflex.

In the United States, deafness affects millions of people. It is generally divided into two main types. The first is *conduction deafness*, or middle ear deafness, in which a mechanical impediment prevents sound from reaching the cochlea. The impediment may be a torn eardrum, blockage of the auditory canal, or some other cause. The most common cause, however, is otosclerosis, in which the stapes of the middle ear becomes fixed in the cochlea and cannot transmit its vibrations. The second type is *sensorineural deafness*. As its name implies, it is

**Figure 14–1**

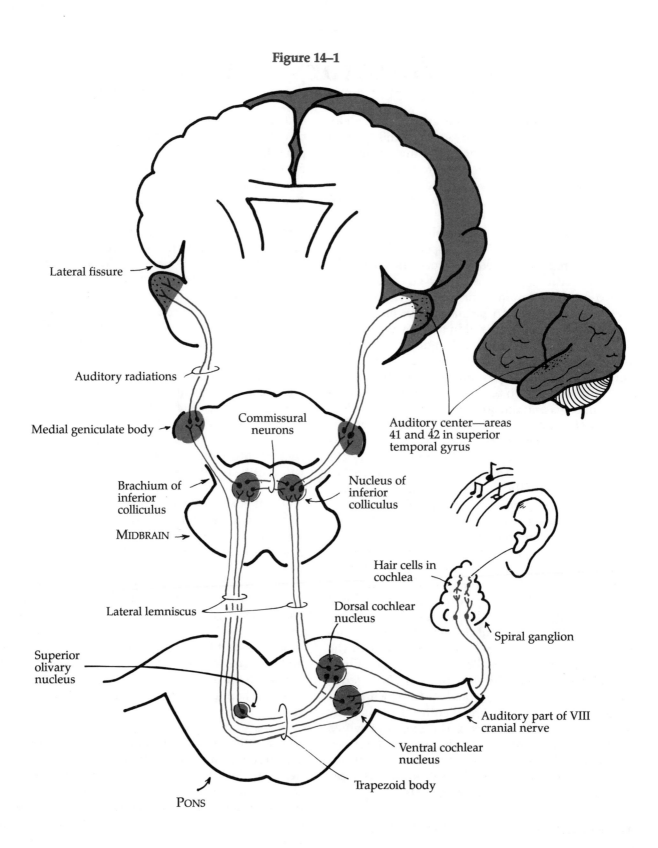

Lateral fissure

Auditory radiations

Medial geniculate body

Commissural neurons

Auditory center—areas 41 and 42 in superior temporal gyrus

Brachium of inferior colliculus

Nucleus of inferior colliculus

MIDBRAIN

Hair cells in cochlea

Spiral ganglion

Lateral lemniscus

Dorsal cochlear nucleus

Superior olivary nucleus

Auditory part of VIII cranial nerve

Ventral cochlear nucleus

Trapezoid body

PONS

caused by damage to either the cochlea or cranial nerve VIII.

The distinction between these two types is important from both a diagnostic and a treatment point of view. In conduction or middle ear deafness, a patient will hear poorly or not at all a vibrating tuning fork that is placed near the ear. However, the patient will hear the tuning fork if it is placed against the skull, because now the vibrations bypass the middle ear and are transmitted directly to the cochlea. On the other hand, in sensorineural deafness the patient will have difficulty hearing a vibrating tuning fork via both air conduction and bone conduction.

In recent years great progress has been made in the treatment of middle ear deafness, especially in otosclerosis. By means of microsurgery, the fixed stapes can be made mobile or even replaced, and the majority of patients show great improvement in their hearing. There are many causes for sensorineural deafness, but the following list (not in order of frequency) mentions only the most common:

- *Rubella infection* in a pregnant woman very often causes her child to be born totally deaf.

- Some *antibiotics* (eg, streptomycin, gentamycin, and neomycin), when given in large doses, may cause partial or total deafness, often accompanied by vestibular disturbances.
- *Atrophy* of the cochlea is one of the most common causes of deafness in the aged.
- *Tumors* such as acoustic neuroma of cranial nerve VIII can produce deafness (see Figures 11 and 14 in Appendix IX).
- There are many forms of *hereditary deafness* caused by genetic defects.

For patients who once heard and then became deaf (sensorineuronal type), scientists and physicians developed an ingenious "bionic ear." The patient wears a small electronic microphone that picks up sound waves and converts them to electric impulses that are then relayed to a small amplifier he or she wears. From this a special wire is implanted into the individual's cochlea, and the amplified sound is heard clearly. The results have been good except for those individuals who were born deaf or developed sensorineuronal deafness early in life.

# Chapter 15

# Visual Pathways and Optic Reflexes

## VISUAL PATHWAYS

The visual pathways are among the most important pathways of the nervous system, and, because injuries to them are common, the physician must know and understand them "cold."

Light rays from an object in the visual field enter the eyeball (see Appendix VIII, Figure 6), are inverted by the lens, and strike the nervous layer, the *retina*. The retina is composed of several layers and types of neurons, including the light-sensitive *rods* and the *cones*. Each eye has a temporal and a nasal visual field, and, because of the inversion by the lens, *the temporal visual field is projected onto the nasal retinal field, and the nasal visual field falls on the temporal retinal field* (Figure 15–1). *Loss of vision is always described with reference to the visual fields, not the retinal fields.* These concepts can be quite confusing at first, and it pays for the student to read and review each concept slowly and attentively.

Axons from nerve cells in the retina pass posteriorly in the optic nerve (see Appendix VIII, Figure 6). At the chiasma, those from the nasal retinal field cross over to join the axons from the temporal retinal field, which do not cross (Figure 15–1). Together they continue posteriorly in the optic tract and end in the lateral geniculate body of the diencephalon. Here they synapse with neurons that sweep out to form the optic radiations, which end in the visual cortex of the occipital lobe. This cortex begins at the occipital pole and is situated on the cuneus and lingual gyrus, which border on the calcarine fissure (Figures 15–1 and 15–2). *Thus the left visual field of each eye is represented on the right occipital cortex, whereas the right visual fields are represented on the left occipital cortex* (Figure 15–1). The lens also inverts the upper visual field onto the lower part of the retina and vice versa (Figure 15–2). This pattern is maintained throughout the pathway, so that the cuneus, which is above the calcarine fissure, receives impulses from the lower visual field and the lingual gyrus, which is below the fissure, gets impulses from the upper visual field (Figure 15–2). Finally, the *macula*, the central area of the retina where vision is the sharpest, sends its impulses to the occipital poles (Figure 15–1).

## CLINICAL NOTES

In an eye examination, the fields of vision of each eye are tested and mapped out. If, for example, the right optic nerve is damaged (Example 1, Figure 15–1) both fields of vision of that eye are affected; in short, *anopsia* or *blindness* of the right eye results.

Example 2 in Figure 15–1 illustrates how an aneurysm of the right internal carotid artery, which lies adjacent to the lateral part of the optic chiasma, can interfere with the temporal axons from the right retina, thus producing *hemianopsia* (half-blindness) in the right eye. Because the visual field affected is the nasal field, we speak of a nasal hemianopsia of the right eye, or right nasal hemianopsia.

Example 3 in Figure 15–1 shows how the pituitary gland, lying below the optic tracts near the chiasma, can develop an expanding tumor that presses on the decussating nasal axons. This can produce hemianopsia in the temporal visual field of both eyes—a *bitemporal hemianopsia*. Homonymous hemianopsia is a result of a lesion beyond the optic chiasm (eg, in the optic tract, radiations, etc). It affects the visual fields of both eyes; in a left homonymous hemianopsia it is the left visual fields of both eyes that are affected, whereas in a right homonymous hemianopsia it is the right visual fields that are affected.

Examples 4, 5, and 6 in Figure 15–1 illustrate how a lesion in the right optic tract, the right optic radiations, or the right visual cortex can produce loss of vision in the left visual fields of both eyes, which is called a *left homonymous hemianopsia*.

Because the visual field of each eye is divided into nasal and temporal parts plus upper and lower parts, the term *quadrant* is used to denote them (eg, upper quadrants or lower right quadrant; Figure 15–3). There can also be various quadratic anopsias.

## OPTIC REFLEXES

If light from a small source, such as a pencil flashlight, is shone into one eye from a short distance,

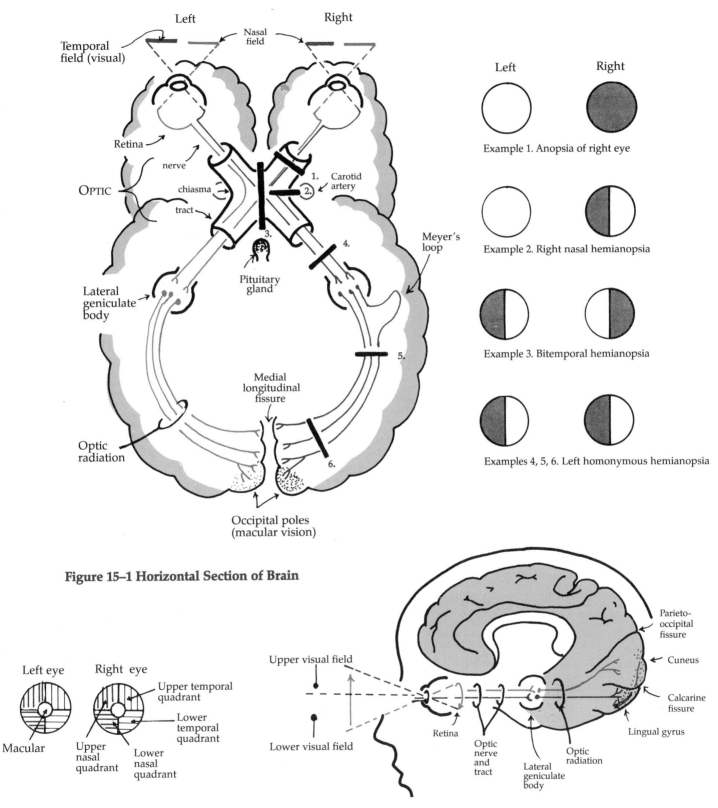

Left    Right

Temporal field (visual)

Nasal field

Retina

nerve

OPTIC

chiasma

tract

1. Carotid artery
2.

3.

Pituitary gland

4.

Meyer's loop

Lateral geniculate body

Medial longitudinal fissure

5.

Optic radiation

6.

Occipital poles (macular vision)

**Figure 15–1 Horizontal Section of Brain**

Left    Right

Example 1. Anopsia of right eye

Example 2. Right nasal hemianopsia

Example 3. Bitemporal hemianopsia

Examples 4, 5, 6. Left homonymous hemianopsia

Left eye    Right eye

Upper temporal quadrant

Lower temporal quadrant

Macular

Upper nasal quadrant

Lower nasal quadrant

**Figure 15–3 Map of Visual Fields**

Upper visual field

Lower visual field

Parieto-occipital fissure

Cuneus

Calcarine fissure

Lingual gyrus

Retina

Optic nerve and tract

Lateral geniculate body

Optic radiation

**Figure 15–2 Midsagittal View of Brain**

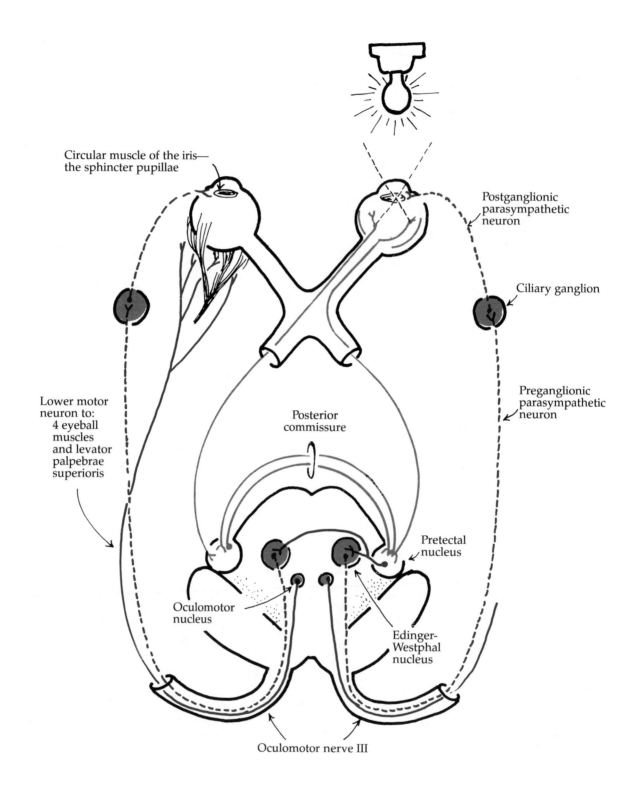

Circular muscle of the iris—
the sphincter pupillae

Postganglionic
parasympathetic
neuron

Ciliary ganglion

Lower motor
neuron to:
4 eyeball
muscles
and levator
palpebrae
superioris

Posterior
commissure

Preganglionic
parasympathetic
neuron

Pretectal
nucleus

Oculomotor
nucleus

Edinger-
Westphal
nucleus

Oculomotor nerve III

**Figure 15–4**

there will be pupillary reflex constriction in both eyes, a reaction known as a *consensual reflex*. As you have just learned, optic tract fibers end in the lateral geniculate body. However, about 1% of them peel off just before reaching the geniculate body and terminate in the pretectal nucleus of the midbrain (Figure 15–4). From here, internuncial fibers pass to the parasympathetic Edinger-Westphal nucleus, which then automatically discharges motor stimuli to the circular muscle of the iris, causing pupillary constriction (Figure 15–4). Therefore, there are three ways that light impulses from one eye can cause reflex constriction in both pupils:

1. Some optic fibers from the right eye's nasal retinal field cross in the chiasm to reach the contralateral pretectal nucleus (Figure 15–4).
2. The right and left pretectal nuclei are interconnected by commissural neurons that pass through the *posterior commissure*. Therefore, a stimulus reaching one nucleus is relayed to the other (Figure 15–4).
3. Each pretectal nucleus sends out fibers to both the right and the left Edinger-Westphal nuclei (Figure 15–4).

## CLINICAL NOTES

The pupillary light reflex is one of the most useful and important reflexes in medical practice, and it occurs even when a person is unconscious. If it cannot be elicited, a serious condition in the central nervous system, especially the brain stem, is indicated. Also, a unilateral dilated pupil that doesn't react to light is a serious sign suggesting cerebral herniation pressing on the oculomotor nerve and midbrain. The neurosurgeon should be called in immediately.

Morphine should not be given to patients with head injuries or increased intracranial pressure for two reasons: First, morphine causes fixed, pinpoint pupils and thereby interferes with normal or abnormal pupillary reflexes that indicate to the physician what's happening in the cranium. Second, morphine produces brain edema, and in a head injury this added volume may cause serious damage.

Pupillary reflexes—dilation (*mydriasis*) and constriction (*miosis*)—are also important in general anesthesia. Here, according to the degree of dilation or constriction (as well as other signs), the anesthetist knows accurately what stages and planes of anesthesia the patient is in (stages and planes refer to the degrees of depth of unconsciousness).

The Edinger-Westphal nucleus is also concerned with the accommodation reflex, whereby the lens of the eye accommodates itself for near and far vision. From this nucleus, motor stimuli are sent out over the preganglionic and postganglionic fibers to reach the ciliary muscle, which controls the anteroposterior (front-to-back) diameter of the lens. This is a complex reflex that involves cortical areas as well as the *nucleus of Perla*, which is concerned with the convergence of the eyes.

In Chapter 12 it was mentioned that physicians often put an atropine solution in the eye to dilate the pupil and so have a larger "window" to look through.* However, it is important first to make sure that the patient doesn't have glaucoma because dilation in these patients can bring a rapid, sharp increase in the intraocular pressure and cause damage to the sensitive retina.

*Glaucoma* is a group of acute or chronic diseases of the eye involving increased intraocular pressure. If left untreated, it can result in blindness (even with detection and treatment, it is a major cause of blindness in the United States). A frequent pathognomonic sign is the patient's complaint of seeing haloes around light sources. However, not all patients experience this phenomenon, and some do not even know that they have the disease. A routine screening test for glaucoma involves the measurement of intraocular pressure by placement of a tonometer on the corneal surface. The intraocular pressure normally ranges between 13 and 29 mm Hg.

---

*Atropine causes prolonged accommodation paralysis. Many shorter-acting derivatives of atropine are now available.

# Chapter 16

# The Olfactory System

Many lower animal forms, such as dogs, deer, amphibians, and certain birds, depend primarily on the sense of smell to locate food, to distinguish friend from foe, and to attract the opposite sex. Consequently, the olfactory system is highly developed in these animals and is closely connected to the aggressive drive necessary to obtain the above-mentioned objects. In humans, the sense of smell is probably the least important of the major senses, but its pathways, carried over from lower forms, are probably the most complex of the nervous system. There is a great deal of contradictory data based on experiments in animals, and beginning students who open most neuroanatomy texts find themselves immersed in a welter of conflicting theories couched in the most obtuse and strange terminology. This chapter discusses the basic, generally agreed-upon facts concerning the olfactory system and touches lightly on the experimental data.

In the epithelial tissue of the nasal cavity are located receptor cells sensitive to smell. These first-order neurons, which are *bipolar*, pass up into the olfactory bulb, where they synapse with second-order neurons whose axons form the *olfactory tract*. This tract runs posteriorly and then bifurcates into lateral and medial olfactory tracts, or *striae* (Figures 16–1 and 16–2). The area between the bifurcating striae forms the *anterior perforated area* (Figure 16–2). The axons of the medial olfactory stria terminate in the *paraolfactory (septal) area* and the *anterior perforated area*; some enter the anterior commissure and cross over to terminate in the contralateral septal area (Figures 16–1 and 16–2). The fibers of the lateral olfactory stria end in the *cortex of the uncus* and in the underlying *amygdaloid nucleus* (Figures 16–1 and 16–2). It is believed that the septal area, the anterior perforated substance, and the cortex of the uncus are the cerebral areas concerned with the "interpretation" of smell (ie, they are the primary olfactory areas or centers).

In humans the sense of smell can trigger memories, various emotions, and their related reflexes. For example, the smell of good food causes pleasure and salivation, whereas that of rotten eggs causes disgust, nausea, and even vomiting. An enticing perfume may result in sexual arousal (isn't that its basic purpose?), whereas other odors may elicit long-forgotten memories.*

The major reflex pathways and centers that constitute the *limbic system* are as follows: From the amygdaloid nucleus, fibers collect in a bundle, the *stria terminalis*, which loops around and terminates in the hypothalamus (Figure 16–3). The amygdala also sends short fibers to the adjacent *hippocampus*, where they synapse with neurons that form a large bundle, the *fornix*. This distinctive tract curves up and around to end in the *mamillary bodies of the hypothalamus* (Figure 16–3). Finally, from the septal or paraolfactory area, short fibers pass to terminate also in the hypothalamus (Figure 16–3). It isn't surprising that all these reflex pathways end in the hypothalamus, for, as shown in the following chapter, this is the main coordination and reflex discharge center for many sensations, such as smell, taste, and emotions, as well as the control center of the autonomic nervous system. Reflex discharge pathways carry smell sensations from the hypothalamus to the appropriate motor nuclei and reticular areas in the brain stem. The two main tracts are the *mamillotegmental* and the *dorsal longitudinal fasciculi* (Figure 16–3). Finally, from the mamillary bodies there is a large bundle, the *mamillothalamic tract*, which ends in the *anterior group of the thalamic nuclei*. From here the impulses are relayed to the *cingulate gyrus* (Figure 16–3). In spite of much experimental work, the functional significance of this pathway remains poorly understood.

## ACCESSORY DETAILS

The limbic system refers to the numerous olfactory reflex centers and their various pathways. These include the amygdala, hippocampus, pyriform area, fornix, stria terminalis, stria medullaris thalami, indusium griseum, median forebrain bundle, habenula, habenular commissure, fasciculus retroflexus, diagonal band of Broca, and so forth. These structures have attracted great interest from theoretical and experimental points of

---

*A well-known case in literature is Proust's *Remembrance of Things Past.*

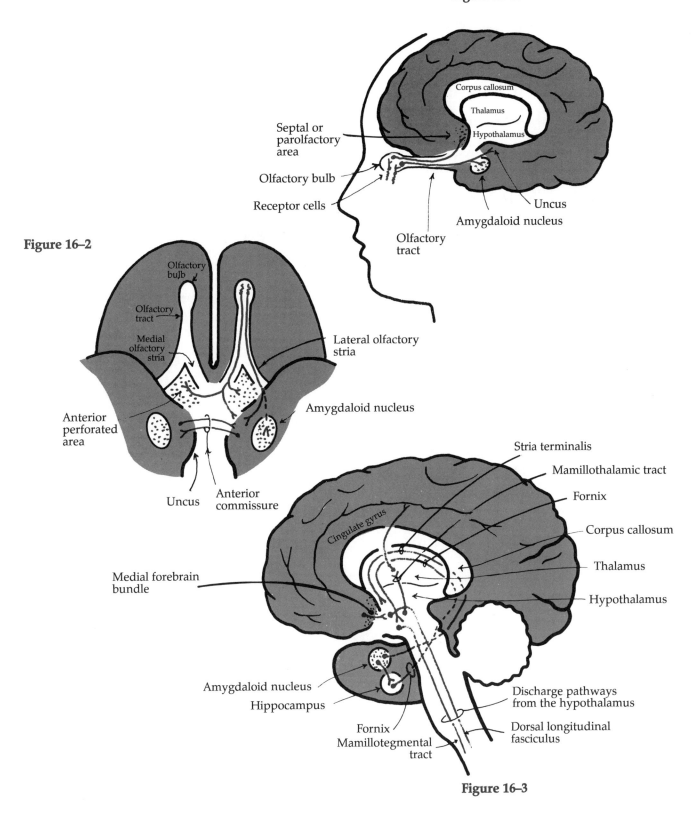

**Figure 16–1**

Corpus callosum

Thalamus

Septal or parolfactory area

Hypothalamus

Olfactory bulb

Receptor cells

Uncus

Amygdaloid nucleus

Olfactory tract

**Figure 16–2**

Olfactory bulb

Olfactory tract

Medial olfactory stria

Lateral olfactory stria

Anterior perforated area

Amygdaloid nucleus

Uncus

Anterior commissure

Stria terminalis

Mamillothalamic tract

Fornix

Corpus callosum

Cingulate gyrus

Thalamus

Medial forebrain bundle

Hypothalamus

Amygdaloid nucleus

Hippocampus

Discharge pathways from the hypothalamus

Fornix

Mamillotegmental tract

Dorsal longitudinal fasciculus

**Figure 16–3**

63

view. However, it was Mike Liebman's view (and in all honesty I cannot disagree with him), that medical students should not be required to know all these complicated pathways and connections. What is shown in the drawings and discussed above is sufficient.

## CLINICAL NOTES

Loss of smell usually results from damage to the receptor cells, the olfactory bulb, or the olfactory tract and is known medically as *anosmia*. Lesions of the temporal lobe in the area of the uncus and the amygdala often produce olfactory hallucinations, epileptic seizures, or a combination of both; these are known as *uncinate fits* when the epileptic fit is preceded by an unpleasant olfactory aura.

In monkeys the removal of the amygdala results in a docile, somnolent animal, whereas in cats the same procedure results in aggressive behavior in unprovoked situations, a condition known as sham rage. However, in both species the procedure causes a greatly increased sexual drive.

## DIAGNOSTIC TESTS

The sense of smell is tested separately in each nostril. Close one nostril and then successively pass vials containing various nonirritative substances, such as pine oil, coffee, and perfume, under the open nostril. Ask the patient if he or she smells the substance and can identify it. A gradual unilateral loss of smell may indicate the presence of a tumor in the frontal lobe. A good sense of smell is also a useful diagnostic tool for the physician or paramedic. For example, the underlying cause of a patient's coma may be deduced by the odor of the breath. In diabetic coma, the breath smells like sweet-spoiled fruit. Alcohol has its own well-known smell (vodka being excepted), whereas uremic coma produces a uriniferous odor. In hepatic coma there is a stinking, musty smell to the breath.

# Chapter 17

# The Reticular System

Phylogenetically, the reticular system is an old system. It is divided anatomically and physiologically into two parts: a descending and an ascending formation.

## DESCENDING RETICULAR FORMATION

The descending reticular formation is a system concerned with:

1. relaying impulses from the hypothalamus to preganglionic neurons of the autonomic nervous system
2. relaying involuntary motor impulses from the extrapyramidal systems to voluntary muscles

Scattered deep in the brain stem are the groups of diffuse nuclei or areas (some authors and investigators call them "formations") belonging to this system. In the midbrain they are called the *deep* and *dorsal tegmental nuclei*, in the pons they are called the *central tegmental nucleus*, and in the medulla they are the *central* and *inferior nuclei*. Some books also mention other descending reticular nuclei or call them by different names, but the main point to grasp is not the exact number of nuclei but the fact that they exist and their functions.

These nuclei or formations receive stimuli from the hypothalamic fiber tracts, such as the dorsal longitudinal fasciculus and the mamillotegmental tract (Figure 17–1). In addition, various basal ganglia, such as the globus pallidus, the substantia nigra, and the subthalamic nucleus, project fibers that terminate in these nuclei. Last, the vestibular system, which is also extrapyramidal, sends some of its fibers to the reticular nuclei (see Chapters 10 and 11).

These incoming fibers synapse with neurons whose axons then leave the reticular nuclei and form the lateral and medial *reticulospinal tracts*. These are descending, crossed, and uncrossed multisynaptic pathways that travel down to all levels of the spinal cord in the lateral and ventral white columns. In the cord they synapse either on the ventral horn cells, which form the final common pathway, or on the preganglionic neurons in the intermediate gray horn.

## ASCENDING RETICULAR FORMATION

The ascending reticular formation, better known as the *reticular activating system*, is concerned with degrees of conscious alertness as well as with sleep. Situated in the medulla, pons, and midbrain are groups of poorly defined nuclei connected to each other by a chain of multisynaptic neurons. Because the nuclei and their interconnecting chain have a diffuse and poorly defined appearance, they were given the name *reticular system*.

All the major sensory pathways (eg, the spinothalamic, for pain, temperature, touch, and pressure; the auditory; and the visual) send collateral axons that end in the nuclei of the reticular activating system. These nuclei then send the sensory stimuli they have received up the multisynaptic chain, which ends primarily in a group of nuclei of the thalamus known as the *midline group*. As has already been shown, the thalamus serves as a relay center for many sensory pathways as well as for motor ones, and it is not surprising that it also serves as a relay for the reticular activating system. From the thalamic midline nuclei, impulses are relayed up to the cerebral cortex, where they influence states of mental alertness and sleep. Exactly how these impulses are relayed and what specific regions of the cerebral cortex they reach are not well defined.

Sleeping animals and humans exhibit characteristic wave patterns on electroencephalography (EEG). If the reticular activating nuclei of sleeping animals are stimulated experimentally, the animals awaken, and we see that the change from sleep to wakefulness is accompanied by a change in the EEG wave pattern. In animals that are already awake, stimulation of the reticular activating nuclei produces states of greater alertness, which are also accompanied by characteristic changes in the EEG pattern. It is therefore assumed that alertness and sleep are largely dependent on the number of stimuli reaching the cerebral cortex via the reticular activating system. If the number of stimuli from the outside world is reduced, there will be a lowering of alertness, and sleep may result. On the other hand, an increase in the amount of stimulation reaching the cerebral cortex via the

**Figure 17–1 Schematic Diagram of the Descending Reticular Formation**

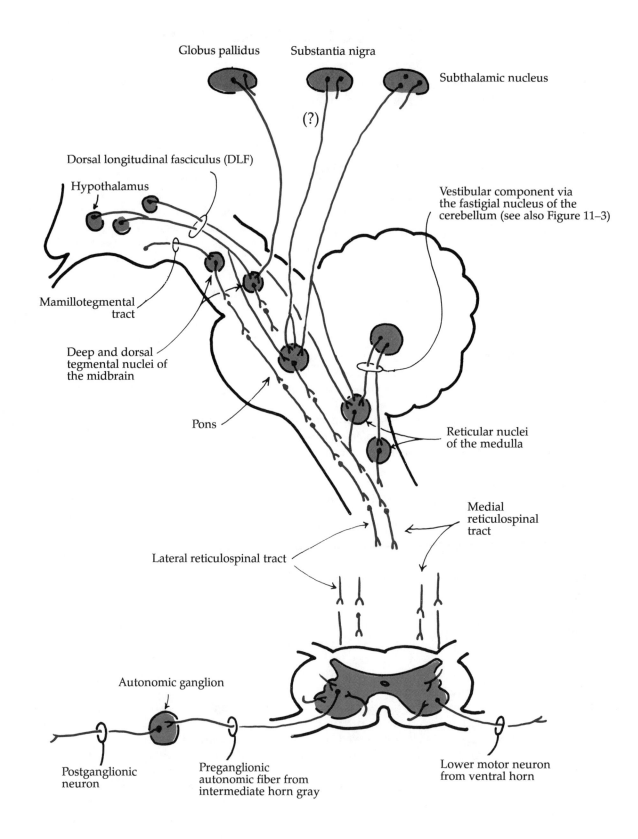

ascending reticular formation results in greater alertness. In a nutshell:

> ↓ stimulation from various sensory systems into reticular nuclei → ↓ amount of stimulation to the thalamic midline nuclei → ↓ stimulus to cerebral cortex → ↓ alertness and/or sleep

This simple outline is just one aspect of an extremely complex picture, most of which is still unknown to us. One should not conclude that sleep or alertness is totally dependent on the state of the reticular activating system; there are many other factors (eg, metabolic and psychologic factors) that play a part in alertness and sleep.

## CLINICAL NOTES

Although there is no known center for sleep or consciousness, it is believed that the reticular formation in the brain stem is primarily involved because damage to it often produces states of unconsciousness or coma (this is suggested by postmortem examination of the brain). Mike Liebman had a friend who was sitting in a car that had stopped for a red light. It was struck from behind by another car, and the driver experienced a severe whiplash, with no other known injuries, and was in a coma for more than 2 years.

### Concussion

This is usually defined as a transient state of unconsciousness caused by a sudden sharp blow to the head. Upon awakening, there may be episodes of vomiting.

### Stupor

This is a state of unconsciousness from which the patient is aroused with difficulty and, when awake, is mentally confused.

### Coma

This is a state of unconsciousness resembling sleep from which the individual cannot be aroused even by the strongest stimuli. Coma varies in degree. For example, in deep coma there is a complete absence of response to stimuli, and most reflexes are lost. In lighter stages the patient may respond to sounds, some reflexes and movements are present, and the eyes may be open. Many pathologic conditions can produce coma or comatose states, but the three most common causes are alcoholism or other drug intoxications, injuries to the head, and cerebrovascular accidents (CVAs; strokes). From a diagnostic perspective the etiology of coma falls into three main groups:

1. *Traumatic and vascular (CVA):* Pupillary reflexes are nearly always absent or abnormal; intracranial pressure is usually increased; the EEG is usually normal.
2. *Substance abuse or toxic substances (alcohol, drugs, poisons):* Pupillary reflexes are usually (but not always) present; intracranial pressure is usually normal; the EEG is usually normal
3. *Metabolic (diabetic acidosis, hypoglycemia, hepatic problems, Addisonian crises, etc):* Pupillary reflexes are usually present; cerebrospinal fluid pressure is usually normal; the EEG is nearly always abnormal. (Remember that your sense of smell can help you deduce the cause; see diagnostic tests in Chapter 16.)

---

From a treatment point of view, and in all circumstances of loss of consciousness, remember:

### ABCD

**A**—Maintain *airway* and avoid aspiration by correct positioning of the patient.
**B**—Maintain and monitor *blood pressure.*
**C**—Avoid *cardiac and circulatory* collapse.
**D**—Attempt to reach a *diagnosis*, remembering the limitations and difficulties of examination of the unconscious patient, and withdraw blood for hematologic, biochemical, and toxicologic analyses.

---

Dr Andres Kanner of University of Wisconsin Hospital reported a case where a man who had been in a vegetative state for 8 years came out of his condition after the administration of diazepam. The patient was lucid and remembered his name, occupation, and so forth. After a few hours, he relapsed into his vegetative state but again regained consciousness when given diazepam. Whether this is an isolated, idiosyncratic reaction remains to be seen. This report underscores two points: first, how little we know about these conditions; and second, that we shouldn't quickly give up hope and "throw in the sponge." As Yogi Berra once said, "The game ain't over 'til it's over." In medicine, as you know, it's sometimes over, but if you work fast you can start it again.

# Chapter 18

# The Hypothalamus

The hypothalamus is one of the smallest areas of the brain, yet no other region is known to have quite so many different and vital functions. It is seen well in a midsagittal section (Plates III and IV in Appendix II). As its name indicates, it lies beneath the thalamus, where it extends from the lamina terminalis to the midbrain. Separating it from the overlying thalamus is a shallow groove, the *hypothalamic sulcus*. The hypothalamus thus forms the lateral wall of the lower part of the third ventricle and is also seen in cross-sections (Plate VI in Appendix II). If one looks at the base of the brain, the hypothalamus is seen as forming the area that lies posterior to the optic chiasm and includes the infundibulum and mamillary bodies. Packed into this small region are many nuclei and areas (Figure 18–1) that are concerned with such functions as temperature control, sleep, water metabolism, secretion of hormones, control of blood pressure, hunger, and maintenance of balance between the sympathetic and parasympathetic divisions. It also plays a part in emotional reactions and possibly other situations.

## HEAT REGULATION

The *anterior hypothalamic area* is concerned with heat regulation of the body. When there is an increase in body temperature, the heated blood passes through the anterior hypothalamic area and sets off a mechanism that facilitates heat loss (Figure 18–2). Fibers leave the anterior hypothalamic area and join the *dorsal longitudinal fasciculus* (DLF), which is the major descending pathway from the hypothalamus. The DLF terminates in the descending reticular nuclei of the brain stem, where it synapses with neurons of the medial and lateral reticulospinal tracts. These then descend the cord and stimulate the sympathetic nervous system and voluntary muscles. Other fibers of the DLF terminate in and stimulate the cardiac and respiratory centers in the medulla. The results of all these stimuli are the following reactions, which serve to reduce body temperature:

- dilation of peripheral blood vessels beneath the skin with a subsequent increase in heat radiation

- an increase in sweating, which reduces heat (evaporation is a cooling process)
- an increase in respiratory rate, with "blowing off" of hot air from the lungs
- a decrease in the body's metabolic rate
- an increase in peripheral blood flow accompanied by increased heat dissipation

If we experimentally destroy an animal's anterior hypothalamic region, it becomes unable to respond to heat increases in its environment. Thus, when the temperature rises, body temperature rises, and eventually death occurs from heat prostration (hyperthermia).

Cold regulation is controlled by the posterior hypothalamic area. When the temperature of the environment drops, the body becomes cooler. The cooled blood passes through the posterior hypothalamic area (Figure 18–2) and sets off a mechanism that is directly the opposite of the one just discussed. The pathways are basically the same: the DLF, reticular nuclei, and reticulospinal tracts. The reactions that are set off to conserve body heat are as follows:

- peripheral vasoconstriction with a subsequent decrease in the amount of heat lost by radiation (therefore, the body seems cold)
- a decrease in peripheral blood flow
- an increase in body metabolism
- shivering of voluntary muscles; shivering is work in which energy, in the form of heat, is produced
- a decrease in the respiratory rate

Experimental lesions in the *posterior hypothalamic area* of animals prevent them from adjusting to cold environments, and their bodies become as cold as the surroundings (poikilothermic).

## WATER BALANCE (OSMOREGULATION)

The hypothalamic mechanism for maintaining water balance is one of the most interesting regulatory mechanisms of the body. It is known that a hormone from the posterior pituitary body, called *antidiuretic hormone* (ADH), acts on the distal convoluted tubules of the kidney, causing resorption of

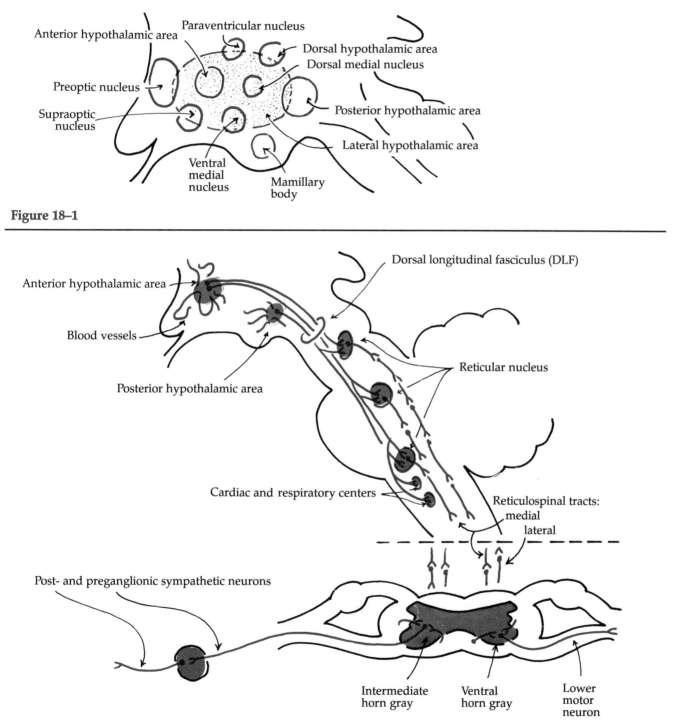

**Figure 18–1**

Anterior hypothalamic area

Paraventricular nucleus

Dorsal hypothalamic area

Dorsal medial nucleus

Preoptic nucleus

Supraoptic nucleus

Posterior hypothalamic area

Ventral medial nucleus

Mamillary body

Lateral hypothalamic area

Dorsal longitudinal fasciculus (DLF)

Anterior hypothalamic area

Blood vessels

Reticular nucleus

Posterior hypothalamic area

Cardiac and respiratory centers

Reticulospinal tracts:
medial
lateral

Post- and preganglionic sympathetic neurons

Intermediate horn gray

Ventral horn gray

Lower motor neuron

**Figure 18–2**

water. If the amount of ADH produced is reduced, a pathologic condition known as *diabetes insipidus* results. In this disease the patient can urinate 18 to 20 L of urine per day instead of the normal 1 to 2 L and also drinks large amounts of fluids (polydipsia) to replace the loss. The regulatory mechanism in the production and release of ADH is a function of the *supraoptic nucleus* of the hypothalamus. The cells of this nucleus and possibly those of the *paraventricular nucleus* produce ADH, and this *neurosecretion* passes down the axons of the neurons, via axonal transport, to reach the cells of the posterior pituitary (Figure 18–3), where the ADH is either stored or released into the capillary network.

If there is a reduction in the amount of water in the blood, the cells of the supraoptic nucleus, which are sensitive to such a change, will produce and release more ADH. This results in more water being resorbed by the kidney tubules and its conservation by the body. On the other hand, if there is a state of hydration, the cells of the supraoptic nucleus react by decreasing the production and release of ADH. This decrease in the production and release of ADH results in a decrease in the amount of water resorption by the kidneys, and therefore a greater amount is urinated (polyuria).

## INFLUENCE OF THE HYPOTHALAMUS ON THE SECRETION OF HORMONES FROM THE ANTERIOR LOBE OF THE PITUITARY

There is much evidence that cells of the hypothalamus *can in part* influence the secretion of various hormones of the anterior lobe of the pituitary gland. The mechanism resembles that of water metabolism. Neurosecretory cells of the hypothalamus are sensitive to the blood concentration of the various anterior lobe hormones. In response to a decrease, these neurons produce a neurosecretion that passes down the axons. However, the axons terminate in the region of the infundibulum, and here the neurosecretion is "picked up" by a pituitary portal system (Figure 18–4). This carries the neurosecretion to the anterior lobe, where it stimulates the cells to produce the various hormones. One must not conclude that the hypothalamus is the only, or principal, regulator of hormones from the anterior lobe. There are other mechanisms, such as a direct feedback control, as well as mechanisms that are not yet clearly understood.

## HYPOTHALAMIC DISCHARGE IN EMOTIONAL STATES

Various emotional states, such as well-being, result in physiologic reactions. The hypothalamus is a center for the control and discharge of such reactions. For example, when one sees or hears something that evokes an angry reaction, the stimuli first reach various areas of the cerebral cortex, such as the visual or auditory centers, the memory centers, or the personality area of the frontal lobe, all of which are interconnected by association tracts. From the cerebral cortex, especially its frontal lobe, there is a discharge pathway to the hypothalamus. From the latter, the major descending pathway is the *dorsal longitudinal fasciculus*, which arises from all the hypothalamic nuclei and areas except the supraoptic and ventral medial nuclei (a minor pathway is the mamillotegmental tract). The dorsal longitudinal fasciculus leaves the hypothalamus and passes down the length of the brain stem, where it gives off branches to all the descending reticular nuclei; all the parasympathetic nuclei of cranial nerves III, VII, IX, and X; the respiratory and cardiac centers; and the motor nuclei of the cranial nerves (Figure 18–2). From the reticular nuclei emerge the lateral and medial reticulospinal tracts, which descend the cord to supply the autonomic nervous system as well as the voluntary muscles. Thus we see the complex interrelationship that exists among various parts of the brain, and one must proceed with great caution in applying new surgical or other techniques, such as lobotomies.

The hypothalamus is also involved in the olfactory reflex system (see Chapter 16). Finally, experimental work in animals has demonstrated that destruction of the ventral medial nucleus produces a voracious, almost insatiable, appetite, whereas destruction of the lateral hypothalamic area produces animals that have no appetite. Clinically, we see that some patients who have tumors of the hypothalamus lose their appetites and become emaciated.

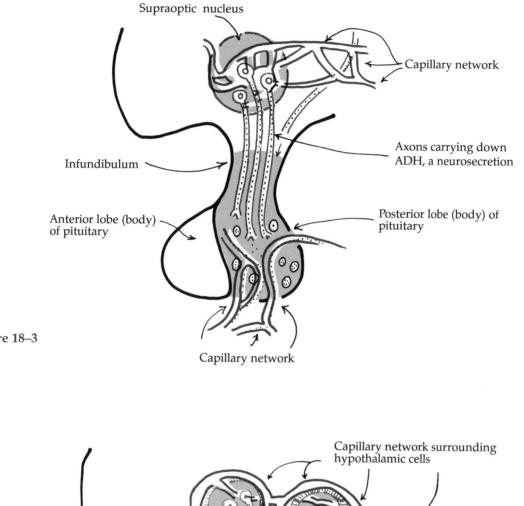

Supraoptic nucleus

Capillary network

Infundibulum

Axons carrying down
ADH, a neurosecretion

Anterior lobe (body)
of pituitary

Posterior lobe (body) of
pituitary

**Figure 18–3**

Capillary network

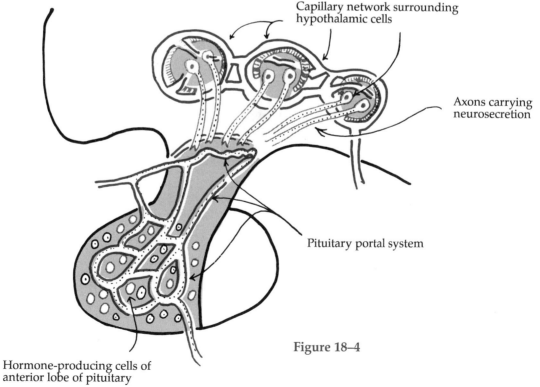

Capillary network surrounding
hypothalamic cells

Axons carrying
neurosecretion

Pituitary portal system

**Figure 18–4**

Hormone-producing cells of
anterior lobe of pituitary

# Chapter 19

# The Cerebral Cortex

The cerebral cortex is most highly developed in humans. It is responsible for the qualities that distinguish humans from other animals, for example the ability to use the hand for skilled and intricate movements, a high level of speech, symbolic thought, personality, and conscience. We know this because damage to certain areas of the cortex results in loss or diminution of specific functions or qualities.

In submammalian species, the cerebral cortex is small and concerned quite extensively with smell, which is for them one of the most important sensations (see Chapter 16). This cortex is the *archicortex* and *paleocortex*. The thalamus is the main sensory receptor area, and the basal ganglia and subthalamic nuclei serve as the motor discharge areas. Because fine, complicated, voluntary movements are not seen in these lower forms, the cerebellum is primarily a center for equilibrium, which is a function of its flocculonodular lobe.

As one ascends the evolutionary ladder, the cerebral cortex enlarges and takes on other functions; this is the *neocortex*. The main sensory area is now localized in the postcentral gyrus, and its former center, the thalamus, now becomes a center that relays the sensory impulses from the body to the cortex. With the appearance of the cerebral motor cortex, the basal ganglia in humans become areas of crude motor activity. Parallel with the development of this motor cortex, there is a great development of the cerebellum as a coordination center for muscle activity, but the floccular nodulus remains the center for body equilibrium. In humans some functions, such as smell, decrease greatly in importance, although the complicated pathways remain.

With the increase in complexity and functions, there is an increase in the number of neurons of the neocortex, and they are arranged in six characteristic layers. The area of the cerebral cortex increases to such a degree that the cortex, to expand in the same volume area, is thrown into folds, giving the characteristic appearance of gyri and sulci (see Appendix VIII, Figures 1 through 5; in lower forms, such as the rat, the surface of the cerebral cortex is smooth). This same principle is used by restaurant owners in high-rent areas: Instead of having straight counters, they make them convoluted and thus squeeze in more customers.

As has been mentioned throughout this text, certain areas of the cortex have specific functions (see Appendix VII). The precentral gyrus (area 4) is concerned with initiating voluntary movements, whereas the postcentral gyrus (area 3,1,2) is the primary somatic sensory reception center. The occipital pole and the area on both sides of the calcarine fissure (area 17) form the primary visual receptor center. Areas 41 and 42, Heschl's gyri, situated on the superior temporal gyrus, represent the primary auditory reception center. Damage to any of these areas may result in a loss of function, such as paralysis, anesthesia, or blindness. In addition, area 8, lying anterior to area 6 in the frontal lobe (Figure 19–1), is concerned with voluntary conjugate movements of the eyes. The frontal poles and the areas surrounding them are the site of personality. A person who has an injury to this area—say, after a car accident—will probably undergo personality changes. There was a case of a friendly and pleasant social worker who suddenly, and for no apparent reason, became argumentative and abusive until her death a short while later. Autopsy revealed an expanding tumor in the frontal lobe that had caused both her death and the marked changes in character.

In the mid-1930s a Portuguese neurosurgeon, Moniz, introduced the procedure of cutting or removing parts of the frontal lobes—lobotomy—as a means of treating severely psychotic patients. With hardly a murmur of dissent, this procedure was widely hailed (Moniz received the Nobel prize for it in 1949) and widely practiced. True, after the operation many of the patients were quieter and more docile, but they also lost all initiative, became indifferent to their surroundings, defecated and urinated in public, and showed other behavioral disturbances. Moniz was almost murdered by a former patient who was distraught over his new state. This was one case where the operation was a success but the surgeon nearly died! Today this barbarous operation has been thoroughly discredited.

Surrounding each of the primary cortical areas, and closely allied with them, are the so-called *as-*

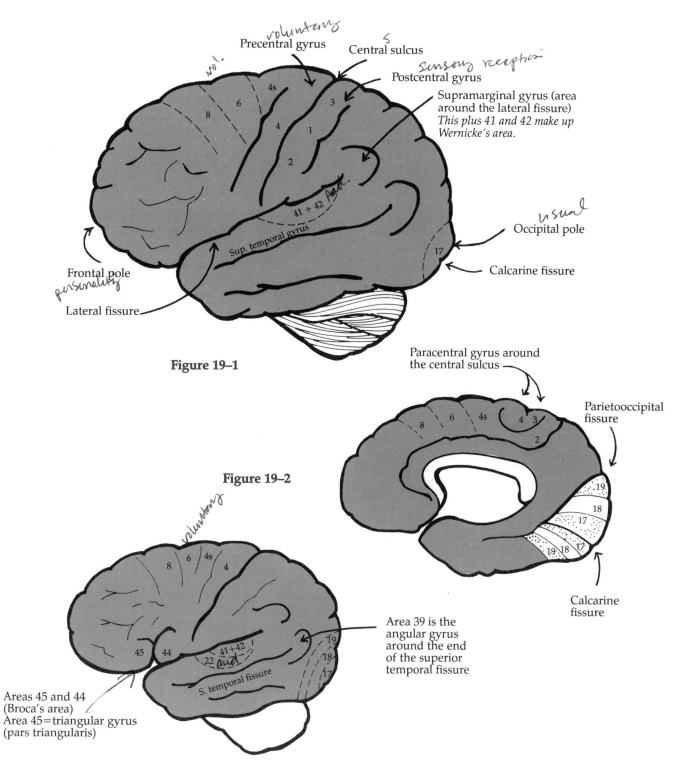

*voluntary*
*vol.*
Precentral gyrus
*s*
Central sulcus
*sensory reception*
Postcentral gyrus
Supramarginal gyrus (area around the lateral fissure) *This plus 41 and 42 make up Wernicke's area.*

*visual*
Occipital pole
Calcarine fissure

Sup. temporal gyrus
41 + 42 *Aud.*

Frontal pole
*personality*
Lateral fissure

**Figure 19–1**

Paracentral gyrus around the central sulcus
Parietooccipital fissure
Calcarine fissure

**Figure 19–2**

*voluntary*

Area 39 is the angular gyrus around the end of the superior temporal fissure

41 + 42
*and*
22
S. temporal fissure

Areas 45 and 44 (Broca's area)
Area 45=triangular gyrus (pars triangularis)

**Figure 19–3**

sociation areas. Around the visual area (area 17) there are areas 18 and 19, which have several functions. First, they are concerned with "interpreting" the visual impulses that reach area 17. We see round, red objects in front of us, and areas 18 and 19 interpret them as apples. This interpretation is called *gnosis*, from the Greek word meaning "to know."* Area 19 is concerned with automatic following movements of the eyes, which occur when an object, such as a jet, suddenly comes into the visual field and the eyes "lock in" and follow it. Associated with area 4 is area 4s, the suppressor band, and area 6, which helps with voluntary movements. Area 22 is the auditory association area. If this area is damaged on the dominant side (the left hemisphere is the dominant one for speech and language in most people, including those who are left-handed), the result is the condition known as *word deafness* or *auditory aphasia*, which is discussed in the following section.

## SENSORY (RECEPTOR) APHASIA

Aphasia is defined as the inability to understand or express the symbols connected with language that the person once knew, and there are two basic kinds: sensory and motor. If one traces the superior temporal sulcus to its posterior end, the gray matter surrounding this end is the *angular gyrus* (area 39) of the parietal lobe (Figure 19–2). Damage to this area on the dominant cerebral hemisphere produces a condition known as *visual aphasia*, "word blindness," or *alexia*. In this condition the patient sees the printed words but cannot read them; they are meaningless lines. This condition is equivalent to a Westerner looking at Chinese writing; all the Westerner sees are curved lines and characters that have no specific meaning.

Area 22, surrounding the primary auditory reception areas (41 and 42), is the auditory reception area. If it is damaged, again on the dominant cerebral hemisphere, *auditory aphasia* results. A patient with this condition experiences sound without any meaning, the same thing as when you hear speech in a completely foreign language. The patient can hear you speaking but cannot understand what is being said. *Wernicke's aphasia* is a condition of both auditory and visual aphasia.

---

*An agnostic is one who doesn't know.

## MOTOR APHASIA (VERBAL APHASIA)

On the inferior frontal gyrus, in the triangular and opercular regions, are found areas 44 and 45, also known as *Broca's area* (Figure 19–3). If these areas are injured in the dominant hemisphere in an adult, they produce a condition in which the patient is unable to talk even though the vocal muscles are not paralyzed. The patient knows what he or she wants to say, but all that comes out is garbled sound or one word repeated over and over again. One might speculate that the memory engrams connected with speech have been destroyed. If the damage occurs in childhood, the child can be taught to speak by utilizing the nondominant cerebral hemisphere.

## APRAXIA

Apraxia is the inability to carry out learned, voluntary acts although there is no paralysis present. It also involves the association areas. When told to take out his or her keys and open the door, the patient might pull out a coin or comb and try to put it into the keyhole. If the damage involves the loss of writing ability, it is known as *agraphia*.

## AGNOSIA

Agnosia is the inability to recognize things even though one sees them. For example, a patient can walk down the street, see some broken glass in the way, and walk around it. However, when you ask what it is the patient walked around, the patient doesn't know.

These conditions may sound strange, but many things concerning the cerebral cortex are so.** As can be readily appreciated, aphasias and apraxias, as well as other cerebral conditions such as epilepsy, are not as simple as has been presented here but rather are complex matters that have psychologic aspects as well. Our "hard fact" knowledge is restricted, and because experiments can't be performed easily on the human cortex what little information we have comes from pathologic cases and autopsies. The reader who wishes to learn more about the telencephalon should consult *Correlative*

---

**For fascinating reading on such conditions, may I suggest you read the best-selling *The Man Who Mistook His Wife for a Hat*, by the noted neurologist Oliver Sacks, who writes with great clarity, sensitivity, and insight.[1]

*Anatomy of the Nervous System*, by Crosby, Humphrey, and Lauer,[2] which has nearly 200 pages on the subject and more than 1300 references. There are also books available that are devoted to individual subject matters, such as epilepsy and electroencephalography (EEG).

**REFERENCES**

1. Sacks O. *The Man Who Mistook His Wife for a Hat.* London: Picador; 1986.

2. Crosby EC, Humphrey T, Lauer EW. *Correlative Anatomy of the Nervous System.* New York: Macmillan; 1962.

# Chapter 20

# The Meninges

Brain tissue, having the consistency of a heavy pudding or custard, is the most delicate of all body tissues. For protection, this vital organ is located in a sealed bony chamber, the *skull*.* To protect it further from the rough bone and from blows and shocks to the head, the brain is enveloped by three membranes, called the *meninges*. The outermost covering is the tough, thick dura mater, which is adherent to the inner surface of the bone (Figure 20–1). In fact, it forms the periosteal layer of the calvarium. Beneath the dura mater is the middle covering, the thin and filamentous *arachnoid*. The third and innermost layer is the very thin, delicate, and capillary-rich *pia mater*, which is attached directly to the brain and dips down into the sulci and fissures (Figure 20–1; the trigeminal nerve and C-1 to C-3 are the sensory nerves to the dura).

Although the dura mater is closely applied to the inner bone surface, it can in certain instances separate from it, creating an area between the two known as the *epidural space* (see "Clinical Notes" at the end of Chapter 21). Between the dura mater and the underlying arachnoid is a narrow subdural space filled with a small amount of serous fluid that acts as a lubricant, preventing adhesion between the two membranes (Figure 20–1). Separating the arachnoid from the pia mater is a relatively large gap, the *subarachnoid space*, which is filled with cerebrospinal fluid (CSF; Figure 20–1). This clear, lymphlike fluid fills the entire subarachnoid space and thus surrounds the brain with a protective cushion that absorbs shock waves to the head. As a further means of protection, there are fibrous filaments known as the *arachnoid trabeculations*, which extend from the arachnoid to the pia and help "anchor" the brain to prevent it from excessive movement in cases of sudden acceleration or deceleration (Figure 20–1). In the fluid-filled subarachnoid space are situated the cerebral arteries and veins (Figure 20–1). The pia mater is so closely attached to the underlying brain that there is no space, potential or otherwise, between the two. In this manner the pia mater acts as a restraining

*The English word *skull* comes from the Scandinavian word *skulla*, and the drinking toast *skol* is also a derivative. The Vikings used to cut off the top part of their victims' skulls, invert them, and use them as drinking cups in their victory celebrations.

agent that holds the brain tissue together and prevents it from separating.

The dura mater dips down into the median longitudinal fissure, and this dural fold, lying between the cerebral hemispheres, is called the *falx cerebri* (Figures 20–1 and 20–2; see also Appendix VIII, Figures 2 through 5). The dura also dips into the space between the cerebellum and the overlying occipital lobes, forming the *tentorium cerebelli* (Figures 20–1 and 20–2), a tentlike covering over the cerebellum. Finally, the dura mater dips between the two cerebellar hemispheres to form the *falx cerebelli* (Figure 20–2). All the meninges, the subarachnoid space, and the CSF pass through the foramen magnum at the base of the skull (Figure 20–1) and extend down the vertebral canal to enclose the spinal cord and nerves. In the vertebral canal the spinal cord most often ends at the level of the second or third lumbar vertebra. However, its surrounding pia extends down as the filum terminale, which is attached to the coccygeal ligament that serves to anchor the spinal cord (Figure 20–3). In addition, the pia mater has, on each side of the entire cord, toothlike extensions called the dentate ligaments (Figure 20–3). These are attached to the arachnoidea and dura and also serve to anchor and stabilize the spinal cord. All the spinal nerves, including those of the cauda equina, are covered by the pia mater, and upon exiting they "pick up" the arachnoidea and dura (Figure 20–3).

## CLINICAL NOTES

*Meningitis* is an infection of the meninges (see Chapter 23); usually it is the arachnoid and pia mater that are attacked (leptomeningitis). As you probably know from personal experience, an infected and inflamed area is sensitive, and any pressure on or stretching of it causes great pain. In meningitis, when there is an attempt to flex (bend) the neck and thereby stretch the meninges, the muscles of the neck contract strongly to prevent the bending and consequent pain. This phenomenon of muscle contraction to prevent stretching of inflamed structures is known as *guarding*. In cases of suspected meningitis, the physician tries to bend the neck of the supine patient. If the neck cannot be bent or if bending is accompanied by pain, this is a key sign that meningitis may be present.

**Figure 20–1 Frontal Section**

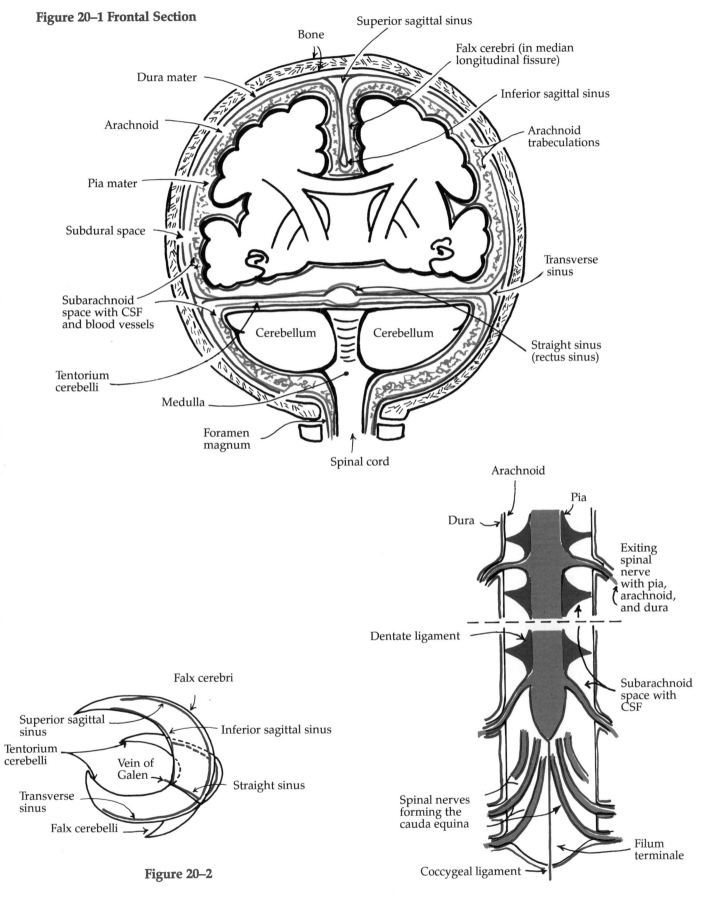

- Bone
- Superior sagittal sinus
- Dura mater
- Falx cerebri (in median longitudinal fissure)
- Arachnoid
- Inferior sagittal sinus
- Arachnoid trabeculations
- Pia mater
- Subdural space
- Transverse sinus
- Subarachnoid space with CSF and blood vessels
- Straight sinus (rectus sinus)
- Tentorium cerebelli
- Cerebellum
- Cerebellum
- Medulla
- Foramen magnum
- Spinal cord

Falx cerebri

Superior sagittal sinus
Tentorium cerebelli
Vein of Galen
Transverse sinus
Falx cerebelli

Inferior sagittal sinus
Straight sinus

**Figure 20–2**

- Arachnoid
- Pia
- Dura
- Exiting spinal nerve with pia, arachnoid, and dura
- Dentate ligament
- Subarachnoid space with CSF
- Spinal nerves forming the cauda equina
- Filum terminale
- Coccygeal ligament

**Figure 20–3**

# Chapter 21

# Blood Supply to the Brain

## ARTERIAL SUPPLY

As mentioned in Chapter 1, nerve cells do not regenerate. They also need a constant, adequate supply of blood, and any interruption of it or injury to the vascular tree can quickly lead to irreparable damage or death. Because such injuries are commonly encountered in medical practice, knowledge and understanding of central nervous system vascularity are essential. Two pairs of arteries, the vertebrals and the internal carotids, are the only suppliers of blood to the brain. The *vertebral arteries* enter the skull through the foramen magnum and pass along the ventral surface of the medulla (Figure 21–1). After giving off the *anterior* and *posterior spinal arteries* as well as the *posterior inferior cerebellar artery*, they join together to form the basilar artery. The basilar artery passes up to the beginning of the pons, where it bifurcates into the *posterior cerebral arteries*. These sweep back to supply the posterior part of the cerebral hemispheres, especially the medial and basilar surfaces (Figures 21–1 through 21–3). In its course, the basilar artery gives off the *anterior inferior cerebellar artery*, the *pontine branches*, the *labyrinthine artery*, and the *superior cerebellar artery*.

The *internal carotid arteries* enter the skull through the carotid canals and lie adjacent to the lateral border of the optic chiasm (Figure 21–1). Here they bifurcate into the *anterior* and *middle cerebral arteries*. The anterior cerebral arteries pass forward into the medial longitudinal fissure and then sweep back to the parietooccipital fissure, thus supplying the medial surface of the hemisphere (Figures 21–1 through 21–3). The *middle cerebral arteries* pass laterally between the temporal and frontal lobes. They emerge at the lateral fissure and fan out to supply most of the lateral surface of the hemisphere (Figures 21–1 and 21–2). In their course between the temporal and frontal lobes, the middle cerebral arteries give off the very important *striate arteries*, which help supply the internal capsule with its descending motor tracts (Figure 21–1). Because the striate arteries are the frequent site of cerebrovascular accident (CVAs), they are known as the "arteries of stroke."

The anterior cerebral arteries are connected to each other by the *anterior communicating artery*. There is also a *posterior communicating artery*, which links the middle cerebral artery with the posterior cerebral artery (Figure 21–1). Thus at the base of the brain an anastomotic ring is formed between the vertebral and internal carotid arteries. This ring is called the *circle of Willis* and is important clinically because, if one of the arteries becomes occluded, the blood can pass around to reach the deprived area, a phenomenon known as collateral circulation. In addition, the circle of Willis is a frequent site for *aneurysms*. An aneurysm forms when blood pressure at a weakening in the wall causes the artery to balloon out. This can press on adjacent structures, such as the optic chiasm, causing visual disturbances (Figure 21–1; also refer to Chapter 15); if it bursts, it causes a CVA.

## VENOUS DRAINAGE

Venous blood takes a roundabout circuit in its drainage to the neck. Most of the veins reach the surface of the brain and join larger cerebral veins. These, the bridging veins, cross the subarachnoid space and empty into large venous sinuses located within the dura mater. The superior cerebral veins drain into the superior sagittal sinus, whereas the inferior cerebral veins drain into the transverse sinus as well as the superficial middle cerebral vein (Figure 21–4). In addition, there are anastomotic veins that connect the superficial middle cerebral vein with the sinuses (Figure 21–4). Blood from the center of the brain flows into the deep cerebral veins and then into the straight sinus (Figure 21–5). There is a confluence of these sinuses into each other: The superior sagittal and straight sinuses flow into the transverse, which continues into the sigmoid, which drains into the internal jugular vein of the neck. The superficial middle cerebral vein flows into the cavernous sinus located at the base of the brain (Figure 21–6), and, because of its location and the structures found in it (cranial nerves III, IV, V, and VI), an infection of the cavernous sinus is very dangerous.

## CLINICAL NOTES

If an artery becomes occluded by a thrombus or embolus or through vasospasm, the area distal to the occlusion is deprived of its blood supply, and the cells quickly die, forming an infarct. This usu-

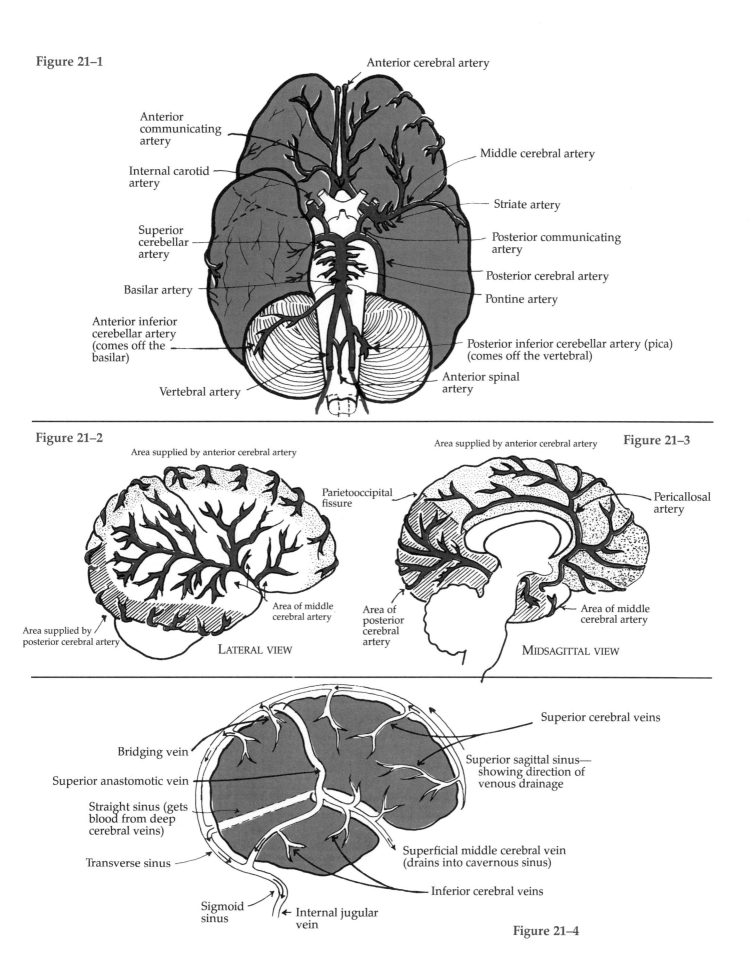

**Figure 21–1**

Anterior cerebral artery

Anterior communicating artery

Internal carotid artery

Superior cerebellar artery

Basilar artery

Anterior inferior cerebellar artery (comes off the basilar)

Vertebral artery

Middle cerebral artery

Striate artery

Posterior communicating artery

Posterior cerebral artery

Pontine artery

Posterior inferior cerebellar artery (pica) (comes off the vertebral)

Anterior spinal artery

**Figure 21–2**

Area supplied by anterior cerebral artery

Area supplied by posterior cerebral artery

Area of middle cerebral artery

LATERAL VIEW

**Figure 21–3**

Area supplied by anterior cerebral artery

Parietooccipital fissure

Pericallosal artery

Area of posterior cerebral artery

Area of middle cerebral artery

MIDSAGITTAL VIEW

Bridging vein

Superior anastomotic vein

Straight sinus (gets blood from deep cerebral veins)

Transverse sinus

Sigmoid sinus

Internal jugular vein

Superior cerebral veins

Superior sagittal sinus—showing direction of venous drainage

Superficial middle cerebral vein (drains into cavernous sinus)

Inferior cerebral veins

**Figure 21–4**

Figure 21–5 Deep Cerebral Veins

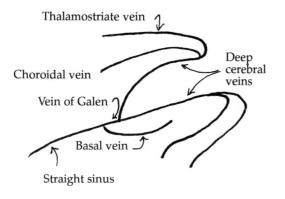

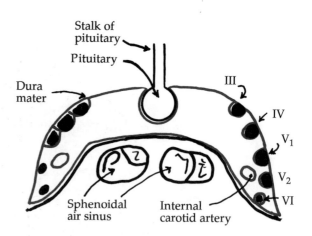

Figure 21–6 Cross-Section of Cavernous Sinus

ally results in a stroke, the severity of which depends on the site of occlusion as well as other factors, including the patient's native clot-lysing capabilities (fibrinolytic system). Stroke can also occur if an artery ruptures, and, if the hemorrhage is massive, death can occur quickly. After 3 to 4 minutes of arterial deprivation, neurons begin to die, with those of the cerebral cortex being most sensitive and those of the lower "vegetative" or brain stem centers being hardier. Thus there can be a short halt in the cerebral blood flow, and, after resumption, the individual is a "vegetable" for life because the neurons of the higher centers, such as personality, memory, and so forth, have died; whereas the lower, life-sustaining ones are still viable. Another way of illustrating the importance of the blood supply is that, although the brain is only 2% of the total body weight, it uses 15% to 20% of the total cardiac output.

The middle meningeal artery supplies not the brain but rather the dura of the middle cranial fossa. It lies between the dura mater and the skull, and in cases of trauma to the head (as in car accidents) jagged bone splinters, especially from the inner part of the bone, can cut the artery. Here the patient may have no complaints or visible injuries for the first hour or two. However, arterial blood, which is under high pressure, flows out rapidly between the dura and the bone, forming a rapidly expanding pool (an *epidural* or *extradural hematoma*) that presses on the underlying brain and brain stem containing the cardiac and respiratory cen-

ters. Unconsciousness and a progressively deepening coma can ensue, and therefore immediate surgical intervention is necessary, involving clamping the artery and draining the blood (see Appendix VIII, Figure 11). This condition and others are beautifully illustrated by Netter in the Ciba collection of atlases.[1]

Because the veins of elderly people are less resilient and more fragile than those of younger individuals, a mild blow to the head can cause a cerebral vein (especially one of the superior cerebral veins at its junction with the superior sagittal sinus) to rupture. Because venous pressure is low, seepage is slow, and the blood usually accumulates between the dura and the arachnoid, forming what is known as a *subdural hematoma*. Weeks later, after the blow has been forgotten, the slowly expanding hematoma presses on the brain, causing *various insidious and nonspecific symptoms*, such as dizziness, headaches, apathy, falling, confusion, and drowsiness. Indeed, this constellation of complaints and symptoms in an elderly person should immediately alert the physician to the possibility of this condition. (In the past the mental complaints occasionally resulted in the patients being sent to a psychiatric hospital.) Today, in the great majority of cases, a computed tomography (CT) scan can accurately and easily pinpoint the condition (see Appendix VIII, Figure 19). Subdural hematomas may also occur in newborns because great pressure on the head during delivery may rupture a cerebral vein.

REFERENCE

1. Netter FH. *The Ciba Collection of Medical Illustrations Volume 1. The Nervous System.* West Caldwell, NJ: Ciba Pharmaceutical Co; 1986.

# Chapter 22

# Cerebrospinal Fluid and the Ventricular System

Cerebrospinal fluid (CSF) is a clear fluid filling the entire subarachnoid space; its volume is about 130 to 150 mL. It acts as a protective "liquid cushion" around the brain and spinal cord by absorbing shock waves from blows and falls. In addition, it is a valuable diagnostic aid: By means of a relatively simple procedure known as a *spinal tap (lumbar puncture)*, the physician can obtain a fresh sample of the fluid, quickly examine it, and identify a number of pathologic processes within the skull and brain.

Deep inside the brain is a series of interconnecting chambers, the ventricular system, and it is here that CSF is produced. In each cerebral hemisphere there is a large space, the *lateral ventricle* (see Appendix VIII, Figures 2 through 5), that is made up of an *anterior horn*, lying in the frontal lobe; the *body* or main part, lying in the frontal and parietal lobes; a *posterior horn*, in the occipital lobe; and an *inferior horn*, which sweeps down into the temporal lobe (Figures 22–1 and 22–2). In each lateral ventricle there is a delicate, lacelike structure, the *choroid plexus* (Figure 22–3; see also Appendix VIII, Figure 3), which is composed of pia mater enveloped by the thin membranous ependyma. As a result of diffusion and active transport, the CSF passes from the capillary-rich choroid plexus into the ventricular space and is therefore similar to lymph. The accumulating CSF fills the lateral ventricles and then flows out of them via the interventricular *foramen of Monro* and into the third ventricle (see Appendix VIII, Figures 3 and 4). This narrow, slitlike space lies in the midline between the walls of the right and left diencephalons (Figures 22–1 and 22–2; see also Plates IV and VII in Appendix II). The choroid plexus in the third ventricle also produces CSF, and all the fluid flows into the narrow *aqueduct of Sylvius (cerebral aqueduct)*, located in the midbrain (Figures 22–1 and 22–2; see also Plates IV, X, and XI in Appendix II). The aqueduct then empties into the fourth ventricle in the pons and medulla (Figures 22–1 through 22–3; see also Plate IV in Appendix II and Figure 4 in Appendix VIII). Here also there is the choroid plexus, which produces CSF. In the thin roof of the fourth ventricle are three openings: the medial *foramen of Magendie* and the two lateral *foramina of Luschka.** It is through these openings that the CSF leaves the ventricular system and flows into and completely fills the subarachnoid space around the brain and cord (Figures 22–2 and 22–3). In certain regions, the arachnoid is situated far from the pia mater, and the enlarged subarachnoid space forms areas known as *cisterns*, for example the cisterna magna (Figure 22–3 and Appendix IX, Figure 16).

An important question is: If CSF is constantly being produced at the rate of 30 mL/hour, what happens to the excess fluid? In the area of the superior sagittal sinus, the arachnoid projects through small openings in the dura mater into the sinus. The accumulating CSF creates a pressure that forces the excess fluid out of the arachnoid projections and into the dural venous blood, which carries it away (Figures 22–3 and 22–4). In gross preparations these fine arachnoid projections resemble granules of sugar or salt and are therefore called *arachnoid granulations*.

## CLINICAL NOTES

### Hydrocephalus

Most often in newborn infants, a blockage may form somewhere in the ventricular system. Consequently, the CSF is unable to flow out and instead accumulates in the ventricles, where it presses on the nervous tissue, causing a thinning out of the brain with a widening of the ventricles (see Appendix VIII, Figure 8). Because the cranial bones of the newborn have not yet fused, the expanding, fluid-filled brain separates the bones, and the head enlarges tremendously. The exact cause of hydrocephalus isn't always known, but it may be due to failure of the foramina or aqueduct to develop; or they may become blocked by a tumor. Hydrocephalus may follow *encephalitis* (infection of the brain), or it may result from inadequate CSF resorption into the venous sinuses. Therefore, examination of infants must include a measurement of the circum-

---

*Magendie is median; Luschka is lateral.

Figure 22–1

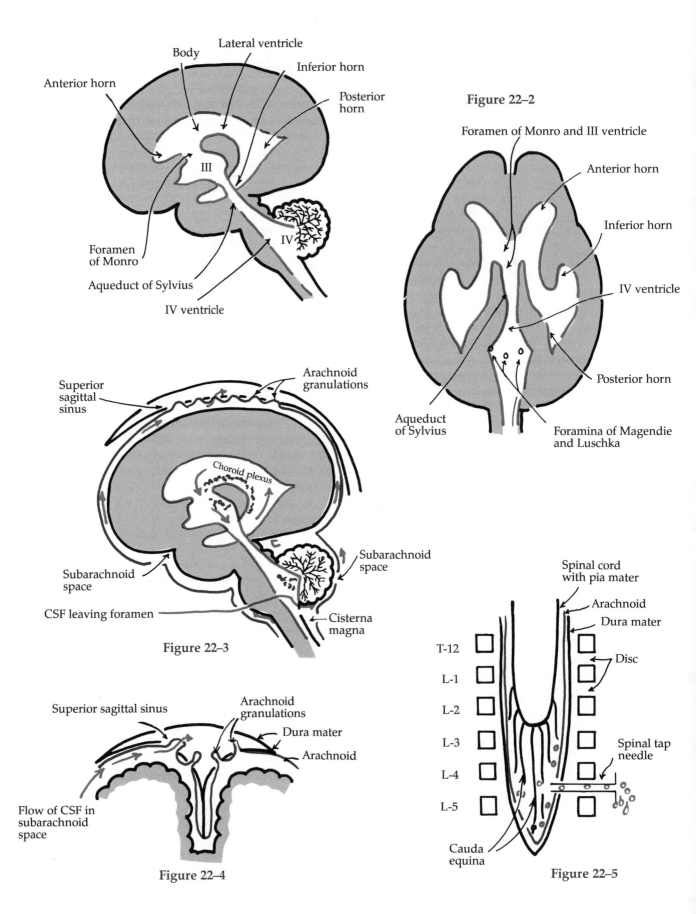

**Figure 22–1**

Anterior horn
Body
Lateral ventricle
Inferior horn
Posterior horn
III
IV
Foramen of Monro
Aqueduct of Sylvius
IV ventricle

**Figure 22–2**

Foramen of Monro and III ventricle
Anterior horn
Inferior horn
IV ventricle
Posterior horn
Aqueduct of Sylvius
Foramina of Magendie and Luschka

Superior sagittal sinus
Arachnoid granulations
Choroid plexus
Subarachnoid space
Subarachnoid space
CSF leaving foramen
Cisterna magna

**Figure 22–3**

Superior sagittal sinus
Arachnoid granulations
Dura mater
Arachnoid
Flow of CSF in subarachnoid space

**Figure 22–4**

Spinal cord with pia mater
Arachnoid
Dura mater
Disc
T-12
L-1
L-2
L-3
L-4
L-5
Spinal tap needle
Cauda equina

**Figure 22–5**

ference of the head, and, if it exceeds normal limits, diagnostic tests should be done.

Today, excellent therapeutic results are obtained in the treatment of hydrocephalus by neurosurgically implanting a tube (catheter) from the anterior horn of the lateral ventricle to the abdominal (peritoneal) cavity or pleural cavity, and the excess CSF is thereby shunted off and absorbed.

## Spinal Tap (Lumbar Puncture [LP])

Because the spinal cord is shorter than the vertebral column, it generally ends at the level of the first or second lumbar vertebra (Figure 22–5). Therefore, the subarachnoid space below this level can be tapped with no danger of injuring the cord. After giving a local anesthetic, the physician inserts a sterile, hollow needle between the third and fourth or fourth and fifth lumbar vertebrae, punctures the dura mater, and enters the subarachnoid space filled with CSF. The hollow needle has a plunger, which is pulled out so that the CSF can then drip out. The physician first measures the pressure of the CSF, which normally can reach 200 mm $H_2O$. In certain brain diseases, the CSF pressure is greatly elevated. However, one must NEVER attempt to reduce the pressure by letting out the CSF through a spinal tap, because the sudden downward flow of the released fluid may pull the brain stem into the foramen magnum, causing the almost instantaneous death of the patient.

The CSF obtained by spinal tap is examined grossly for pus or blood and microscopically for the presence of white blood cells, red blood cells, bacteria, and fungi. It is also examined for the levels of chloride, protein, and sugar (in bacterial infections there is a decrease in sugar levels because CSF acts as a great energy source for the proliferating bacteria).*

In certain operations in which general anesthesia is contraindicated, local anesthetic fluid can be injected through the spinal tap needle into the epidural or subarachnoid space, producing what is known as a sacral or lumbar block. The anesthetist employs techniques that prevent the anesthetic fluid from flowing up the vertebral canal and silencing nerves to vital organs.

## Increased Intracranial Pressure

Many pathologic conditions (eg, tumors, trauma, and strokes) can produce an increase in intracranial pressure. This is often indicated by a patient's complaints of headaches, but it must be emphasized that most headaches are not the result of an increase in pressure. Increased intracranial pressure may be detected by looking with an ophthalmoscope into the patient's eye and observing the configuration of the optic disc of the retina. Normally, the optic disc is sharp and distinct, but when there is an increase in CSF pressure, the borders of the disc may become blurred, there is congestion or hemorrhage of the peripapillary veins, and the entire optic disc may bulge. This is known as *papilledema*. The underlying cause should be sought to relieve the pressure and to prevent brain damage, coma, or death.

After a spinal tap, some of the CSF may leak out into the surrounding tissues. This produces a decrease in intracranial pressure, which is often accompanied by severe headaches.

---

*See Appendix III for normal and abnormal CSF values.

# Chapter 23

# Pathologic Conditions of the Central Nervous System

This chapter is designed to give the reader a short introductory overview of the most common neuropathologic conditions that he or she will encounter. In no way is it a substitute for more detailed study of the subject. These diseases can be classified according to general etiology as vascular, infectious, traumatic, (auto)immune, metabolic, idiopathic and degenerative, neoplastic, substance abuse and toxins, and congenital.

## VASCULAR

It should be remembered that neurologic events of vascular origin are generally of sudden onset, unlike the degenerative and metabolic diseases, which are usually much more insidious.

### CEREBROVASCULAR ACCIDENT

Cerebrovascular accident (CVA) may be defined as damage to the brain as a result of a pathologic condition of the blood vessels, especially the arteries. CVAs, or strokes, are the third most common cause of death in the United States, after heart attacks and cancer, and more than 1 million survivors are left disabled each year.

As mentioned in Chapter 1, the brain is sensitive to oxygen deprivation. If the arterial supply to an area is cut off, it will undergo a process of degeneration and death, producing what is known as an ischemic infarcted area (see Appendix VIII, Figure 9). The arterial blockage may be the result of thrombus formation, emboli, or vasospasm, and these cases account for 70% to 80% of all CVAs. The clinical picture that one sees depends on the area that is affected, but what is seen most often is some kind of upper motor neuron paralysis. Embolism is the most common cause of stroke, and most emboli come from the heart as a result of atrial fibrillation, complications of myocardial infarction, and valvular disease.

As one gets older the arteries become less elastic and more fragile; these changes, often combined with hypertension, can result in the rupture of a vessel. The subsequent hemorrhage (see Appendix VIII, Figure 10) often results in rapid death or permanent disablement.

### RUPTURE OF ANEURYSM

An aneurysm is a local ballooning out of an arterial wall. Aneurysms in the brain are most often located in and around the circle of Willis and are known as berry aneurysms. Eighty percent arise from the internal carotid artery or its branches, including the middle meningeal arteries. Before rupture, most berry aneurysms are asymptomatic, but if suspected they can be located and removed by microneurosurgery. If a berry aneurysm ruptures, there will be hemorrhaging into the subarachnoid space, which is fatal in a large percentage of cases.

### HEMORRHAGE FROM ARTERIOVENOUS MALFORMATION

Arteriovenous (AV) malformation is a congenital anomaly where there is a Medusa-like tangle or mass of arteries and veins with no capillaries in between (see Figure 10 in Appendix IX). The danger is that there is a high chance of rupture with hemorrhage. The Swedes developed a technique of nonsurgical radiation intervention that has produced excellent results in obliterating the malformation. Many sources of low gamma radiation are focused precisely on the AV mass, and the accumulation of beams at that point is strong enough to cause its slow obliteration without damaging the surrounding brain tissue through which each individual beam passes. The beams cause a massive proliferation of the endothelial lining, which eventually "stops up" the arteries and veins.

Finally, it should be mentioned here that intraventricular hemorrhage is the most common neurologic complication in low–birth weight infants.

### TRANSIENT ISCHEMIC ATTACK

A transient ischemic attack (TIA), or "little stroke" in layperson's terms, occurs when a spasm or occlusion of an artery causes temporary neurologic deficits lasting minutes or hours followed by complete recovery of function. This condition can recur over a period of months or years and can sometimes signal an oncoming full stroke. The etiology of TIAs is primarily embolic (eg, from a complicated atherosclerotic carotid artery in the neck).

# INFECTIOUS

## BACTERIAL INFECTIONS

*Meningitis* is an infection of the cerebral and/or spinal meninges (usually the arachnoid and pia). In 80% to 90% of cases it is caused by one of three bacteria: *Neisseria meningitidis*, pneumococci, or *Hemophilus influenzae*, with the latter being a more frequent pathogen in children. In infants younger than 1 year the most common organism is *Escherichia coli*. The triad of fever, headache, and stiff neck should immediately alert the physician to the possibility of the disease, and a spinal tap (lumbar puncture [LP]) should be considered at once for this medical emergency. Broad-spectrum antibiotics should be administered immediately after the spinal tap until accurate microbiologic identification permits a more focused regimen.

*Brain abscess* is a pocket or pockets of pus that have formed in the brain tissue (see Appendix VIII, Figure 12). They are rarely primary infections but mostly secondary ones from sites elsewhere in the body, with the most common ones being middle ear infections, sinusitis, or purulent pulmonary conditions. The most common agents are *Staphylococcus* and *Streptococcus* species and pneumococci, and they spread either by direct extension or via the blood stream. Computed tomography (CT) and magnetic resonance imaging (MRI) have dramatically improved the correct diagnosis and treatment, which involves the use of antibiotics or surgical removal. More recently we have witnessed a marked increase in the frequency of tuberculous meningitis and brain abscesses. This is due, in part, to the high incidence of mycobacterial infections among patients with acquired immunodeficiency syndrome (AIDS).

*Tetanus* occurs when a cut or wound is invaded by anaerobic *Clostridium tetani* or its spores. Once in the tissue, the bacteria produce a powerful neurotoxin that causes severe muscular spasms. The best "cure" is prevention by immunization.

*Infection of the dural venous sinuses*, like brain abscess, is most often secondary to an infection elsewhere in the body. Infection of the cavernous sinus, because of its location at the base of the brain and the structures in it,* is particularly dangerous.

*Syphilis* is caused by the spirochete *Treponema pallidum*. The last, or tertiary, stage of the illness occurs many years after the initial infection and may also affect the nervous system, causing a multiplicity of symptoms, many of them mental (eg, delusions of grandeur).

*Lyme disease* is a spirochete infection (*Borrelia burgdorferi*) that is transmitted by the bite of the deer tick and is named after the city of Lyme in Connecticut, where it was first reported. Shortly after being bitten, the patient will develop a red rash around the area and mild flulike symptoms, which then disappear. A few weeks to months later, arthritis sets in. There may be cardiac manifestations, and various kinds of neurologic symptoms may develop (eg, cranial nerve neuritis leading to bilateral Bell's palsy or symptoms associated with a more severe meningoencephalitis). The disease is endemic in lower Connecticut (upper Westchester county) and in areas of Wisconsin and Minnesota, but it has been identified in other areas as well (remember that a person doesn't have to live in these areas to get the disease; he or she might have vacationed there). Diagnosis is based on a high index of suspicion, a careful history, and a positive serologic report. Treatment is based on early administration of oral antibiotics (penicillin or tetracycline) or high-dose intravenous therapy if the disease is diagnosed in later stages.

*Botulism* is a rare but headline-making form of food poisoning caused by the contamination of canned foods by the anaerobic bacteria *Clostridium botulinum*. The exotoxin of this bacterium, one of the most powerful poisons known, blocks the release of acetylcholine at the voluntary motor end plate and at the postganglionic parasympathetic endings. As a result, one sees first a weakness and paralysis of skeletal muscles, including orbital muscles, which produces diplopia (double vision). Paralysis of throat musculature may produce loss of speech or difficulty swallowing (dysphagia) and slowing down of peristalsis, which results in constipation. The paralysis characteristically spreads downward, and there is danger of death due to paralysis of respiratory muscles. Treatment is based on a quick diagnosis and consists of the use of antitoxins and appropriate respiratory support where necessary.

Ophthalmologists in the United States devised an ingenious use for the toxin. In cases of spasms of the eye muscles, they carefully inject measured amounts of the toxin into the muscle, and the toxin acts on the muscle and reduces the contractions. Also, in cases of strabismus (crossed eyes), espe-

---

*Cranial nerves III, IV, V, VI and the internal carotid artery. See Figure 21–6.

cially in children, where one muscle is stronger than its antagonist, some will inject the toxin into the stronger muscle, thereby weakening it and bringing it into balance with its weaker antagonistic muscle.

## VIRAL INFECTIONS

*Encephalitis* is inflammation and infection of the brain tissue by any one of a large number of organisms. Viral infections of the nervous system (brain, spinal cord, or peripheral nerves) may enter by way of the oral or intestinal route (poliomyelitis and other diseases caused by enteroviruses), the respiratory tree (measles and mumps), the genital tracts (AIDS), the placenta (German measles and cytomegalovirus), or directly through contact (herpes simplex) or bite wounds (rabies and others). Other common types of encephalitis are St Louis encephalitis, Eastern encephalitis, Japanese B encephalitis, and encephalitis lethargica. Mortality rates vary from type to type.

*Poliomyelitis*, once a highly prevalent and dreaded disease, specifically attacks the cell bodies of lower motor neurons, leaving in its wake a trail of death or paralysis.* In developed countries it has been virtually eliminated by a vaccine developed by the great work of Enders, Salk, and Sabin. Nonetheless, several cases are still seen each year in unvaccinated children or unvaccinated adults exposed to vaccinated children.

*Measles* may rarely cause an acute meningoencephalitis, but it may also give rise to a slowly developing process called *subacute sclerosing panencephalitis (SSPE)*, which may surface even many years later. SSPE is characterized by seizures, which may be focal or generalized with accompanying disorders of gait. Antibodies to measles are markedly elevated. The disease is usually fatal, but with the widespread measles vaccination few cases have been identified recently. Mumps used to be the most common cause of acute meningoencephalitis of viral origin, being more frequent in males. However, its incidence has declined with the recent vaccination programs, and that of herpes simplex types 1 and 2 (genital) has markedly increased.

*Herpes simplex* encephalitis can be quite severe, ranging from headache and fever to stupor, coma, and death. Nonetheless, the most common mani-

festation by far of herpes simplex infection is the cutaneous ulcers (eg, cold sores on the lip or ulcers on the penis or vulva). Once a patient is infected, such ulcers usually recur, and the virus is thought to remain between episodes in a latent state within cell bodies of the sensory nerves supplying the affected area. To date, no effective treatment has been developed for the cutaneous manifestations of herpes simplex, although there have been reports of a shortened time course with administration of acyclovir. On the other hand, acyclovir has significantly reduced the morbidity and mortality of herpes encephalitis when administered early in the disease process.

*AIDS* is caused by the *human immunodeficiency virus* (HIV), which, in addition to its other devastating systemic effects, attacks the brain in two ways: indirectly and directly. In the first case, the virus weakens and destroys certain of the T lymphocytes, which are part of the body's defense mechanism, and as a result the brain is vulnerable to attack by various rare but lethal yeasts, molds, or fungi for which there is no effective therapy. The virus also directly attacks and destroys the neurons, glia, and white matter of the brain, and the patient's first symptoms and complaints resemble those of multiple sclerosis (ie, weakness of the muscles, loss of coordination, numbness and tingling of the skin, etc). The differential diagnosis can be made on the basis of laboratory examination, which in AIDS will reveal the presence of HIV antibodies.

Although clinical evidence of involvement of the central nervous system (CNS) or peripheral nerves is found in only about 30% of patients in the terminal stages of AIDS, CNS involvement is present in virtually all such patients at autopsy. Neurologic involvement later in the disease process is highly variable and includes meningoencephalitis, dementia, focal brain and/or spinal cord lesions from superimposed opportunistic infections, acute and chronic inflammatory changes in peripheral nerves, and even demyelinating and inflammatory changes within the innervated muscles themselves.

*Rabies* was once one of the most feared diseases because, once infected, the patient always died, with death being preceded by the most terrifying symptoms, including excitability, refusal to drink water (hydrophobia) because of painful laryngeal spasms, and convulsions. The disease is transmitted via the saliva of an infected warm-blooded animal, such as a dog, cat, squirrel, or fox. Because the virus travels along axons to reach the brain, those

---

*Prior to the development of the vaccine there were approximately 30,000 to 50,000 deaths per year. This rate has been reduced to under 100 deaths per year.

bites closer to it (eg, on the face) will have a shorter incubation time than bites farther away (eg, on the leg). The incubation period varies from 10 days to many months and sometimes more than a year. Animals that have bitten humans should be quarantined for 10 days. If the animal does not die during this period, it is considered not rabid. If the animal does die, the brain should be examined microscopically, especially the hippocampal area, where the neurons contain characteristic inclusions in the cytoplasm known as Negri bodies. Treatment consists of vaccination, but once symptoms have set in there is no cure.

## SPONGIFORM ENCEPHALOPATHIES

This is a group of rare, degenerative diseases of the brain. The symptoms and signs of the different diseases are similar. They are uniformly fatal, and, on microscopic examination, the brain, especially the cerebellum, is so riddled with vacuoles that it resembles a sponge (hence the name *spongiform*). The diseases include kuru, found among brain-eating cannibals in New Guinea; scrapie, found in sheep; cow-madness, found in cattle; and Creutzfeldt-Jakob disease, a rare disease in humans found throughout the world. Now the reader may think: "All well and good, but what's this got to do with me and my future patients? New Guinea is a long way off, and the chances of my meeting such a cannibal are nil."

Until recently, it was thought that the smallest self-replicating transmissible agent capable of causing pathology was the virus, small strands of encapsulated DNA or RNA. However, in the last decade, much smaller agents have been discovered that have been reported to consist either of nucleic acid–containing material (the virus or virino hypothesis) or unencapsulated proteins (the prion hypothesis). These so-called subviral particles are almost certainly the causative agents of the above-mentioned diseases. The properties of these particles are different from those of other infectious agents, such as bacteria and viruses: In the infected animal or human, they don't produce antibodies or induce any other immune response, and they don't produce an inflammatory reaction. How they replicate is unknown, and there is a relatively long incubation period varying from months to years. They are resistant to boiling, ultraviolet light, and formalin (hence the added potential danger to anatomists and pathologists). They are uniformly fatal, and there is no known cure. From the affected brain tissue, the particles can be removed, concentrated, and injected into rabbits, which will produce antibodies against it. It is these antibodies that are used in immunologic tests to confirm the presence or absence of the disease.

Chimpanzees will develop kuru if given the infected brain tissue of natives who died of it. In Britain, thousands of heads of cattle are dying from cow-madness, and although the carcasses are burned local beef consumption has dropped off drastically in fear that the dressed beef of unaffected cattle may harbor prions and that its consumption may produce the disease in humans in the future (because the incubation time is relatively long). For the same reason, countries such as France, Germany, and Russia have slapped a total embargo on the importation of British beef.

The discovery of subviral particles and prions has led scientists to question whether other chronic, degenerative diseases such as Alzheimer's, Parkinson's, and so on might be caused by similar subviral particles.[1-3]

## FUNGAL INFECTIONS

Fungal infections of the CNS are rare, but once established they are difficult to treat, and the mortality rate is high. They often attack individuals whose immune system has been weakened or destroyed (eg, people taking immunosuppressive drugs, AIDS patients, etc).

# TRAUMATIC

In modern medical practice it is common to see trauma to the brain and/or spinal cord from various causes, such as accidents (eg, automobile, work, home, or sports) and violence (eg, blows, bullets, knife wounds; approximately 1% of the population). In these cases the skull and/or vertebral column is often fractured, and the delicate nervous tissue is compressed, lacerated, or destroyed, leading to death or permanent neurologic disabilities. Trauma to the brain is often accompanied by tearing of blood vessels followed by hemorrhage and the damage it can produce.

After an accident, clear or pink-tinged fluid seeping from the ear or nose often indicates a skull fracture with escaping cerebrospinal fluid (CSF). A skull fracture may exist without escaping CSF, however. Therefore, X-rays must be taken for confirmation. A palpable steplike deformation on physical examination often accompanies a skull fracture.

# AUTOIMMUNE

## MYASTHENIA GRAVIS

This is an insidious disease characterized by intermittent weakness and fatigability of voluntary (striated skeletal) muscle, especially the muscles of the eyelids (ptosis), eyeballs (diplopia or strabismus), face, jaws (drooping jaw), and limbs. These may be associated with difficulties in swallowing (dysphagia) and speech (dysphonia) and changes in facial expression. Proximal muscles are affected more than distal ones, but the tendon reflexes may be normal. It was mentioned in Chapter 1 that the junction between the axon and the voluntary muscle is the motor end plate and that the neurotransmitter is acetylcholine. This reacts with the acetylcholine receptor site to cause further transmission of the nerve impulse, which results in contraction. The enzyme acetylcholinesterase breaks down acetylcholine, enabling the motor end plate and muscle fiber to repolarize and be ready to contract again. If repolarization did not occur, then the contracted muscle would eventually become fatigued, and paralysis would follow.

Myasthenia gravis has been considered an autoimmune disease. The acetylcholine receptor sites on the motor end plate are proteins, and in some individuals they act as antigens, producing antibodies that react with and destroy many of these receptor sites and reduce the efficiency of many others. Indeed, immune complexes have been identified on the postsynaptic receptor sites, and antibodies to acetylcholine receptor proteins can be identified in the serum of these patients. The amount of acetylcholine released is normal, but because the number and efficiency of sites are lowered muscles are weakened, and they tire quickly. Treatment consists of prolonging the life of acetylcholine by giving agents such as neostigmine, which blocks the action of cholinesterase in breaking down acetylcholine, thymectomy in the appropriate patient, corticosteroids and/or other immunosuppressive agents (eg, azathioprine), and possibly plasmapheresis to reduce the immune complex load.

Clinically, neuromuscular blocking agents can be divided into three types, with each having its own characteristics and medical application. The first kind is exemplified by *curare*, a drug used by South American natives (and mystery writers) to kill their prey and enemies. It is a powerful poison that blocks neuromuscular transmission by competitive inhibition; that is, the curare molecules, rather than acetylcholine, occupy the receptor sites on the motor end plate. Paralysis of voluntary muscles may include those of respiration; if respiration is not supported, the patient may die quickly.

*Succinylcholine*, an example of the second kind of blocking agent, causes prolonged depolarization of the motor end plate, and one therefore sees initial muscle contraction followed by flaccid paralysis. Clinically it is widely used in general surgery to relax muscles so that the surgeon can operate without interference. It is also virtually undetectable, being the closest thing to a perfect poison; not surprising, it was at the center of one of the most sensational murder cases in the United States in the 20th century. Dr Coppolino, an anesthetist, was tried and found guilty of murdering his wife by injecting her with a large dose of succinylcholine so that he could marry his mistress. Six months before this case, he was tried but acquitted on the charge of murdering, by suffocation, the husband of yet another mistress. In this first case, everything hung on the condition of the cricoid cartilage in the neck: Was it broken before or after the murder? For fascinating accounts of these trials, one from the prosecution's point of view and the other through the eyes of the defense, I suggest you read *Autopsy—The Memoirs of Milton Helpern, the World's Greatest Medical Detective*, by Milton Helpern, MD, who was the major prosecution witness in both cases, and *The Defense Never Rests*, by F. Lee Bailey, who defended Dr Coppolino in both trials.[4,5]

The third and last type of neuromuscular blocking agent works by "knocking out" or neutralizing acetylcholinesterase, thereby producing a build-up of acetylcholine. The best examples of these anticholinesterases are neostigmine and physostigmine, which are used in the treatment of myasthenia gravis and are classified as reversible agents. In addition, there are certain organophosphorus anticholinesterases whose action is irreversible; these are used to make the deadly nerve gases. In addition to resulting in a wide range of excessive autonomic activity, these cause the muscles to contract abnormally (muscle fasciculations) and then to become paralyzed; the paralysis may involve the respiratory muscles and cause death. The principal antidote to these gases is the quick injection of atropine, whose purpose is to block the action of the excess acetylcholine at its receptor site.

## REYE'S SYNDROME

This is a condition of unknown etiology that often follows viral infections in children and teenagers.

Vomiting, lethargy, disorientation, personality changes, and possibly coma and decerebration are associated with marked cerebral edema. Fatty changes of the liver are common. Mortality rates are high (35% to 40%), and treatment is aimed at reducing brain swelling and providing intensive supportive care. Damage to the liver results in the loss of a wide variety of functions, including the ability to detoxify ammonia. It has been suggested that administration of salicylates, such as aspirin, to young children with respiratory infections might be a precipitating factor to this syndrome.

## ACUTE POLYNEURITIS OR GUILLAIN-BARRÉ

This, again, is a disease of unknown etiology that can affect all age groups. In most cases, it follows soon after an upper respiratory illness and starts with progressive, usually symmetric muscle weakness and/or paralysis, usually involving the legs first. This is often followed by an ascending paralysis, which may reach brain stem levels. CSF proteins are elevated, but no or few white blood cells are seen. Recovery varies in length of time, but most patients eventually recover completely, and the mortality rates are low. Treatment is based on respiratory support if necessary as well as administration of immune globulin or plasmapheresis. The use of corticosteroids has been disappointing.

## DEMYELINATING DISEASES

This group includes such diseases as multiple sclerosis, which is discussed in detail in Chapter 1. Also included in this group is postvaccinal encephalomyelitis, which may occur after an individual has received a vaccination.

# METABOLIC

Metabolic diseases of the CNS are divided into two main groups: the acquired and the inherited. The former are really metabolic diseases of other organs that secondarily affect the brain. For example, hypothyroidism in children (cretinism) produces, among other things, severe mental retardation. Hypoglycemia can also adversely affect the brain, with signs ranging from restlessness to seizures and coma. Recently in New York City a man was convicted of having attempted to murder his wealthy socialite wife by injecting her with a massive dose of insulin. She survived but became comatose. Because the liver is a vital organ involved in the metabolic process, damage to it can produce CNS symptoms that may end in coma and death.

The inherited or inborn metabolic diseases are due to an enzyme defect that alters the metabolism of various substances. As there are now more than 100 such diseases, many with such quaint names as *gargoylism* and *maple syrup urine disease*, only the most common are mentioned here. Most of these enzyme deficiencies are transmitted by autosomal recessive inheritance.

*Phenylketonuria* (PKU) is an autosomal recessive disorder caused by the absence of the enzyme phenylalanine hydroxylase, which normally converts phenylalanine to tyrosine. Phenylalanine and its derivatives build up in the body and, if not detected in time, will produce severe mental retardation with disorders of movement and coordination. A standard, but relatively primitive, screening test involves taking the newborn infant's diaper and placing a little ferric chloride on it. If a bright green appears, then phenylpyruvic acid is present in the urine, and the infant probably has PKU. To confirm this, one should always check the serum for elevated phenylalanine levels. Once the infant has the disease, it can be controlled by providing a diet low in phenylalanine.

*Tay-Sachs disease* is also an inherited autosomal recessive disorder seen almost exclusively (95%) in Jewish infants with an eastern European background. Because of the absence of the enzyme hexosaminidase A, there is an accumulation of lipids known as gangliosides in the brain. The disease begins at 4 to 6 months with retardation of emotional and mental development, seizures, and the development of blindness. Because there is no means of control or cure, the disease progresses and ends fatally by age 3 or 4 years. A cherry-red macula in the retina of the eye is pathognomonic of the illness. The carriers of the disease can be identified through screening tests, and thereby the appearance of the disease can be prevented by genetic counseling.

*Gaucher's disease* is really a heterogeneous complex of diseases associated with a deficiency of beta-glucosidase (glucocerebrosidase). This enzyme is responsible for the conversion of glucosylceramide to ceramide and glucose. Several mutations have been identified within the gene encoding for the enzyme, and this is responsible for the heterogeneity of clinical symptoms in this autosomal recessive disease. Clinical symptoms are related to the buildup of cerebrosides with the cells of the bone marrow, liver, spleen, and brain. Large histiocytes known as Gaucher cells are characteristic microscopic findings in this condition. Untreated, the disease runs a progressively downhill course. A recent, major breakthrough in the treatment of this disease is based on home-administered intravenous replacement therapy of this enzyme. This replacement, alglucerase, has been reported to result in improvement in the hematologic picture, reduces organomegaly, and lowers the frequency of severe bacterial infections and neurological deficits.[6,7]

*Wilson's disease (hepatolenticular degeneration)* is a rare genetic disorder involving copper metabolism. As a result of decreased levels of serum ceruloplasm, which normally binds copper, there is an abnormal deposit of it in the liver and lentiform nucleus of the brain. The disease begins between the ages of 10 and 20 years with tremors and symptoms resembling Parkinson's disease. In addition, there are psychic and emotional disturbances, which can lead to a misdiagnosis of mental illness. A greenish-brown ring (Kayser-Fleischer ring) in the cornea of the eye is pathognomonic of the disease. Once detected, the disease can be controlled by giving a chelating agent such as penicillamine, which removes the excess copper.

# IDIOPATHIC AND DEGENERATIVE

## EPILEPSY

This is a common neurologic condition that affects more than 1 million people in the United States. Once, and perhaps even now, a sense of shame was attached to epilepsy, but it is a disease like any other, and many famous people in history had a form of epilepsy, including Old Testament prophets, Julius Caesar, Dostoyevski, Byron, Alexander the Great, Peter the Great, Pascal, and Napoleon.

Epilepsy is characterized by sudden, uncoordinated discharges from cerebral neurons. These seizures have many forms and are categorized in various ways, but about 95% of all seizures fall into two main groups: the *generalized seizure* and the *partial seizure*. In the first group are the *grand mal* and *petit mal* seizures. In the grand mal seizure, the individual often has a visual or olfactory aura preceding the attack. He or she often lets out a cry, loses consciousness, and enters the *tonic phase* of the attack. This consists of sustained muscle contraction without relaxation that lasts for about 1 or 2 minutes. The body is stiff and rigid with arms and forearms flexed against the body. This is followed by the *clonic phase*, lasting for 3 to 5 minutes, which consists of waves of violent muscle spasms, biting of the tongue, foamy and often bloody saliva, loss of bladder and bowel control, rolling of the eyeballs, and often interruption of breathing with cyanosis—a truly frightening sight to the inexperienced. When the contractions stop, the individual often enters a deep sleep for several hours.

Petit mal epilepsy occurs most often in children between the age of 4 and puberty. The seizures, which can number between 50 to 100 a day, consist of a much briefer loss of consciousness than those of the grand mal, lasting from 1 to 3 seconds without closure of the eyes or any muscle spasms. In fact, the child is often unaware of his or her condition, and the child's teachers may complain that the subject often doesn't pay attention and is daydreaming (*absence seizure*). Electroencephalography (EEG) is useful in reaching a diagnosis. In most cases the symptoms disappear after puberty, but if they do not the petit mal seizure frequently evolves into the grand mal type.

The partial, or focal, seizures often have a physical cause, such as a glial scar or tumor that acts as a cerebral irritant and center for electrical discharge. The symptoms here can be quite variable, but they usually reflect the location of the discharging focus. The specific location can be identified by correlative studies with EEG followed by CT and/or MRI. Partial seizures may be classified into the *simple* and the *complex*. In the simple, consciousness is not lost, unlike the case for the complex. Two types of partial seizures worthy of note here are the psychomotor and the Jacksonian. In the psychomotor, which is sometimes called temporal lobe epilepsy, the patient first has visual or olfactory hallucinations followed by altered states of consciousness but does not lose consciousness. These altered states of consciousness involve such psychic phenomena as feelings of unreality or déjà vu (familiarity) combined with anxiety. The attack then usually ends with some inappropriate motor phenomena (eg, undressing in public, smacking of the lips, or walking in a daze).

The focal or Jacksonian seizure starts from a generally known motor focus on the precentral gyrus, and one sees such manifestations as finger jerks and dorsiflexion of the foot. The excitement can spread in succession to adjacent motor areas of the precentral gyrus, and one then sees a progression or "marching" of the contractions as various groups of muscles are excited (the Jacksonian march).

Although much research has been and is being done, the cause of epilepsy is still unknown. In many cases, there is a definite physical focus, such as a glial scar or tumor. Fortunately, in the majority of cases, epileptic seizures can be prevented by the proper use of the appropriate anticonvulsive drug.

Two main principles underlie drug treatment. The first is tailoring the drug and dosage to the individual; if one drug doesn't work, consider another. The second is that one never withdraws anticonvulsant drugs suddenly, for this can precipitate an attack of status epilepticus (see below), which is a life-threatening situation.

### Drugs Used for Grand Mal Attacks

Carbamazepine (Tegretol) has been used recently as a drug of choice. Other drugs include phenytoin (Dilantin, which can cause hypertrophied gums as an unpleasant side effect), primidone, and phenobarbital; the latter two have relatively low toxicity.

### Drugs Used for Petit Mal Attacks

In petit mal attacks, ethosuximide or valproic acid have been the drugs of choice. In partial seizures, carbamazepine has been considered appropriate for the psychomotor as well as the focal attacks.

### Status Epilepticus

This is an acute, life-threatening situation in which the individual is racked by a continuous series of violent spasms that most often end in death. The underlying cause is often the sudden withdrawal or too low a dose of an anticonvulsive drug. Treatment consists of first giving diazepam (Valium) intravenously. If this doesn't stop the seizures, then paraldehyde or phenobarbital is used. If either of these proves unsuccessful, then general anesthetic is administered.

### Underlying Causes

Finally, it should be remembered that epileptic seizures can be caused by tumors, infections such as meningitis or encephalitis, toxicity such as lead poisoning or drug overdose, toxic metabolic substances from other diseases, high fever (especially in infants and children), hypoglycemia, water and electrolyte imbalances, and subdural hematomas. Thus with any epileptic seizure, the physician should always rule out the presence of an underlying disease process.

## ALZHEIMER'S DISEASE

Alzheimer's disease is the most common degenerative disease of older people. In recent years, it has assumed epidemic proportions, with more than 4 million Americans affected by it (nearly 5% of the population older than 60 years). Microscopically one sees widespread neuronal death in the cerebral cortex. The two characteristic pathologic features of Alzheimer's disease are *senile plaques* and *neurofibrillary tangles*. The cerebral hemisphere undergoes marked atrophy with a characteristic widening of the sulci and lateral ventricles that can be seen on CT scan or MRI.

As with all degenerative diseases, the onset of Alzheimer's disease is insidious. Impairment of memory is often limited to recent events at first, but this may worsen as the disease progresses. As the disease advances, speech may be impaired, and there may be progressive disorientation and confusion. A wide variety of other specific disorders of neurologic function also may be present. Motor disabilities may cause the patient to become bedridden. On top of all this, a slow, progressive dementia generally appears with paranoia and hostility. Thus Alzheimer's disease, in addition to destroying the individual slowly, puts tremendous emotional, psychologic, and financial strains on the family and society. Despite widespread research, the cause remains uncertain, and there is no known cure or means of prevention. It is known, however, that a high percentage of the cases have a familial association.

## PARKINSON'S DISEASE (PARALYSIS AGITANS)

Parkinsonism is a slow, progressive disease that generally affects people older than 50 years. More than half a million Americans are affected. Its cause is uncertain, and there is no effective cure or means of prevention. Microscopically one sees a degeneration of the neurons of the substantia nigra and sometimes the caudate nucleus or globus pallidus. The disease is characterized by resting tremors; marked hypertonicity of muscles, which produces cramps; a masklike face; jerky movements and rigidity; and, often in final stages, loss of movement and inability to swallow (for a detailed discussion of this and Huntington's chorea, see Chapter 9).

# NEOPLASTIC

*Brain tumors* may be derived from nervous tissue, nonnervous tissue of the CNS, or primary sites outside the CNS. Tumors of the last-named type are called metastatic in origin (see Appendix VIII, Figure 15). Malignancy depends not only on the histology of the tumor cell but also on the location of the tumor. For example, a growth that is benign from a morphologic point of view may be so located that it cannot be reached surgically (eg, a tumor in the midbrain) and will therefore be fatal.

Because developed neurons do not undergo mitosis, the vast majority of tumors derived from nervous tissue are glial in origin and are known as gliomas. Gliomas constitute approximately 50% to 60% of all intracranial tumors. Histologically the most common are astrocytomas, which are graded on a scale of I to IV according to their malignancy. Type IV, the glioblastoma multiforme, is the most common and malignant type. Cerebral gliomas are rare in children, whereas cerebellar ones are the most common, often being situated in the roof of the fourth ventricle. Other gliomas include oligodendrocytomas, ependymomas, and the fast-growing, highly malignant medulloblastomas of the cerebellum that are found virtually only in children, especially in the 4- to 8-year age group (see Appendix VIII, Figure 16).

About 30% of intracranial tumors arise from nonnervous tissue in the CNS, the most common being the benign, slow-growing meningioma, which is found most often in older people (peak age, 45 years); it is twice as common in women than men (see Appendix VIII, Figure 13). Some other types of nonnervous intracranial tumors are pinealoma, craniopharyngioma, acoustic schwannoma, angioma, and pituitary adenoma (see Appendix VIII, Figure 17).

Last, tumors of the brain may be metastatic in origin (see Appendix VIII, Figure 15), and these account for approximately 10% of all intracranial growths. In such cases, the main site of growth is an organ, from which tumor cells have broken off and reached the brain via the circulatory system. The most common primary sites are lung, kidney, prostate, gastrointestinal tract, and skin (melanoma).

In adults, 85% of tumors are located in the cerebral hemispheres or the regions above the tentorium cerebelli (ie, they are *supratentorial*). In children, most tumors are situated in the cerebellum and regions below the tentorium (ie, *infratentorial*) in the posterior fossa. The most common types of tumors in children are astrocytomas of the brain stem, medulloblastomas, and ependymomas derived from the ependymal cells lining the fourth ventricle. One of the most common and early signs of a tumor is ataxia.

To understand symptoms of tumors, it is helpful to remember the following:

- Tumors are space-occupying lesions that also produce edema. Therefore, they cause an increase in intracranial pressure that gives rise to headaches, papilledema, vomiting (often projectile in nature), and/or drowsiness.
- Tumors expand and irritate the brain matter, which in turn may cause epilepticlike seizures.
- Tumors impinge on the brain and can therefore produce specific (focal) signs depending on where the tumor is located. If in the cerebellum, ataxia, falling, or other cerebellar signs are seen. If in the frontal pole, there may be personality changes or loss of smell (anosmia). A pituitary adenoma can press on the optic chiasm and produce diplopia or other visual disturbances.

In the past, the prognosis for brain tumors was poor, but with CT and MRI being able to reveal 95% of all intracranial growths, better surgical techniques, and radiation therapy and chemotherapy, the results now are much more favorable. The most common and serious postoperative complications are infection, bleeding, edema, seizures, and focal signs.

# SUBSTANCE ABUSE AND TOXINS

## ALCOHOL

Alcoholism is, by far, the most common form of substance abuse. Alcoholism is one of the most prevalent diseases in the United States: An estimated 12 to 15 million people are alcoholics or have a drinking problem, and alcohol-related deaths occur at a rate of more than 100,000 per year (ie, about 5% of total deaths). Alcoholism has many causes, and a genetic predisposition has been identified in some patients.* Most of us have seen the havoc it wreaks upon the individual, the family, and society. There is no known cure, but practicing complete absti-

---

*An interesting research paper on this topic was written by D. Goodwin and colleagues.[8] Recently researchers have suggested the involvement of a mutation on chromosome 11.

nence and joining Alcoholics Anonymous give the best chance for avoidance of relapse.

Clinical manifestations of alcohol toxicity include excitation, uninhibited behavior, slurred speech, and unbalanced gait followed, in more severe cases, by stupor, coma, and respiratory depression, which may be fatal. Withdrawal from prolonged alcohol abuse may give rise to a variety of symptoms, ranging from nausea and vomiting to sleep disorders, hallucinations, and seizures. *Delirium tremens (DTs)*, which usually begins 2 to 4 days after stopping drinking, consists of severe coarse tremor, hallucinations, and confusion and may be associated with high fever and tachycardia. About 10% of patients with delirium tremens die of complications of alcohol withdrawal. Pregnant women who are heavy drinkers have a 35% risk that their newborn child will have fetal alcohol syndrome, consisting of cerebral dysfunctions, abnormal facies, and growth deficiencies.

Methyl alcohol poisoning occurs most often when illegal distillers "cut" expensive, nontoxic, ethyl alcohol with cheap, lethal, methyl alcohol. The latter is degraded in the body to formaldehyde, and this is then broken down to formic acid, which produces blindness, circulatory collapse, and high mortality rates.

## COCAINE

Cocaine toxicity has recently become a major cause of neurotoxicity due to substance abuse. This, in part, is due to its recent widespread availability, particularly in the form of "crack" or "free base" cocaine. Severe intoxication may be associated with restlessness and seizures followed by stupor, coma, and death. Cocaine users have also been shown to have a tendency toward premature coronary artery disease.

## HEROIN

Heroin, a derivative of the opiate morphine, affects the CNS by producing a sense of well-being or "high." This euphoria, however, is rapidly followed by nausea, vomiting, and fainting. These symptoms are relieved by follow-up injections, which forms the basis for the initiation of addiction. Addicts will sometimes resort to heinous crimes to obtain their next "fix." Death from opiate poisoning is often caused by miscalculation of the dose. Such an overdose results in reduced responsiveness, shallow breathing, and finally respiratory arrest.

## OTHER TOXINS

In this category are included many exotic substances that are found more often in mystery and espionage stories than in real life, but when found in the latter they often outdo fiction.

Deaths from the *venom* of snakes, spiders, and scorpions are rare but always stir the imagination. Several years ago in California, a man was convicted of attempted murder for placing a rattlesnake in the mailbox of his intended victim, who barely survived after reaching in to get the morning mail. (The author disclaims responsibility for planting this idea, or any like it, in the minds of his readers.) Some venoms are neurotoxins that depress the cardiac and/or respiratory centers, whereas others prevent the transmission of nervous impulses.

*Heavy metals* can also be lethal. Lead poisoning occurs most often in children, especially those in poor urban areas, who often chew on lead-based paint that has peeled from walls. Symptoms occur a few weeks after ingestion and are varied, insidious, and nonspecific. They may include loss of appetite, irritability, loss of alertness, and, later, drowsiness, seizures, and coma. Mercury, manganese, and arsenic, as well as many industrial compounds, can cause neuropathy. For this reason, an accurate, detailed history of a patient's occupation, place of residence, and daily habits is important.

There are a variety of *neurotoxins from plants* (eg, curare, ergot, and some species of mushrooms). Finally, thousands of people in the United States die every year of *barbiturate* poisoning, and it is still a major cause of toxic death.

# CONGENITAL

Congenital neuropathologic conditions may arise from a number of different causes, including radiation, anoxia, maternal infections, and other unidentified events that may be associated with chromosomal abnormalities, such as Down syndrome.

## SPINA BIFIDA

*Spina bifida* is a congenital malformation that occurs in about 1 per 1000 births in which the arches of one or several vertebrae, usually in the lumbosacral region, have failed to develop or fuse in the midline. In some cases there is no protrusion of the meninges, but in others the meninges protrude and push up under the skin, often forming a rounded sac known as a meningocele (see Appendix VIII,

Figure 18). If, in addition to the meninges, the cord and/or the spinal nerves also push out, this is called a meningomyelocele.

## ANENCEPHALY

*Anencephaly* (failure of brain development) is the most common CNS developmental malformation. This, as well as other open neural tube defects, can be detected by the increased levels of alfa-fetal proteins in the amniotic fluid or in the mother's serum after 12 weeks of pregnancy, when the neural tube finally closes. Anencephaly can also be identified with ultrasound.

## CONGENITAL RUBELLA

A *rubella infection* may be mild for the pregnant woman herself. However, the virus may also attack the fetus, causing the child to be born deaf and possibly to exhibit other defects.

## SUBSTANCE ABUSE

In a pregnant woman who is a heroin addict, the heroin passes the placental barrier, and the unborn child may become addicted. After birth, the child is cut off from the source of the drug, and severe withdrawal signs are seen. Also, in the pregnant woman who smokes, nicotine and other byproducts pass the placental barrier and affect the fetus adversely, resulting, for example, in intrauterine growth retardation.

# OTHER CONDITIONS OF UNCERTAIN ORIGIN

## DYSLEXIA

*Dyslexia* (word blindness) is the inability to or difficulty in recognizing letters, reading words, spelling, or writing, although the individual is neurologically healthy and is often bright and intelligent. The condition tends to run in families, with four to five times as many males being affected as females. It is now realized that undetected dyslexia may be one reason why a student does poorly in school. Also, poor writing, avoidance of reading, and reading upside-down or sideways may indicate the presence of dyslexia. Once detected, intensive private tutoring helps improve the student's performance.

## STAMMERING

*Stammering* is a worldwide, ancient condition that once again affects males more than females by a ratio of 4:1. (Moses [see Exodus 4:10–16], the Roman emperor Claudius, King George VI of England, and Prince Charles' grandfather were stammerers.) Many children have periods in their life when they stammer, but the majority outgrow it. There are numerous theories of causation and a variety of approaches to therapy, but the results have been generally disappointing. Stress is thought to worsen the condition, but most if not all stammerers are fluent in some situations, such as when they are singing. There have been actors who stammered in private life but on stage were perfectly articulate and gave superb performances.

## ANOREXIA NERVOSA

*Anorexia nervosa* is an increasingly common syndrome in postpubescent girls and young women who voluntarily starve themselves into emaciation, sometimes to the point of death. Nearly all the girls come from middle and upper socioeconomic strata. Few are Asian or African-American. The disease is rarely found among young men.

There have been reports of improvement with antidepressive drugs despite the fact that these patients do not exhibit typical characteristics of depression. Supportive treatment consists of hospitalization and tube feeding if necessary. The etiology is unknown, and therefore the number of theories is large, including one of a possible hypothalamic–pituitary dysfunction. Results with psychotherapy have been poor, and the overall prognosis is uncertain.

## MENTAL RETARDATION

If one plots out the intelligence of the population (as measured by IQ tests), one gets a bell-shaped curve, with the lower end of the scale (2% to 3%) having an IQ below 70 and thus being considered mentally retarded. The older classifications of moron, idiot, and imbecile have fortunately been abandoned. The following four gradations based on the standard IQ test have been used. Although this method of classification has been criticized by many for various reasons, it is useful for simplification and comparative purposes.

- *Mild mental retardation* has been used for those individuals with an IQ of 54 to 69. These individuals can be taught, hold jobs, support themselves, and live independently. Indeed, there is a fine Hollywood movie actor who is mildly retarded and openly acknowledges the fact.

- *Moderate mental retardation* has been used for those persons with an IQ between 40 and 54. Some can be taught to do useful skills and can look after themselves, but usually in a structured situation.

- *Severe mental retardation* has been used for persons with an IQ of 25 to 39.

- *Profound mental retardation* is used for persons with an IQ less than 25.

The severe and profound categories constitute 10% of all the mentally retarded, and they usually require institutionalization. Their condition is often associated with other physical symptoms, and the cause of their retardation is often known.

In 40% to 50% of all mentally retarded, there is no known cause (ie, it is idiopathic), and their brains show no gross or microscopic lesions. Behaviorally each case varies, and one sees some individuals who are apathetic or dull and others who are hyperactive or aggressive or have obsessive movements.

The leading known cause of mental retardation is *Down syndrome*, which is a genetic disorder involving chromosome 21: Instead of there being two, there are three chromosomes (*trisomy 21*). Down syndrome is closely associated with the age of the mother and probably also of the father. In women who are 15 to 19 years old, the incidence is 1 per 2400 births; in mothers older than 45 years, the incidence rises to 1 in 40 births. The overall average incidence is 1 in 660 births. The second largest cause of retardation in boys is a genetic defect known as *fragile X syndrome*.

Other possible causes of mental retardation include a variety of infectious (eg, congenital rubella, meningitis, or encephalitis), metabolic (eg, oxygen deprivation during birth, congenital hypothyroidism, or PKU), autoimmune (Rh incompatibility*), toxic (eg, lead poisoning), congenital (eg, microcephalus), and idiopathic (of uncertain cause) factors.

---

*This is an antigen–antibody reaction that occurs when, for example, the father is Rh positive, the mother is Rh negative, and the fetus is Rh positive. The mother will produce antibodies against the Rh-positive red blood cells of her unborn child, which can cause massive hemolysis (destruction) of these cells. The breakdown products of hemoglobin (eg, bilirubin) can then, if in high enough concentrations, cause severe neuronal damage leading to mental retardation.

## REFERENCES

1. Adelman G, ed. *Encyclopedia of Neurosciences.* Boston: Birkhauser; 1984.

2. Gabizon R, Prusiner S. Prion liposomes. *Biochem J.* 1990;266:1–14.

3. Schreuder BE. General aspects of transmissible spongiform encephalopathies and hypotheses about the agents. *Vet Q.* 1993;15:167–174.

4. Helpern M. *Autopsy—The Memoirs of Milton Helpern, the World's Greatest Medical Detective.* New York: St Martin's Press; 1977.

5. Bailey FL. *The Defense Never Rests.* New York: New American Library; 1972.

6. Zimran A, Hollak CE, Abrahamov A, Vans-Oers MH, Kelly M, Beutler E. Home treatment with intravenous enzyme replacement therapy for Gaucher's disease: an international collaborative study of 33 patients. *Blood.* 1993;82:1107–1109.

7. Zimran A, Elstein D, Kannai R, Zevin S, Hadas-Halpern I, Levy-Lahad E, et al. Low-dose enzyme replacement therapy for Gaucher's disease: effects of age, sex, genotype, and clinical features on response to treatment. *Am J Med.* 1994;97:3–13.

8. Goodwin D, et al. Alcohol problems in adoptees raised apart from alcoholic parents. *Arch Gen Psychiatry.* 1973;28:238.

# Special Neuroanatomic Glossary

| WORD | DERIVATION | ILLUSTRATIVE EXAMPLE OR COGNATE |
|---|---|---|
| Agnosia | *a*, not<br>*gnosis*, knowledge | Agnostic |
| Alexia | *a*, not<br>*lexis*, word | Lexicon |
| -algia | Greek, suffix meaning "pain" | Analgesic; nostalgia, the mental pain of returning or going back |
| Aqueduct | *aqua*, water<br>*ductus*, leading | Aquarium; duke, "a leader" |
| Arachnoid | *arachne*, spider<br>*eidos*, resemblance | The arachnoid resembles a cobweb |
| Archi- | Greek prefix meaning "ancient" | Archeology |
| Arcuate | *arcus*, a bow | Arch; archery |
| Astrocyte | *astron*, star<br>*kytos*, cell | Astronomy |
| Ataxia | *a*, not<br>*taxia*, orderly | Taxonomy |
| Ballism | *ballein*, to throw | Ball, ballistics |
| Brachium | *brachium*, arm | Embrace |
| Carotid | *karoo*, to put to sleep | Pressure on the carotid artery results in unconsciousness, as is well known in judo |
| Caudate | *cauda*, a tail | A caudate nucleus has a tail |
| Cerebellum | *Cerebellum* is the diminutive of *cerebrum* (brain), and it means "little brain" | |
| Cerebrum | *cerebrum*, brain | Cerebration is thinking |
| Chiasma | The Greek letter chi (χ) is cross-shaped | A chiasma is an arrangement in the form of a crossing |
| Chorea | *choreia*, dance | People with Huntington's chorea exhibit characteristic ("dancing") movements; choreography |
| Cingulum | *cingulum*, belt | Shingles (the disease) is a verbal corruption because the herpes simplex virus follows the path of the intercostal nerves and forms a beltlike welt of vesicles around the chest wall |
| Cistern | *cisterna*, a well | |
| Claustrum | *claustrum*, enclosure | Claustrophobia; closet |
| Clinoid | *kline*, bed<br>*eidos*, resemblance<br>The four clinoid processes were thought to resemble the four posts of a bed | Clinic |

| WORD | DERIVATION | ILLUSTRATIVE EXAMPLE OR COGNATE |
|---|---|---|
| Cornu | *cornu*, horn | Cornucopia |
| Coronary | *corona*, crown or garland | The coronary arteries encircle the heart; coronation |
| | Also, the *corona radiata* is a fan-shaped ("radiating") fiber mass in the cerebral cortex | |
| Corpus callosum | *corpus*, body | Callus; corporation |
| | *callosum*, hard | |
| Cortex | *cortex*, bark | The cerebral cortex covers the cerebral hemisphere, much as bark covers the trunk of a tree |
| Crista | *crista*, crest | |
| Cuneate | *cuneatus*, wedge-shaped | The cuneiform writing of ancient Babylon had wedge-shaped characters |
| Decussation | The Roman numeral X is called *deca* | A decussation is a crossing |
| Dendrite | *dendron*, branching figure or tree | Rhododendron |
| Dentate | *dens*, tooth | Dentist |
| | *dentatus*, tooth-shaped | |
| Dura mater | *dura*, hard | Durable; alma mater |
| | *mater*, mother (who protects) | |
| Dyskinesia | *dis*, improper | Disorder; disease; kinetics |
| | *kinesia*, motion | |
| Edema | *oidema*, swelling | Oedipus (see Appendix XIII, "Did You Know?") |
| Epi- | Greek prefix meaning "upon, over, above" | An epitaph is inscribed over a grave (*taphos*) |
| Fasciculus | *fasciculus*, a bundle (of rods or fibers) | The symbol of the Italian Fascists was the Roman bundles of rods, the *fascis*, seen on old Mercury head dimes |
| Fornix | *fornix*, arch | In ancient Rome the prostitutes hung around the supporting arches of the viaducts; a man visiting the area was engaged in fornication |
| Genu | *genu*, knee | Genuflect, ie, bend (bow) before royalty |
| Glia | *glia*, glue | Glial cells "hold together" the neurons |
| Glossal | *glossa*, tongue | Glossary |
| Gracilis | *gracilis*, slender | |
| Gyrus | *gyros*, ring, circle | Gyrate; gyroscope |
| Hippocampus | *hippos*, horse | In cross-section this hippocampus resembles a seahorse; hippodrome |
| | *kampos*, sea | |
| Hypo- | Greek prefix meaning "under, below" | A hypodermic goes under the skin (*dermis*) |
| Insula | *insula*, island | Insulin is produced by the islands of Langerhans; insulation |
| Internuncial | *inter*, between | Announce; papal nuncio |
| | *nuncio*, messenger | |
| Lamina | *lamina*, layer or thin plate | Lamination |
| Lemniscus | *lemniskos*, ribbon, band | |
| Lentiform | Lens shaped | *Lens* is the Latin word for "lentil," the lens-shaped vegetable of the bean family |
| Limbic | *limbus*, border or edge | Limbo is the area bordering on Hell |
| Lingula | *lingula*, little tongue | Linguist; language |
| Lumbar | *lumbus*, loin or flank | Lumbago |
| Macula | *macula*, spot | Immaculate; spotless; clean |

| WORD | DERIVATION | ILLUSTRATIVE EXAMPLE OR COGNATE |
|---|---|---|
| Mamillary | *mamma*, breast | Mammary; mammals |
| Mesencephalon | *meso*, middle | Mezzanine |
| | *enkephalos*, the brain | |
| Oligodendroglia | *oligo*, few | Oligarchy, "a few who rule" |
| | *dendron*, branching figure or tree | |
| | *glia*, glue | |
| Paleo- | Greek prefix meaning "old" | Paleontology |
| Pallidus | *pallidus*, pale | The pallidus is pale in comparison to the neighboring putamen |
| Peduncle | *ped*, foot, limb, stalk | Pedal; pedestrian |
| Petrous | *petra*, rock | Petrified; refers to the "rock" on which the Catholic Church stands; Peter is also slang for "penis." |
| Pia mater | *pia*, soft delicate | Pianissimo is a musical term meaning "very soft" |
| | *mater*, mother | |
| Pineal | *pinea*, pine cone | The pineal body is conical |
| Pons | *pons*, bridge | Pontoon |
| Ramus | *ramus*, branch | Ramifications |
| Rectus | *rectus*, straight | Rectify; erect |
| Reticular | *reticulum*, small net | A reticle is the network of lines in a telescopic sight; a lady's reticule is a small net bag |
| Rhinencephalon | *rhin*, nose | Rhinoceros |
| | *enkephalos*, brain | |
| Rubro | *ruber*, red | Ruby |
| Sacral | *sacer*, holy, sacred | The sacral bone was believed to resist decomposition and thus to serve as the basis for resurrection |
| Sagittal | *sagitta*, arrow | Sagittarius is the Archer of the zodiac |
| Sella turcica | *sella*, saddle | The sella turcica resembles a Turkish saddle |
| | *turcica*, Turkish | |
| Septum | *septum*, partition | Separate |
| Substantia nigra | *substantia*, substance | Nigeria; negroid |
| | *nigra*, black | |
| Tapetum | *tapete*, carpet | Tapestry |
| Tectum | *tectum*, roof | Architecture |
| Temporal | *tempus*, time | The temporal area gives evidence of the passage of time; ie, the hair turns gray |
| Tentorium | *tentorium*, tent | |
| Tubercle | *tuber*, swelling or rounded projection | Tubers (potatoes); protuberance |
| Vagus | *vagus*, wandering | The vagus nerve extends into the thorax and abdomen; vagabond; vagrant |
| Velum | *velum*, covering | Veil |
| Venereal | *Venus*, the goddess of love | |
| Ventricle | *ventriculus*, little chamber, cavity, hollow, stomach | A ventriloquist "speaks from the stomach" |
| Vermis | *vermis*, worm | The cerebellar vermis resembles a worm; vermin |
| Vertebra | *vertere*, to turn | Vertigo; vertebra (they turn on themselves) |

## TERMS RELATED TO NEUROPHARMACOLOGY

| | |
|---|---|
| Barbiturate | Emil Fisher first produced barbiturates by condensing malonic acid with urea. The correct name should be *malonylurate*. The urea was extracted from large quantities of urine given to him by a waitress who worked in a coffeehouse he frequented (coffee is a diuretic agent). Not surprisingly, her name was Barbara, and to thank her for her efforts on behalf of science, he named the new drug after her. |
| Belladonna | *Bella donna* is Italian for "beautiful lady." In Italy during the Renaissance, ladies before going to parties would put belladonna (atropine) in their eyes, causing the pupils to dilate and the eyes to sparkle, thus enhancing their beauty. However, the drug greatly blurred their vision, and one can imagine the scene that ensued when such a lady mistook her husband for her lover. |
| Cocaine | Cocaine comes from the leaves of the coca tree. Sigmund Freud discovered its use as a local anesthetic for the eye. For a while, he also used it to get "high," or "euphoric," as he put it. |
| Hashish | This is an Arabic word. In the Middle East during the Crusades, professional killers often smoked hashish before doing a "hit," and for this reason they were called *hash-ha-shans*. The Crusaders could not pronounce this guttural word and corrupted it to "assassins," from which we get the word "assassinate." |
| Heroin | This drug gets its name from the fact that it often gives one transitory heroic feelings. |
| Marijuana | This drug is so called from the belief that it is an aphrodisiac. It is derived from the Spanish names *Maria*, which is feminine, and *Juan*, which is masculine. |
| Morphine | Morpheus was the Greek god of dreams, and taking morphine puts one in a dreamlike state. Shapes and forms appear in dreams, and from this is also derived the word *morphology*, meaning the study of structures or forms. |
| Nicotine | This drug was named after Jean Nicot, who introduced tobacco into France. |

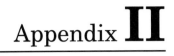

# Atlas of the Brain

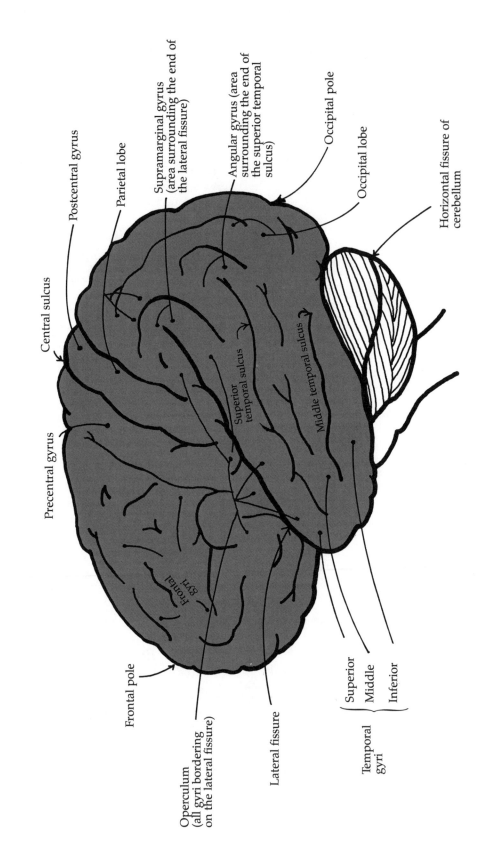

Central sulcus

Postcentral gyrus

Parietal lobe

Supramarginal gyrus (area surrounding the end of the lateral fissure)

Angular gyrus (area surrounding the end of the superior temporal sulcus)

Occipital pole

Occipital lobe

Horizontal fissure of cerebellum

Precentral gyrus

Superior temporal sulcus

Middle temporal sulcus

Frontal gyri

Frontal pole

Operculum (all gyri bordering on the lateral fissure)

Lateral fissure

Superior
Middle
Inferior

Temporal gyri

**Atlas Plate I** Lateral View of the Brain

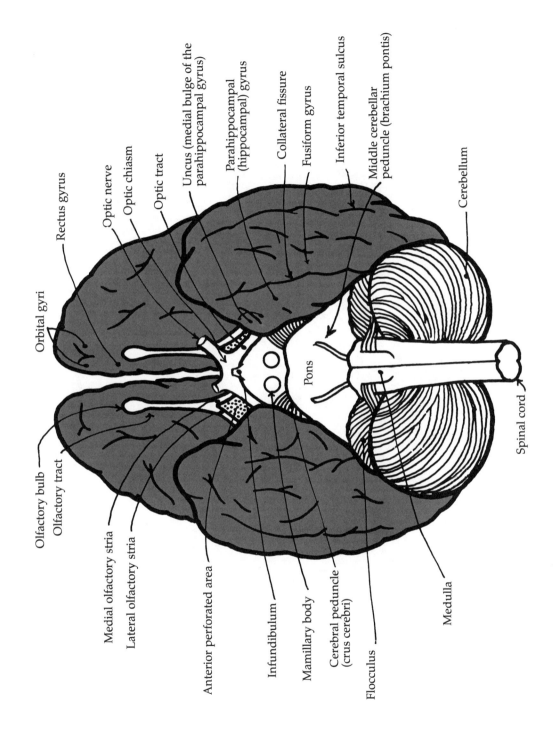

Orbital gyri

Rectus gyrus

Optic nerve

Optic chiasm

Optic tract

Uncus (medial bulge of the parahippocampal gyrus)

Parahippocampal (hippocampal) gyrus

Collateral fissure

Fusiform gyrus

Inferior temporal sulcus

Middle cerebellar peduncle (brachium pontis)

Cerebellum

Olfactory bulb

Olfactory tract

Medial olfactory stria

Lateral olfactory stria

Anterior perforated area

Infundibulum

Mamillary body

Cerebral peduncle (crus cerebri)

Flocculus

Medulla

Spinal cord

Pons

**Atlas Plate II** Basal View of the Brain*

*For a more detailed view of the brain stem with the cranial nerves, see Plate VII of this atlas.

103

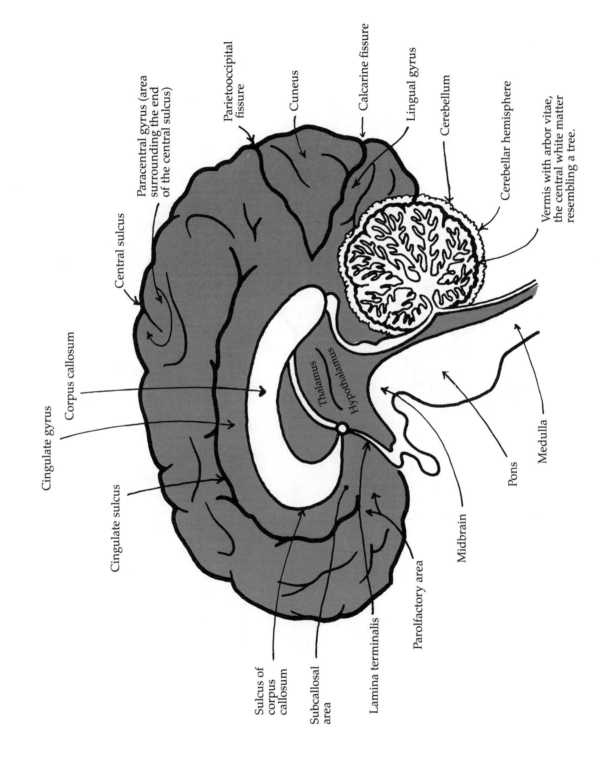

Cingulate gyrus

Corpus callosum

Central sulcus

Paracentral gyrus (area surrounding the end of the central sulcus)

Parietooccipital fissure

Cuneus

Calcarine fissure

Lingual gyrus

Cerebellum

Cerebellar hemisphere

Vermis with arbor vitae, the central white matter resembling a tree.

Cingulate sulcus

Thalamus

Hypothalamus

Sulcus of corpus callosum

Subcallosal area

Lamina terminalis

Parolfactory area

Midbrain

Pons

Medulla

**Atlas Plate III** Midsagittal View of the Brain

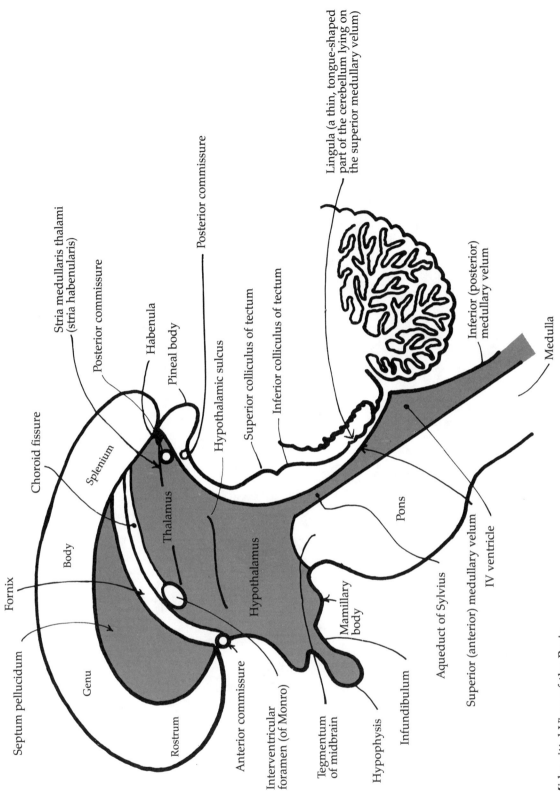

**Atlas Plate IV** Enlarged Midsagittal View of the Brain

Septum pellucidum

Fornix

Choroid fissure

Stria medullaris thalami (stria habenularis)

Posterior commissure

Habenula

Pineal body

Posterior commissure

Lingula (a thin, tongue-shaped part of the cerebellum lying on the superior medullary velum)

Body

Genu

Splenium

Thalamus

Hypothalamic sulcus

Superior colliculus of tectum

Inferior colliculus of tectum

Inferior (posterior) medullary velum

Medulla

Rostrum

Anterior commissure

Interventricular foramen (of Monro)

Hypothalamus

Mamillary body

Pons

Tegmentum of midbrain

Hypophysis

Infundibulum

Aqueduct of Sylvius

Superior (anterior) medullary velum

IV ventricle

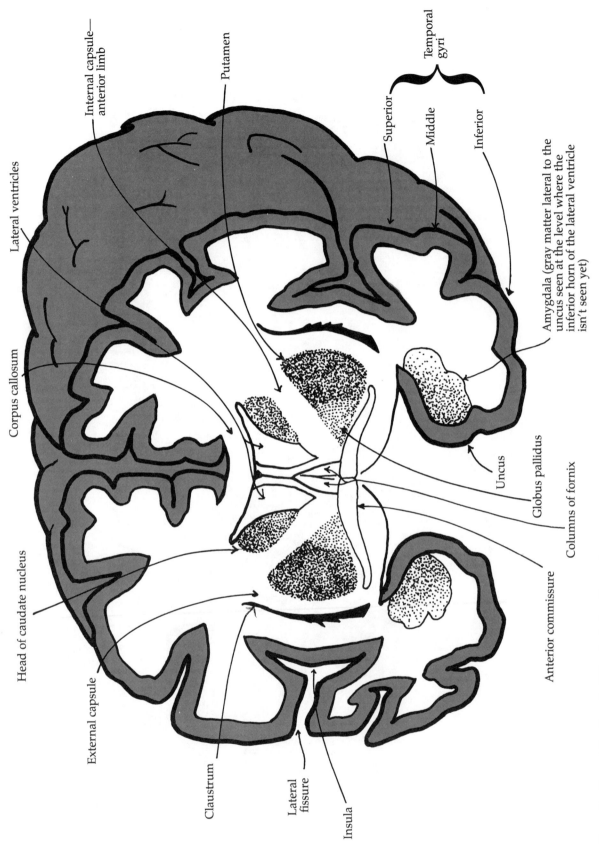

Internal capsule— anterior limb

Putamen

Temporal gyri

Superior

Middle

Inferior

Amygdala (gray matter lateral to the uncus seen at the level where the inferior horn of the lateral ventricle isn't seen yet)

Lateral ventricles

Corpus callosum

Uncus

Globus pallidus

Columns of fornix

Head of caudate nucleus

External capsule

Anterior commissure

Claustrum

Lateral fissure

Insula

**Atlas Plate V** Cross-Section at the Level of the Anterior Commissure

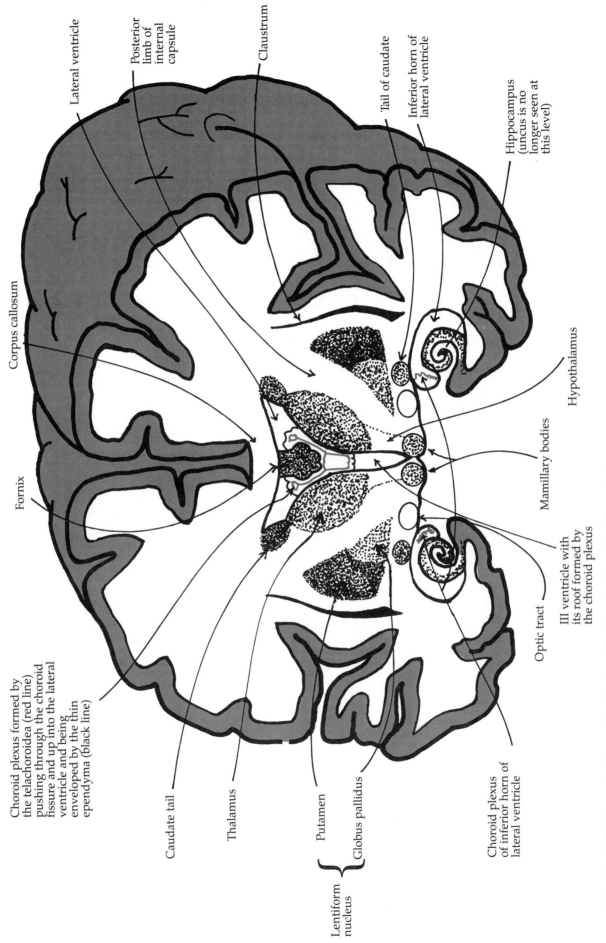

Lateral ventricle

Posterior limb of internal capsule

Claustrum

Tail of caudate

Inferior horn of lateral ventricle

Hippocampus (uncus is no longer seen at this level)

Corpus callosum

Hypothalamus

Fornix

Mamillary bodies

Choroid plexus formed by the telachoroidea (red line) pushing through the choroid fissure and up into the lateral ventricle and being enveloped by the thin ependyma (black line)

III ventricle with its roof formed by the choroid plexus

Optic tract

Choroid plexus of inferior horn of lateral ventricle

Caudate tail

Thalamus

Putamen

Globus pallidus

Lentiform nucleus

**Atlas Plate VI** Cross-Section of the Brain at the Level of the Mamillary Bodies

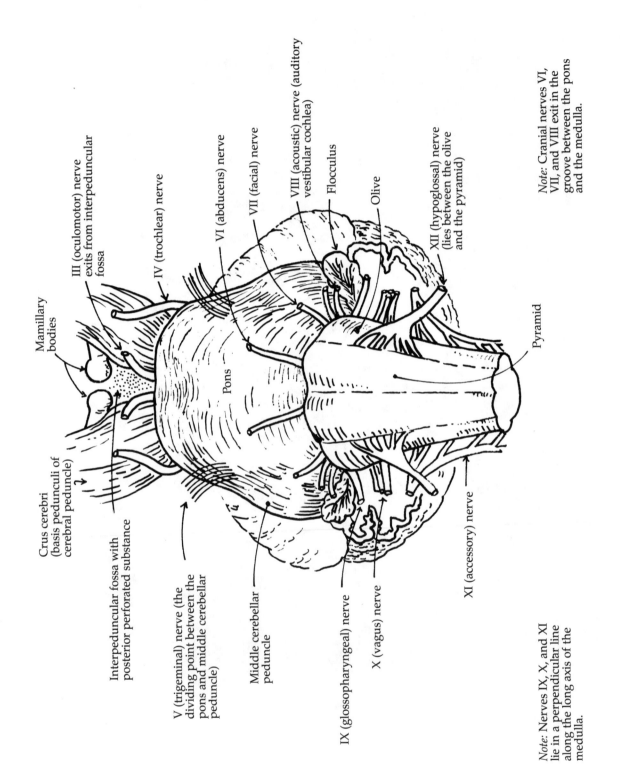

Mamillary bodies

Crus cerebri (basis pedunculi of cerebral peduncle)

III (oculomotor) nerve exits from interpeduncular fossa

IV (trochlear) nerve

VI (abducens) nerve

VII (facial) nerve

VIII (acoustic) nerve (auditory vestibular cochlea)

Flocculus

Olive

XII (hypoglossal) nerve (lies between the olive and the pyramid)

Pons

Pyramid

Interpeduncular fossa with posterior perforated substance

V (trigeminal) nerve (the dividing point between the pons and middle cerebellar peduncle)

Middle cerebellar peduncle

IX (glossopharyngeal) nerve

X (vagus) nerve

XI (accessory) nerve

*Note:* Nerves IX, X, and XI lie in a perpendicular line along the long axis of the medulla.

*Note:* Cranial nerves VI, VII, and VIII exit in the groove between the pons and the medulla.

**Atlas Plate VII** Ventral View of the Brain Stem

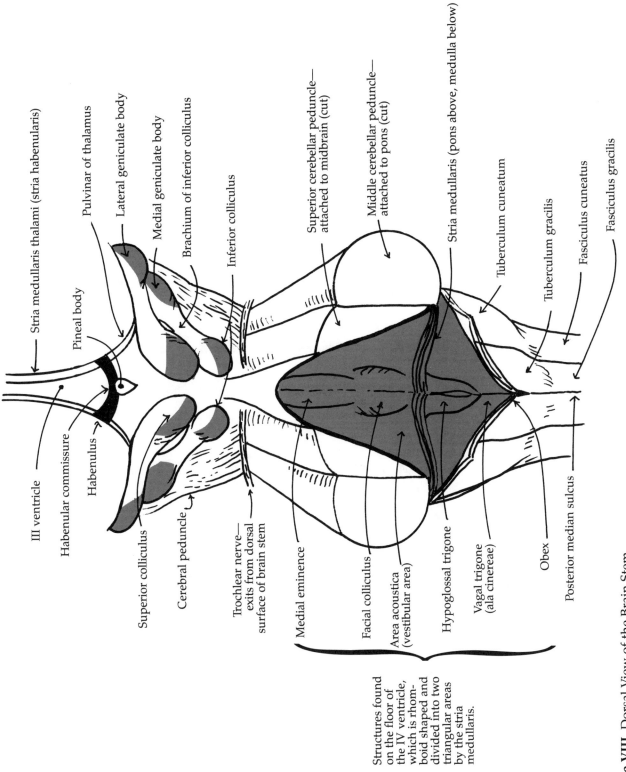

III ventricle

Stria medullaris thalami (stria habenularis)

Pineal body

Habenular commissure

Habenulus

Pulvinar of thalamus

Lateral geniculate body

Medial geniculate body

Brachium of inferior colliculus

Inferior colliculus

Superior colliculus

Cerebral peduncle

Trochlear nerve— exits from dorsal surface of brain stem

Superior cerebellar peduncle— attached to midbrain (cut)

Middle cerebellar peduncle— attached to pons (cut)

Stria medullaris (pons above, medulla below)

Tuberculum cuneatum

Tuberculum gracilis

Fasciculus cuneatus

Fasciculus gracilis

Medial eminence

Facial colliculus

Area acoustica (vestibular area)

Hypoglossal trigone

Vagal trigone (ala cinereae)

Obex

Posterior median sulcus

Structures found on the floor of the IV ventricle, which is rhomboid shaped and divided into two triangular areas by the stria medullaris.

**Atlas Plate VIII** Dorsal View of the Brain Stem

109

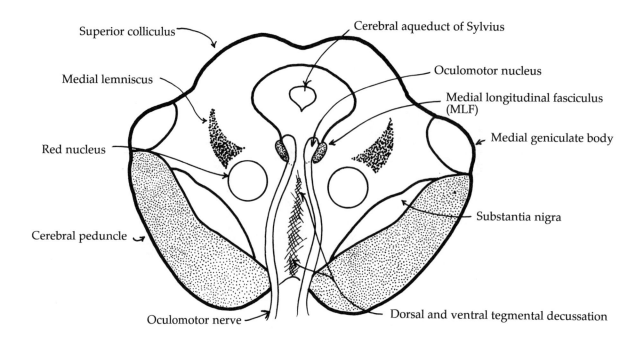

Superior colliculus

Medial lemniscus

Red nucleus

Cerebral peduncle

Oculomotor nerve

Cerebral aqueduct of Sylvius

Oculomotor nucleus

Medial longitudinal fasciculus (MLF)

Medial geniculate body

Substantia nigra

Dorsal and ventral tegmental decussation

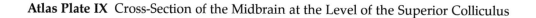

**Atlas Plate IX** Cross-Section of the Midbrain at the Level of the Superior Colliculus

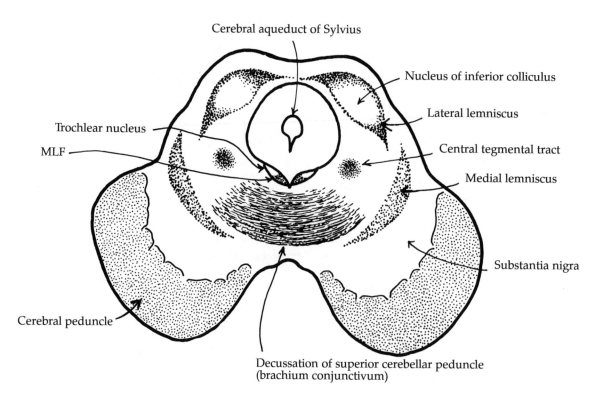

Cerebral aqueduct of Sylvius

Trochlear nucleus

MLF

Nucleus of inferior colliculus

Lateral lemniscus

Central tegmental tract

Medial lemniscus

Substantia nigra

Cerebral peduncle

Decussation of superior cerebellar peduncle (brachium conjunctivum)

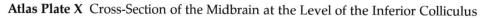

**Atlas Plate X** Cross-Section of the Midbrain at the Level of the Inferior Colliculus

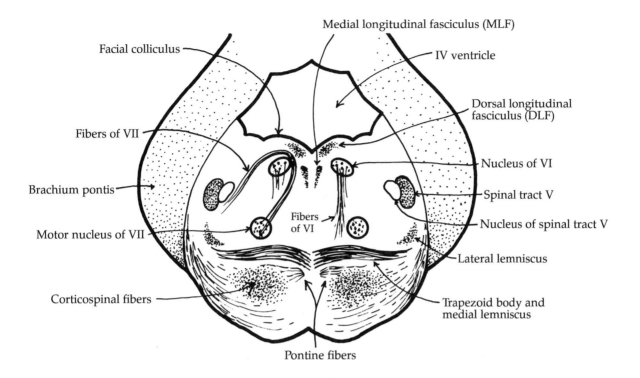

**Atlas Plate XI** Cross-Section of the Pons at the Facial Colliculus

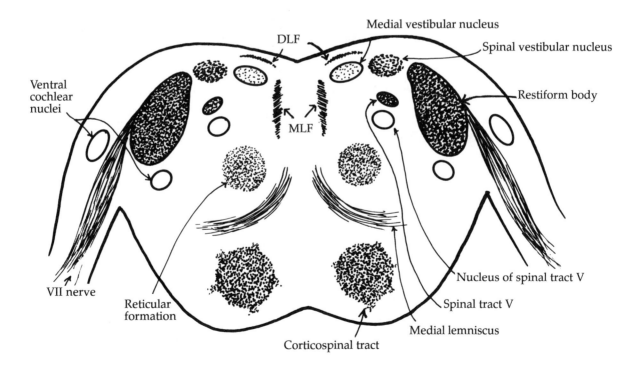

**Atlas Plate XII** Cross-Section of the Lower Pons

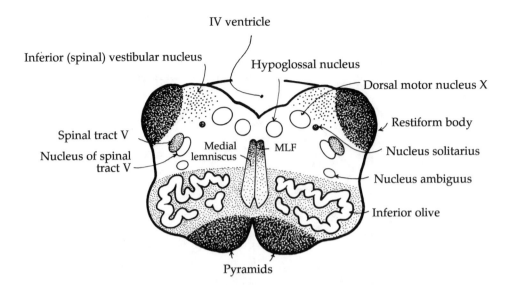

**Atlas Plate XIII** Section through the Upper Medulla

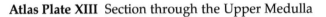
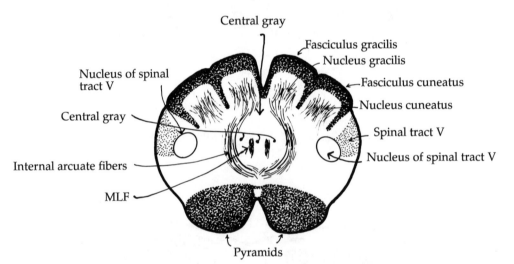

**Atlas Plate XIV** Section through the Lower Medulla

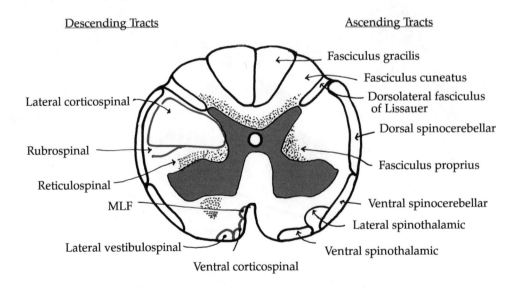

**Atlas Plate XV** Section through the Spinal Cord at the Midcervical Level

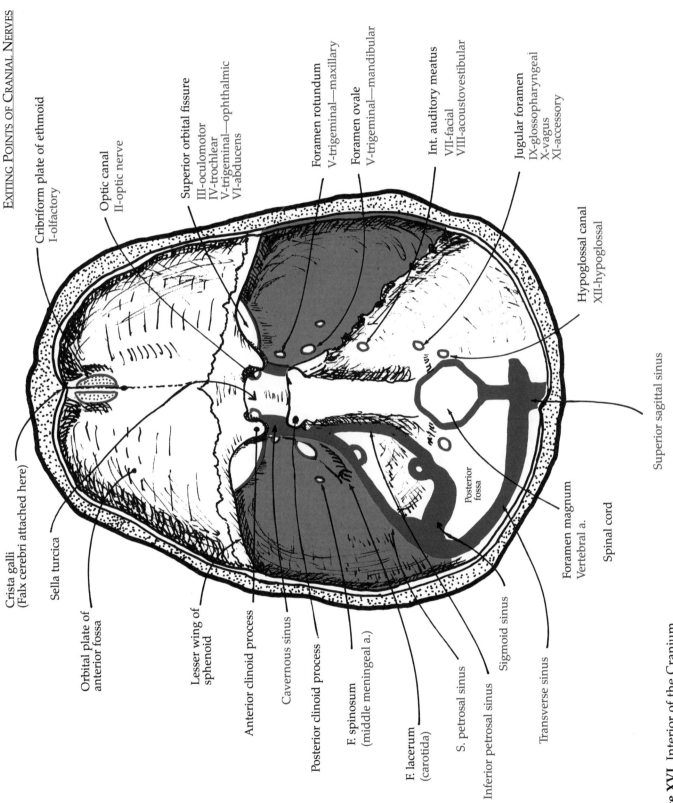

Crista galli
(Falx cerebri attached here)

Sella turcica

Orbital plate of
anterior fossa

Lesser wing of
sphenoid

Anterior clinoid process

Cavernous sinus

Posterior clinoid process

F. spinosum
(middle meningeal a.)

F. lacerum
(carotida)

S. petrosal sinus

Inferior petrosal sinus

Sigmoid sinus

Transverse sinus

Cribriform plate of ethmoid
I-olfactory

Optic canal
II-optic nerve

Superior orbital fissure
III-oculomotor
IV-trochlear
V-trigeminal—ophthalmic
VI-abducens

Foramen rotundum
V-trigeminal—maxillary

Foramen ovale
V-trigeminal—mandibular

Int. auditory meatus
VII-facial
VIII-acoustovestibular

Jugular foramen
IX-glossopharyngeal
X-vagus
XI-accessory

Hypoglossal canal
XII-hypoglossal

Superior sagittal sinus

Posterior
fossa

Foramen magnum
Vertebral a.

Spinal cord

**Atlas Plate XVI** Interior of the Cranium

113

# Clinical References for Cerebrospinal Fluid Values

Normal and Abnormal Values of Cerebrospinal Fluid (CSF)

| | Pressure (mm $H_2O$) | Color | White blood cell count (per $mm^3$) | Red blood cell count (per $mm^3$) | Glucose | Protein |
|---|---|---|---|---|---|---|
| Normal | 70–190 | Clear and colorless | 0–3 | 0–5 | 60–80 mg/100 mL | 15–45 mg/100 mL |
| Acute bacterial meningitis | 250–800 | Usually cloudy yellow or white because of pus | Hundreds to tens of thousands, nearly all neutrophils | 0–5 | Greatly reduced, sometimes to 0 | Greatly increased, as high as 400–500 mg/100 mL |
| Aseptic meningitis | Slight increase | Clear | 50–500, mostly lymphocytes | 0–5 | Normal | Slight increase (up to around 100 mg/100 mL) |
| Viral encephalitis | Slight increase | Clear and colorless | 30–400 | 0–5 | Normal | Slight increase (rarely above 100 mg/100 mL) |
| Cerebrovascular accident (hemorrhagic into ventricles or subarachnoid space) | Up to 500 | Bloody | | | Normal | Normal |

*Remarks:*
1. If manometer reads a pressure of 300 mm $H_2O$ or more, remove it at once and use fluid in it to do a microscopic reading.
2. To differentiate between a traumatic tap and blood in CSF due to subarachnoid hemorrhage, centrifuge the CSF. In a traumatic tap the supernatant is clear; in a subarachnoid hemorrhage the supernatant will be yellowish.
3. A fall in the chloride level of the CSF is characteristic of tuberculous meningitis.
4. In infants younger than 1 year, the most common organism to cause acute meningitis is Gram-negative *Escherichia coli*; in children it is *Hemophilus influenzae*; in adults it is Gram-negative *Neisseria meningitidis*.

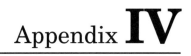

# Dermatome Maps

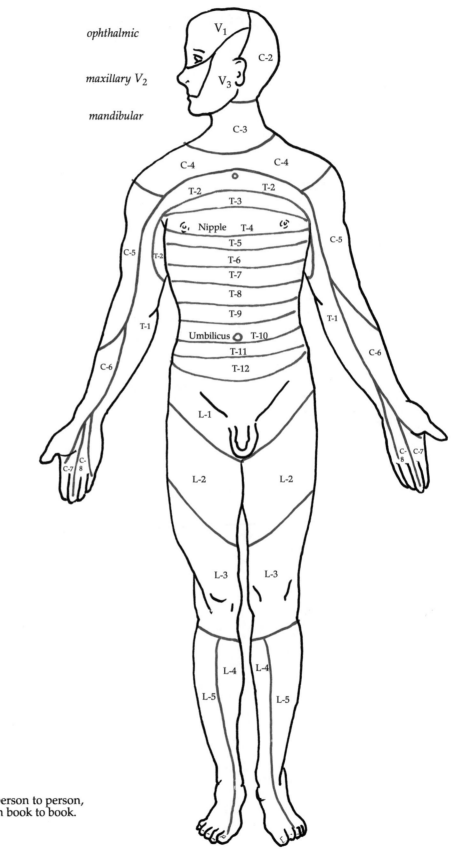

*ophthalmic*

*maxillary* $V_2$

*mandibular*

$V_1$

C-2

$V_3$

C-3

C-4    C-4

T-2    T-2

T-3

Nipple    T-4

T-5

C-5    C-5

T-2    T-6

T-7

T-8

T-9

T-1    T-1

Umbilicus    T-10

T-11

C-6    C-6

T-12

L-1

C-7  C-8    C-8  C-7

L-2    L-2

L-3    L-3

L-4    L-4

L-5    L-5

There is considerable overlap from person to person, and these maps vary somewhat from book to book.

118

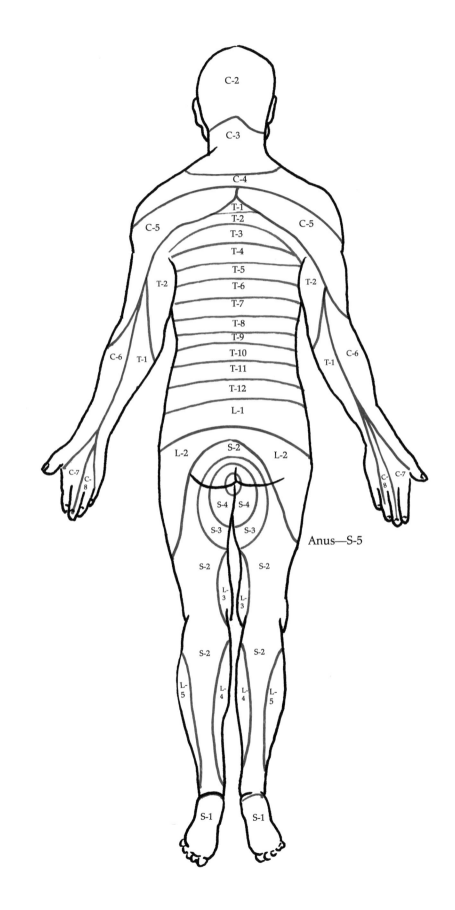

# Muscle Actions and Their Nerve Supplies

## UPPER LIMB

| Muscle and Action | Peripheral Nerves | Spinal Nerves |
| --- | --- | --- |
| **I. SHOULDER** | | |
| *Elevation*: | | |
| 1. Levator scapulae | Branches of C-3 to C-5 from cervical plexus | |
| 2. Trapezius (upper part) | Spinal accessory (cranial nerve XI) and C-3 to C-4 | C-3 to C-4 |
| *Depression*: | | |
| 1. Trapezius (lower part) | Spinal accessory (cranial nerve XI) and C-3 to C-4 | C-3 to C-4 |
| 2. Latissimus dorsi | Thoracodorsal | C-6 to C-8 |
| *Retraction* (draw toward vertebral column—"Pull them shoulders back"): | | |
| 1. Trapezius | Spinal accessory (cranial nerve XI) and C-3 to C-4 | C-3 to C-4 |
| 2. Rhomboid major and minor | Dorsal scapular | C-5 |
| *Protraction*: | | |
| 1. Pectoralis minor | Medial pectoral | C-8 to T-1 |
| 2. Serratus anterior | Long thoracic | C-5 to C-7 |

Note: Serratus anterior also holds shoulder flat on thorax, and if nerve is injured one sees a "winged scapula."

| Muscle and Action | Peripheral Nerves | Spinal Nerves |
| --- | --- | --- |
| **II. ARM** | | |
| *Abduction*: | | |
| 1. Deltoid | Axillary | C-5 to C-6 |
| 2. Supraspinatus (initiates action) | Suprascapular | C-5 |
| *Adduction*: | | |
| 1. Pectoralis major | Medial and lateral pectoral | C-5 to C-8, T-1 |
| 2. Latissimus dorsi | Thoracodorsal | C-5 to C-6 |
| 3. Teres major | Lower subscapular | C-5 to C-8 |
| *Extension* (moving arm front to back, as in swimming): | | |
| 1. Latissimus dorsi | Thoracodorsal | C-6 to C-8 |
| 2. Teres major | Lower subscapular | C-5 to C-6 |
| *Flexion*: | | |
| 1. Pectoralis major | Medial and lateral pectoral | C-5 to C-8, T-1 |
| *Medial rotation*: | | |
| 1. Teres major | Lower subscapular | C-5 to C-6 |
| 2. Subscapularis | Upper and lower subscapular | C-5 to C-6 |
| *Lateral rotation*: | | |
| 1. Teres minor | Axillary | C-5 |
| 2. Infraspinatus | Suprascapular | C-5 to C-6 |
| **III. FOREARM** | | |
| *Extension*: | | |
| 1. Triceps | Radial | C-7 to C-8 |
| 2. Anconeus | Radial | C-7 to C-8 |
| *Flexion*: | | |
| 1. Biceps | Musculocutaneous | C-5 to C-6 |
| 2. Brachialis | Musculocutaneous | C-5 to C-6 |

| Muscle and Action | Peripheral Nerves | Spinal Nerves |
|---|---|---|
| 3. Coracobrachialis | Musculocutaneous | C-6 to C-7 |
| 4. Brachioradialis | Radial | C-5 to C-6 |
| *Pronation*: | | |
|    1. Pronator teres | Median | C-6 to C-7 |
|    2. Pronator quadratus | Median | C-8, T-1 |
| *Supination*: | | |
|    1. Supinator | Radial | C-6 |
|    2. Biceps brachii | Musculocutaneous | C-5 to C-6 |

**IV.  HAND**

| Muscle and Action | Peripheral Nerves | Spinal Nerves |
|---|---|---|
| *Flexion*: | | |
|    1. Flexor carpi ulnaris | Ulnar | C-8, T-1 |
|    2. Flexor carpi radialis | Median | C-6 to C-7 |
|    3. Palmaris longus | Median | C-6 to C-7 |
| *Extension*: | | |
|    1. Extensor carpi radialis longus | Radial | C-6 to C-7 |
|    2. Extensor carpi radialis brevis | Radial | C-6 to C-8 |
|    3. Extensor carpi ulnaris | Radial | C-6 to C-8 |
| *Adduction*: | | |
|    1. Flexor carpi ulnaris contracting with | Ulnar | C-8, T-1 |
|    2. Extensor carpi ulnaris | Radial | C-6 to C-8 |
| *Abduction*: | | |
|    1. Flexor carpi radialis contracting with | Median | C-6 to C-7 |
|    2. Extensor carpi radialis | Radial | C-6 to C-7 |

**V.  FINGERS (digits 2–5)**

| Muscle and Action | Peripheral Nerves | Spinal Nerves |
|---|---|---|
| *Flexion of distal phalanx*: | | |
|    1. Flexor digitorum profundus | Median | C-7, T-1 |
| | Ulnar | C-8, T-1 |
| *Flexion of middle phalanx*: | | |
|    1. Flexor digitorum sublimis | Median | C-7, T-1 |
| *Flexion of proximal phalanx* (at metacarpophalangeal joint): | | |
|    1. Lumbricales,  two lateral | Median | C-6 to C-7 |
|                    two medial | Ulnar | C-8, T-1 |

Note:   The flexor digitorum profundus and sublimis also act as flexors of the proximal and middle phalanges. The fifth digit (little finger) is also flexed by the flexor digiti quinti brevis, supplied by the ulnar nerve (C-8 and T-1).

| Muscle and Action | Peripheral Nerves | Spinal Nerves |
|---|---|---|
| *Extension of all phalanges*: | | |
|    1. Extensor digitorum communis | Radial | C-6 to C-8 |
|    2. Extensor digiti quinti minimi | Radial | C-6 to C-8 |
|    3. Extensor indicis | Radial | C-6 to C-8 |

Note: The lumbricales also extend the middle and distal phalanges of digits 2–5.

| Muscle and Action | Peripheral Nerves | Spinal Nerves |
|---|---|---|
| *Abduction* (through a line of reference drawn through the long axis of the middle finger): | | |
|    1. Dorsal interossei | Ulnar | C-8, T-1 |
|    2. Abductor digiti quinti | Ulnar | C-8, T-1 |

| Muscle and Action | Peripheral Nerves | Spinal Nerves |
| --- | --- | --- |
| *Adduction* (through a line of reference drawn through the long axis of the middle finger): | | |
| 1. Palmar interossei | Ulnar | C-8, T-1 |
| *Opposition*: | | |

Note: The little finger (digit 5) does opposition, and the major muscle is the opponens digiti minimi, supplied by the ulnar nerve (C-8 and T-1).

**VI. FIRST DIGIT (thumb)**

| Muscle and Action | Peripheral Nerves | Spinal Nerves |
| --- | --- | --- |
| *Flexion of distal phalanx*: | | |
| 1. Flexor pollicis longus | Median | C-6 to C-7 |
| *Flexion of proximal phalanx*: | | |
| 1. Flexor pollicis brevis (the flexor pollicis longus also assists) | Median | C-6 to C-7 |
| *Extension*: | | |
| 1. Extensor pollicis longus and brevis | Radial | C-6 to C-8 |
| *Adduction*: | | |
| 1. Adductor pollicis | Ulnar | C-7 to C-8 |
| *Abduction:* | | |
| 1. Abductor pollicis longus | Radial | C-6 to C-7 |
| 2. Abductor pollicis brevis | Median | C-6 to C-7 |
| *Opposition*: | | |
| 1. Opponens pollicis | Median | C-6 to T-1 |

## Tips

For easy memorization, remember that:

1. All the muscles on the posterior aspect (extensor compartment) of the arm are supplied by the radial nerve.
2. All the muscles in the anterior (flexor) compartment of the arm are supplied by the musculocutaneous nerve.
3. All the muscles of the posterior compartment (extensor) of the forearm are supplied by the radial nerve.
4. All the muscles of the anterior compartment (flexor) of the forearm are supplied by the median nerve except for half the flexor digitorum profundus and the flexor carpi ulnaris, which are supplied by the ulnar nerve.
5. All the intrinsic muscles of the hand are supplied by the ulnar nerve except for *LOAF*, which are supplied by the median nerve.

>    **L** — two lateral lumbricals
>    **O** — opponens pollicis
>    **A** — abductor of pollicis brevis
>    **F** — half of flexor pollicis brevis

## Historical Tidbits

The Roman (Latin) names for the fingers were:

1. Little finger—auricularis, because it was put in the ear to clean or scratch it.
2. Ring finger—annularis, because *annulus* means "circular" or "ring." *Annual* means "yearly"; a year circles back on itself, and so does the anus.
3. Middle finger—vulgaris, no explanation needed.
4. Forefinger—indicis, because it is used to indicate or point with.
5. Thumb—pollicis. This word means "strong," and this is the strongest of the five fingers. You can hang by your thumbs but not by any other finger.

Digitalis has been used for centuries to treat heart problems, and it gets its name because it's found in the leaves of the foxglove plant, which resembles fingers.

*Phalanx* means "spear" and comes from the famous battle formation of spears of Alexander the Great.

## LOWER LIMB

| Muscle and Action | Peripheral Nerves | Spinal Nerves |
|---|---|---|

### I.  THIGH (action at hip joint)

*Flexion*:

| | | |
|---|---|---|
| 1.  Iliopsoas | Femoral | L-2 to L-3 |
| 2.  Sartorius | Femoral | L-2 to L-3 |
| 3.  Tensor fasciae latae | Superior gluteal | L-4 to S-1 |

Note:   The adductors longus, brevis, and magnus plus the pectineus and the anterior part of the gluteus medius also help flex the thigh.

*Extension*:

| | | |
|---|---|---|
| 1.  Gluteus maximus | Inferior gluteal | L-5 to S-2 |
| 2.  Gluteus medius | Superior gluteal | L-4 to S-1 |
| 3.  Adductor magnus | Obturator | L-3 to L-4 |

Note:    The biceps femoris, the semitendinosus, the semimembranosus, and the piriformis also help extend the thigh.

*Abduction*:

| | | |
|---|---|---|
| 1.  Gluteus medius | Superior gluteal | L-4 to S-1 |
| 2.  Gluteus minimus | Superior gluteal | L-4 to S-1 |

*Adduction*:

| | | |
|---|---|---|
| 1.  Adductor magnus | Obturator | L-3 to L-4 |
| 2.  Adductor longus | Obturator | L-3 to L-4 |
| 3.  Gradilis | Obturator | L-3 to L-4 |

*Lateral rotation*:

| | | |
|---|---|---|
| 1.  Obturator externus | Obturator | L-3 to L-4 |
| 2.  Obturator internus | Branch of sacral plexus | L-5 to S-2 |
| 3.  Superior gemellus | Obturator | L-3 to L-4 |
| 4.  Inferior gemellus | Branch of nerve to quadratus femoris | L-4 to S-1 |
| 5.  Quadratus femoris | Nerve from sacral plexus | L-4 to S-1 |

*Medial rotation*:

| | | |
|---|---|---|
| 1.  Gluteus minimus | Superior gluteal | L-4 to S-1 |
| 2.  Gluteus medius (anterior part) | Superior gluteal | L-4 to S-1 |

### II. LEG (action at knee joint)

*Flexion*:

| | | |
|---|---|---|
| 1.  Biceps femoris | Sciatic | L-5 to S-3 |
| 2.  Semitendinosus | Branch of sciatic | L-5 to S-2 |
| 3.  Semimembranosus | Branch of sciatic | L-5 to S-2 |
| 4.  Popliteus | Tibial | L-4 to S-1 |
| 5.  Gastrocnemius | Tibial | S-1 to S-2 |

*Extension*:

| | | |
|---|---|---|
| 1.  Quadratus femoris | Femoral | L-2 to L-4 |

Note: When the leg is flexed there is some lateral rotation done by biceps femoris, or medial rotation done by the popliteus.

### III.  FOOT

*Dorsal flexion*:

| | | |
|---|---|---|
| 1.  Tibialis anterior | Deep peroneal | L-4 to S-1 |
| 2.  Extensor hallucis longus | Deep peroneal | L-4 to S-1 |
| 3.  Extensor digitorum longus | Deep peroneal | L-4 to S-1 |
| 4.  Peroneus tertius | Deep peroneal | L-4 to S-1 |

**LOWER LIMB**

| Muscle and Action | Peripheral Nerves | Spinal Nerves |
|---|---|---|
| *Plantar flexion*: | | |
| 1. Gastrocnemius | Tibial | S-1 to S-2 |
| 2. Soleus | Tibial | S-1 to S-2 |
| 3. Plantaris | Tibial | L-4 to S-1 |
| 4. Tibialis posterior | Tibial | L-5 to S-1 |
| 5. Flexor digitorum longus | Tibial | L-5 to S-1 |
| 6. Flexor hallucis longus | Tibial | L-5 to S-2 |
| 7. Peroneus longus | Superficial peroneal | L-4 to S-1 |
| 8. Peroneus brevis | Superficial peroneal | L-4 to S-1 |
| *Inversion (adduction)*: | | |
| 1. Tibialis anterior | Deep peroneal | L-4 to S-1 |
| 2. Tibialis posterior | Tibial | L-5 to S-1 |
| *Eversion (abduction)*: | | |
| 1. Peroneus longus | Superficial peroneal | L-4 to S-1 |
| 2. Peroneus brevis | Superficial peroneal | L-4 to S-1 |
| **IV. TOES** | | |
| *Flexion of distal phalanx* (of four small toes): | | |
| 1. Flexor digitorum longus | Tibial | L-5 to S-1 |
| 2. Quadratus plantae | Lateral plantar | S-1 to S-2 |
| *Flexion of middle phalanx* (of four small toes): | | |
| 1. Flexor digitorum brevis | Medial plantar | L-4 to L-5 |
| *Flexion of proximal phalanx* (of four small toes): | | |
| 1. Interossei | Lateral plantar | S-1 to S-2 |
| 2. Flexor digiti minimi brevis | Lateral plantar | S-1 to S-2 |
| 3. Lumbricales | Lateral and medial plantar | L-4 to S-2 |
| *Flexion of distal phalanx* (of big toe): | | |
| 1. Flexor hallucis longus | Tibial | L-5 to S-2 |
| *Flexion of proximal phalanx* (of big toe): | | |
| 1. Flexor hallucis brevis | Medial plantar | L-4 to S-1 |
| *Extension of distal phalanges* (of all toes): | | |
| 1. Interossei | Lateral plantar | S-1 to S-2 |
| 2. Lumbricales | Lateral and medial plantar | L-4 to S-2 |
| *Extension of all phalanges* (of all toes): | | |
| 1. Extensor digitorum longus | Deep peroneal | L-4 to S-1 |
| 2. Extensor digitorum brevis | Deep peroneal | L-5 to S-1 |
| 3. Extensor hallucis longus | Deep peroneal | L-4 to S-1 |
| *Abduction of toes* (through long axis of 2nd toe): | | |
| 1. Dorsal interossei | Lateral plantar | S-1 to S-2 |
| 2. Abductor hallucis | Medial plantar | L-4 to L-5 |
| 3. Abductor digiti minimi | Lateral plantar | S-1 to S-2 |
| *Adduction of toes*: | | |
| 1. Plantar interossei | Lateral plantar | S-1 to S-2 |
| 2. Adductor hallucis | Lateral plantar | S-1 to S-2 |

| Muscle and Action | Peripheral Nerves | Spinal Nerves |
|---|---|---|
| *Extension*: | | |
| Three muscles in the suboccipital triangle, all supplied by C-1 | | |
| 1. Rectus capitis posterior major | | |
| 2. Rectus capitis posterior minor | | |
| 3. Obliquus capitis superior | | |
| Trapezius | Cranial nerve XI (accessory) and C-2 to C-3 | C-2 to C-3 |
| *Flexion*: | | |
| 1. Longus colli | Branches of C-2 to C-7 | C-2 to C-7 |
| 2. Longus capitis | Branches of C-1 to C-3 | C-1 to C-3 |
| 3. Rectus capitis anterior | Branches of C-1 to C-2 | C-1 to C-2 |
| *Rotation*: | | |
| 1. Obliquus capitis inferior | | C-1 |
| 2. Rectus capitis posterior major | | C-1 |
| *Lateral bending*: | | |
| 1. Rectus capitis lateralis | | C-1 to C-2 |
| 2. Obliquus capitis superior | | C-1 to C-2 |
| *Simultaneous flexion, rotation, and lateral bending*: | | |
| 1. Sternomastoid (on one side) | Cranial nerve XI (accessory) and C-2 to C-3 | C-2 to C-3 |

# Summary of Cranial Nerves: Innervation (by Functional Fiber Type) and Principal Clinical Signs

| CRANIAL NERVE | SENSORY | | | MOTOR | | PRINCIPAL CLINICAL SIGN |
|---|---|---|---|---|---|---|
| | Somatic (skin) | Visceral (organs, includes taste and smell) | Special (sight hearing balance) | Voluntary* (striated skeletal) | Autonomic (parasympathetic; smooth muscle and glands) | |
| I. Olfactory | | + | | | | Anosmia, eg, from damage to ciliated receptors (see also Chapter 16) |
| II. Optic | | | + | | | Blindness: Varies with site and severity of lesion (see also Chapter 15) |
| III. Oculomotor | | | | + All extrinsic ocular muscles except superior oblique and lateral rectus | + Sphincter pupillae†; ciliary muscle of accommodation | Ptosis, outward and downward deviation of eye, dilation of pupil |
| IV. Trochlear | | | | + Superior oblique muscle | | Weakness of downward movement of eye when turning inward, often associated with diplopia |
| V. Trigeminal | + Skin of face; mucous membranes of orbital, oral, and nasal cavities; teeth; meninges; external surface of tympanic membrane; temporomandibular joint; anterior ⅔ tongue (pain, temperature, and touch only) | | | + Muscles of mastication‡ (temporalis, masseter, medial and lateral pterygoids); mylohyoid; anterior digastric; tensor tympani; tensor veli palatini | | Sensory: Loss or pain in territory of supply (eg, teeth, temporomandibular joint); tic doloreux: pain syndrome, usually without sensory loss (often can be provoked by rubbing "trigger zone," eg, lower lip) |
| VI. Abducens | | | | + Lateral rectus muscle | | Medial strabismus with possibility of diplopia |
| VII. Facial | + Skin of external ear | + Taste: anterior ⅔ of tongue and hard and soft palates | | + Muscles of facial expression§ with occipitalis and frontalis; orbicularis oculi; buccinator; posterior digastric and stylohyoid; stapedius | + Lacrimal gland; all major and minor salivary glands except parotid; all mucous glands of oral and nasal cavities | If peripheral CNS lesion, includes all facial muscles with drooping angle of lip, loss of nasolabial folds, inability to close eye or raise brow, possible loss of taste to anterior ⅔ of tongue and palate; if brow can raise and eye close, suggests central lesion involving brain stem connection to facial nucleus |

| Nerve | Somatic sensory | Sensory | Parasympathetic | Motor | Clinical |
|---|---|---|---|---|---|
| VIII. Vestibulocochlear | | + *Hearing* from receptors in organ of corti of cochlea; *balance* from receptors of utricle and saccule of semicircular canals | | | Reduction or loss of hearing: May be *sensorineural* loss involving the cochlear or VIII nerve (eg, by acoustic neurinoma or trauma); to be distinguished from *conductive* hearing loss, involving external or middle ear, and from *central* hearing loss, involving brain stem or temporal lobe structures. Vertigo (dizziness): eg, benign positional vertigo or labyrinthitis associated with a viral infection; symptoms depend on location of lesion |
| IX. Glossopharyngeal | + Skin of external ear | + Mucosa of upper pharynx, middle ear cavity, carotid sinus, posterior ⅓ of tongue (taste, pain, temperature, touch) | + Parotid gland | + Stylopharyngeus muscle | Sensory: pain of otitis media; glossopharyngeal neuralgia is rare (involves pain in tonsilar fossa, upper pharynx, and ear; worsens on swallowing or chewing) |
| X. Vagus | + Skin of external ear | + Lower pharynx, larynx, carotid body, taste in area of epiglottis, afferents from thoracic & abdominal viscera through proximal ⅔ of transverse colon (ie, to end of embyronic midgut) | + Glands and smooth muscle of thoracic and abdominal viscera through proximal ⅔ of transverse colon ‖; modulatory innervation of heart | + All extrinsic and intrinsic muscles of pharynx and larynx except stylopharyngeus | Depends on location: eg, hoarseness after thyroidectomy due to damage to branch of vagus; cutting nerve can result in paralysis of vocal cords |
| XI. Accessory | | | | + Sternocleidomastoid, trapezius | Paralysis or weakness of shoulder shrugging on same side with inability to or difficulty in turning head to opposite side (eg, from trauma or polio affecting lower motor neurons) |
| XII. Hypoglossal | | | | + All intrinsic and all extrinsic muscles of tongue except the palatoglossus (X) | Deviation of tongue to the side of the affected peripheral hypoglossal nerve when asked to stick out tongue |

* Includes striated skeletal muscle derived from somites and from pharyngeal (branchial) arches.

† Innervation of dilator pupillae is sympathetic and originates from the upper segments of the thoracic spinal cord.

‡ The trigeminal nerve is the nerve of the first branchial arch and therefore innervates all muscles that develop from that arch.

§ The facial nerve is the nerve of the second branchial arch and innervates all muscles originating from this arch.

‖ The parasympathetic innervation from the distal 1/3 of the transverse colon, descending, sigmoid, and rectum (ie, structures developing from the hind gut and gut) originates from sacral spinal cord segments S-2, S-3, and S-4.

# General Functions of Selected Regions of the Telencephalon and Diencephalon

| Structure | Function |
|---|---|
| Telencephalon | |
| Precentral gyrus | Primary motor area (areas 4 and 6;* premotor area is just anterior) |
| Superior frontal gyrus | Supplementary motor area |
| Middle frontal gyrus | Frontal eye field (area 8; conjugate gaze) |
| Prefrontal cortical areas | Abstract thinking, judgment, personal control |
| Postcentral gyrus | Primary sensory area (areas 1–3) |
| Superior parietal lobule with precuneus | Somatosensory association area (areas 5 and 7) |
| Calcarine cortex of occipital lobe (cuneus and lingual gyrus around calcarine sulcus) | Primary visual area (area 17) |
| Occipital lobe areas surrounding above | Visual association and perception (areas 18 and 19) |
| Transverse temporal gyrus (Heschl's gyrus) | Primary auditory area (areas 41 and 42) |
| Superior temporal gyrus (lateral surface with part of supramarginal gyrus; Wernicke's area) | Auditory association area (area 22) |
| Inferior frontal gyrus (caudal portion, left side in most; Broca's area) | Motor speech area (area 44) |
| Limbic system (including amygdala, hippocampus, cingulate gyrus, and associated tracts and nuclei) | Modulation of a variety of autonomic and endocrine activities related to emotion, mood, feeding, sexuality; also, learning and recent memory (hippocampus) and retention of sensory impressions (eg, olfactory) and integration with the ideomotor processes of the brain |
| Basal ganglia (including putamen, globus pallidus, and caudate nucleus) | Extrapyramidal motor activity, including facilitation and/or inhibition of primary motor activity |
| Diencephalon | |
| Epithalamus (pineal body) | Mediates some cyclic functions (eg, secretion of melatonin and melanocyte-stimulating hormones involved with gonadotropins) |
| Thalamus (= complex of nuclei) | Integration, processing, and relay of sensory information from ascending tracts to a variety of cortical areas |
| Hypothalamus (= complex of nuclei) | Regulation of autonomic activity and integration with endocrine functions (eg, sexual activity, water balance, temperature control, feeding activity) |
| Subthalamus (corpus Luys) | Associated with extrapyramidal control with connections to basal ganglia |
| Reticular formation | Interconnecting network of neurons (cell bodies and fibers) lying primarily between the level of the decussation of the pyramids to the lower border of the diencephalon with connections to higher and lower centers |

*Numbers refer to areas of Brodmann.

*Note:* This table is designed to give only a general, and intentionally oversimplified, take-home idea of the complex functions associated with the structures listed.

# Atlas of Normal and Pathologic Computed Tomography Scans of the Brain

*Rina Tadmor, MD*

The discovery of X rays by William Roentgen in 1895 was one of the great contributions to medicine. A further revolutionary step was made in 1972 by the physicist Godfrey Hounsfield and the neuroradiologist James Ambrose, who introduced the technique of computed tomography (CT). They, like Roentgen, won the Nobel Prize in medicine for their work.

In conventional radiology, most of the shadows and outlines of the various three-dimensional structures are superimposed on a two-dimensional film. Furthermore, in conventional X-rays of the skull, the brain is not seen because of its low density. However, CT is about 100 times more sensitive than conventional radiography, and enables one to see clearly the brain and its subdivisions. CT images appear in the various shades of gray from black to white. In the negative mode (the one most commonly used in CT), the densest objects and materials, such as bone, appear white, whereas those of low density, such as cerebrospinal fluid, are black. The ventricular system, the cerebral sulci, and similar structures are thus rendered quite visible. This mode of presenting the CT image may at first present some confusion because the gray matter in the basal ganglia, cerebral cortex, and elsewhere appears white on a CT scan because it is packed with cell bodies and is therefore relatively dense. The white matter is lower in density and therefore shows up as gray or black.

A complete CT examination of the brain involves 10 to 12 successive, parallel, horizontal scans or "cuts" of the brain. The injection of intravenous contrast substances enhances the visibility of lesions and thereby facilitates the viewing of such pathologic conditions as tumors and abscesses.

This atlas provides a basic understanding of normal and abnormal CT scans. With this foundation, the student can go on to further reading and practice interpreting more detailed scans. Figures 1 through 4 in this atlas are normal horizontal scans. The drawing below indicates the level at which each cut was taken. The ventricular system is outlined in red in the drawing; it appears in black in the CT images themselves. Figure 5 is a coronal scan, and Figures 6 and 7 are partial horizontal scans showing the orbital areas and the structures of the ear, respectively. The 12 pathologic scans in Figures 8 through 19 represent some of the most common disease conditions seen in the neurologic service.

Finally, the following are three important works related to CT that will give you a deeper understanding of this very important subject:

1. Kieffer SA, Heitzman ER. *Atlas of Cross-Sectional Tomography, Ultrasound, Radiography, Gross Anatomy.* New York: Harper & Row; 1979.

2. Harwood-Nash DC. *Neuroradiology in Infants and Children.* St Louis, Mo: Mosby; 1976; 2.

3. Gonzales CF, Grossman C, Palacios J. *Computed Brain and Orbital Tomography: Technique and Interpretation.* New York, NY: Wiley; 1976.

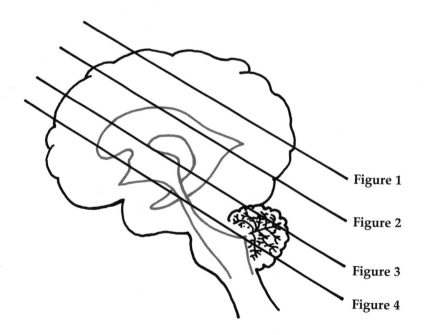

Figure 1

Figure 2

Figure 3

Figure 4

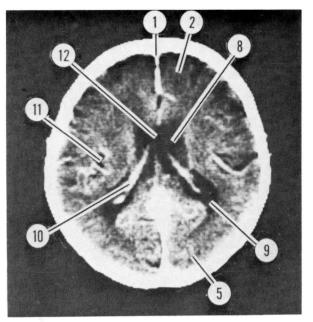

Figure 1. Horizontal section of the superior part of the normal brain.

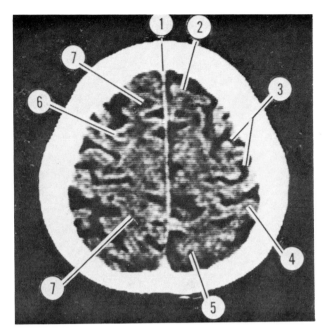

Figure 2. Horizontal (axial) section at a lower (inferior) level.

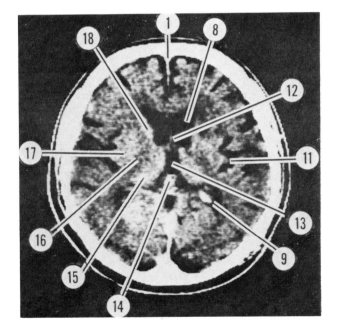

Figure 3. Horizontal section at a still lower level.

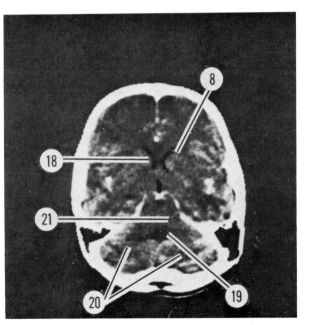

Figure 4. Horizontal section through the basal part of the brain.

Legend: *1*, falx cerebri; *2*, frontal lobe; *3*, sulcus; *4*, gyrus; *5*, occipital lobe; *6*, gray matter; *7*, white matter; *8*, anterior horn of lateral ventricle; *9*, posterior horn of lateral ventricle; *10*, choroid plexus; *11*, insula; *12*, septum pellucidum; *13*, third ventricle; *14*, calcified pineal body; *15*, thalamus; *16*, internal capsule; *17*, lentiform nucleus; *18*, head of caudate nucleus; *19*, fourth ventricle; *20*, cerebellar hemisphere; *21*, pons.

*Note:* Several of the illustrations in this section were provided courtesy of the Elscint Corporation of Haifa, Israel, and are reproduced with their permission.

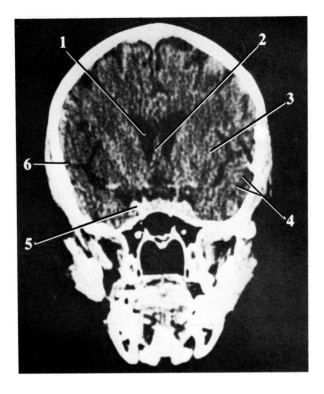

Figure 5. Coronal section of the brain 1 inch anterior to the external auditory meatus. *1*, lateral ventricle; *2*, septum pellucidum; *3*, insula; *4*, temporal lobe; *5*, cavernous sinus; *6*, lateral fissure.

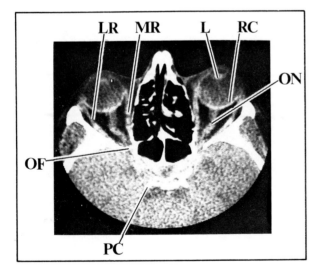

Figure 6. Horizontal cut through the middle of the orbits. *L*, lens; *RC*, retina and choroid; *ON*, optic nerve; *LR*, lateralis rectus muscle; *MR*, medial rectus muscle; *OF*, optic foramen; *PC*, posterior clinoid process of the sella turcica.

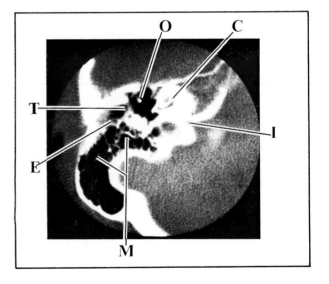

Figure 7. Horizontal section through the middle and inner ear. *E*, external auditory canal; *T*, tympanic membrane (eardrum); *O*, ossicle in middle ear cavity; *C*, cochlea in inner ear cavity; *I*, internal auditory canal; *M*, mastoid air cells.

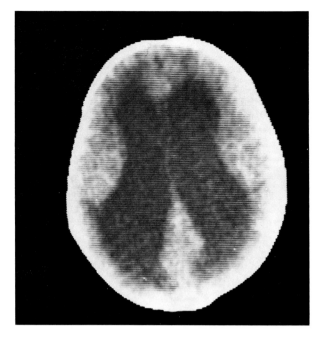

Figure 8.   Hydrocephalus. The accumulated CSF has greatly increased the size of the lateral ventricles.

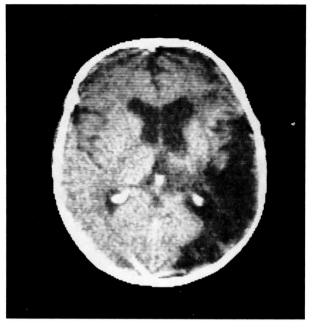

Figure 9.   Infarct. Obstruction of the right middle cerebral artery has produced a dark infarcted area in the parieto-occipital lobes with no displacement of brain structures. Non-displacement is typical in infarcts due to emboli and thrombi. The three white spots are the capillary-rich choroid plexus filled with contrast medium.

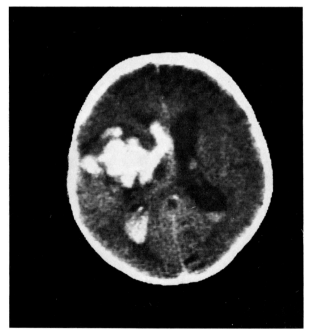

Figure 10.   Intracerebral Hemorrhage. The dense, white, ir-regular mass in the left parietal lobe represents blood, which has also ruptured into the lateral ventricle and caused dis-placement of structures. Displacement will occur in all space-occupying lesions.

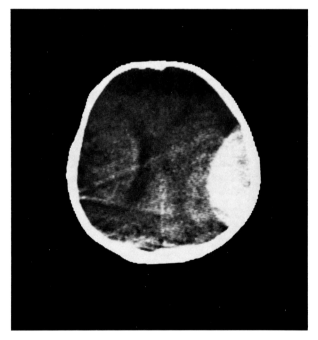

Figure 11.   Epidural Hematoma. The well-delineated white area represents an extracerebral hemorrhage in the right pa-rietal region, causing compression and closure of the lateral ventricle on the same side.

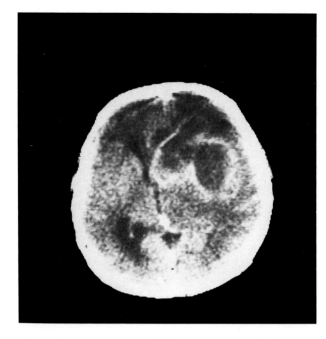

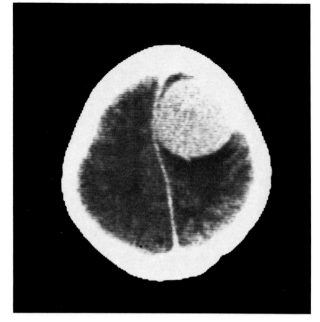

Figure 12.   Abscess. A multilobulated mass in the frontoparietal lobes has caused massive displacement of brain tissues and structure. Abscesses can only be differentiated from gliomas (Figure 14) on the basis of clinical and laboratory findings.

Figure 13.   Meningioma. The round, white, homogeneous tumor in the right frontal lobe has caused a displacement of the falx cerebri. The whiteness, homogeneity, and roundness are quite typical of meningiomas.

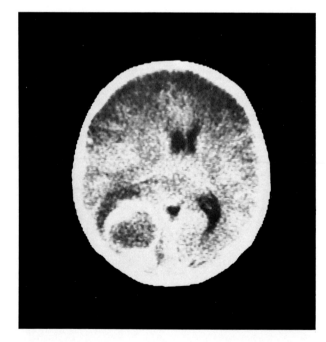

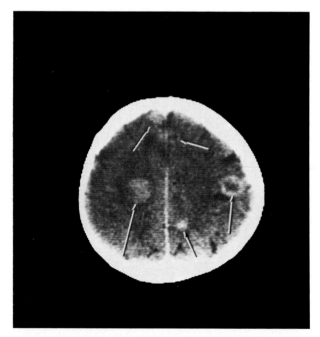

Figure 14.   Astrocytoma. This round, well-delineated, non-homogeneous tumor in the left parieto-occipital lobes is surrounded by a dark edematous area. This growth has caused a shift in structures as seen by the displaced septum pellucidum and obliteration of the posterior horn of the lateral ventricle.

Figure 15.   Metastasis. Multiple round lesions (*arrows*) in both hemispheres represent metastatic spread ("seeding") from a primary tumor elsewhere in the body. The white ring, characteristic of various nonspecific lesions (e.g., tumors, abscesses, fungal diseases) indicates a breakdown of the blood-brain barrier.

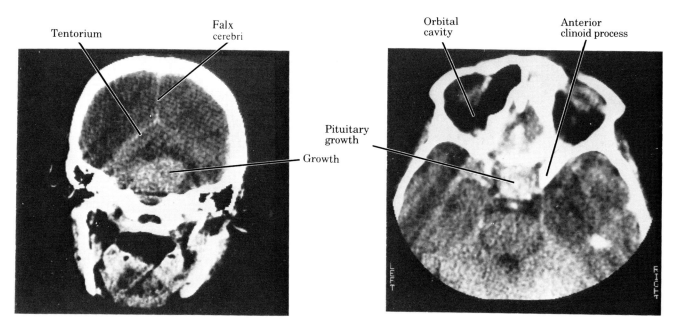

Figure 16.   A CT coronal study of the posterior fossa following intravenous contrast injections showing the falx and tentorium and a hyperdense lesion occupying most of the posterior fossa with surrounding edema (black halo), most probably a medulloblastoma.

Figure 17.   A horizontal section of the head at the level of the sella turcica showing a pituitary growth.

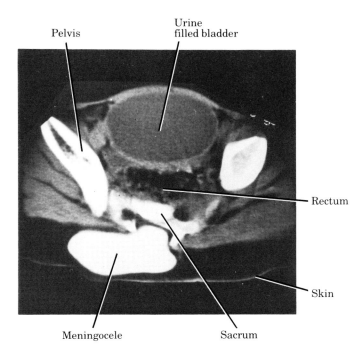

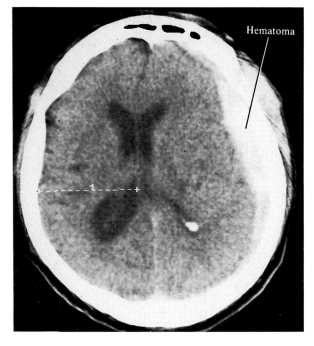

Figure 18.   CT Myelography. Cross section of the pelvis of a child showing spina bifida of the sacrum with a meningocele located beneath the skin but not forming a protruding sac.

Figure 19.   Horizontal section showing subdural hematoma (arrow).

# Normal and Pathologic Magnetic Resonance Imaging of the Brain

*Rina Tadmor, MD*

Magnetic resonance imaging (MRI) is an imaging modality based on the interaction of a magnet, radio-frequency energy, and the protons of molecules. The data obtained are then fed into a computer, and the result is seen as an image on a screen. Because hydrogen is present in all tissues, as well as other considerations, the hydrogen atom has been chosen for imaging (the proton of the hydrogen atom is the one that is measured). However, it is possible to use the protons of other atoms, such as carbon or magnesium, for imaging purposes.

The advantages of MRI over computed tomography (CT) scanning are that it doesn't require the use of ionizing radiation and it is much more sensitive, thus allowing the visualization of smaller anatomic structures and details. It also permits imaging to be done in the sagittal plane. It should be noted, however, that because the proton density of hydrogen in bone and calcified tissue is low their visualization is poor, and thus details in or about them can be missed. It seems that MRI has not replaced CT and other imaging techniques but rather has become a complementary examination, the choice being dictated on a case-by-case basis. Because spectroscopy is another option available by MRI, it has become a valuable tool in research.

It is the author's intention to present readers with introductory pictures of normal MRI scans and some simple pathologic scans to familiarize them with this imaging modality.

*Note:* The basic theoretical work was done in the 1940s by the American physicists Felix Bloch and Edward Purcell, who in 1952 won the Nobel Prize for their work.

All images were obtained with an Elscint Gyrex S-5000 and Gyrex 2T. The authors wish to thank the Elscint Corporation of Haifa, Israel, for the use of these scans and for their generous assistance.

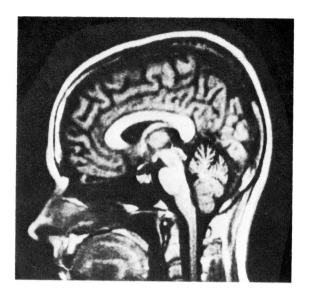

Figure 1a.  Midsagittal section of the brain.

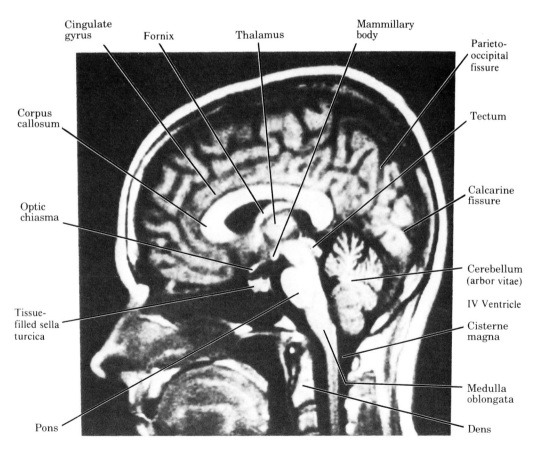

Figure 1b.  Midsagittal section of the brain with identifying leaders.

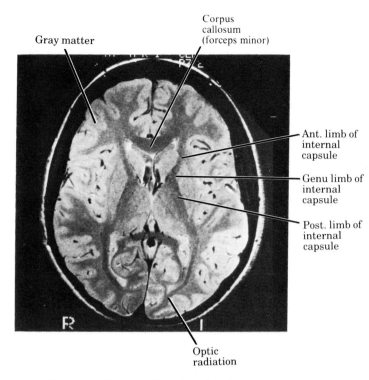

Figure 2.   Horizontal section of the brain.

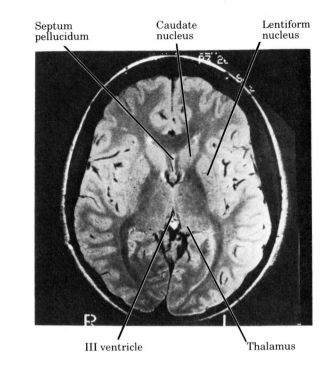

Figure 3.   A horizontal section of the brain, lower (more caudal) than Figure 2.

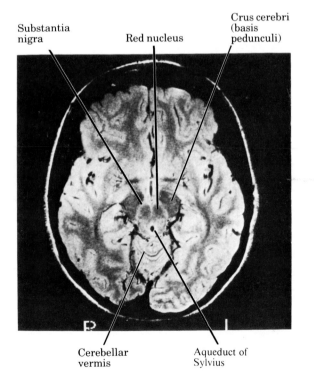

Figure 4.   A horizontal section of the brain lower than Figures 2 and 3 showing the midbrain. In this cut the midbrain resembles Mickey Mouse with the crus cerebri, the ears; the red nucleus, the eyes; and the aqueduct, the mouth. However, as you are learning, neuroanatomy is no "Mickey Mouse" subject.

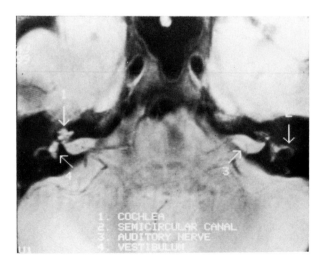

Figure 5.   MRI scan of the inner ear.

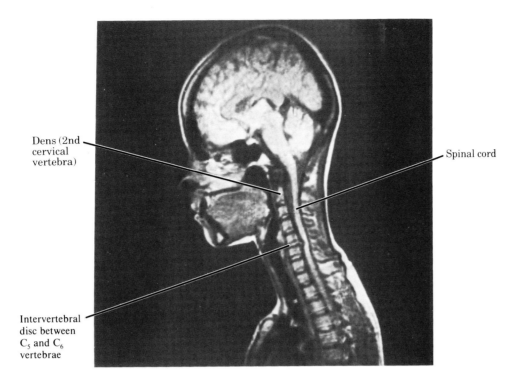

Dens (2nd cervical vertebra)

Spinal cord

Intervertebral disc between C₅ and C₆ vertebrae

Figure 6.  Midsagittal MRI scan of the spinal cord showing a "slipped" disc which is impinging on the cord in the cervical region.

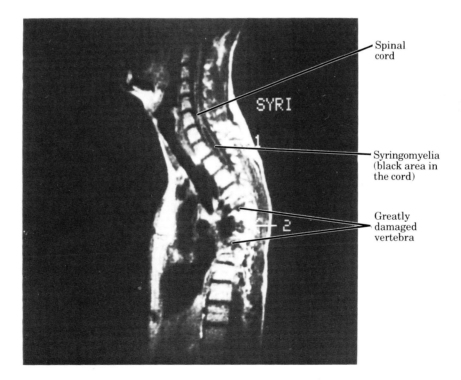

Spinal cord

Syringomyelia (black area in the cord)

Greatly damaged vertebra

Figure 7.  Syringomyelia and damaged thoracic vertebra.

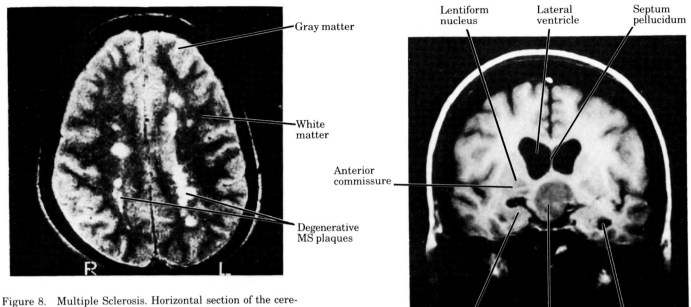

Figure 8. Multiple Sclerosis. Horizontal section of the cerebral hemispheres showing degenerative plaques in the white matter which is black on the picture.

Figure 9. Coronal section of the brain at the level of the anterior commissure showing a growth at the base of brain (also see Plate V, Appendix II for orientation).

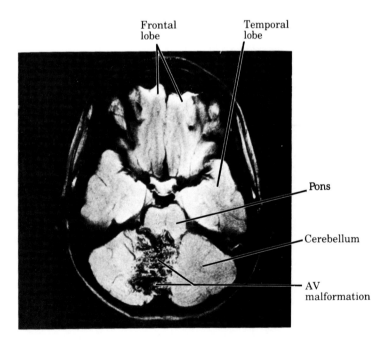

Figure 10. AV Malformation. The black area in the cerebellum represents a mass of arteries and veins.

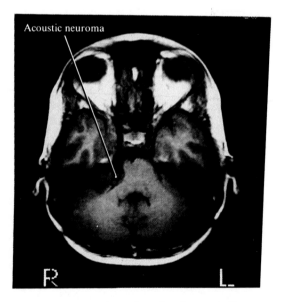

Figure 11. Horizontal section showing acoustic neuroma (arrow).

# CT and MRI in 3D and Color

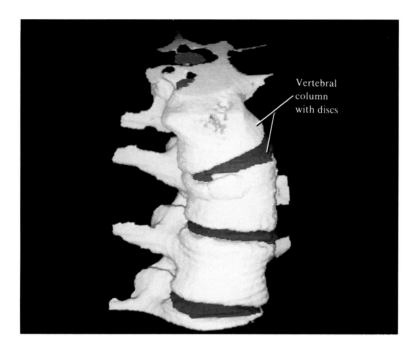

Figure 12.  Vertebral column with discs shown in blue.

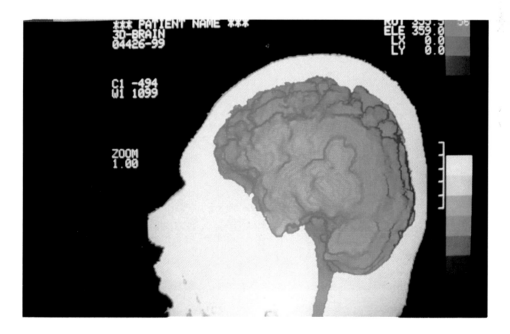

Figure 13.  Lateral view of the brain.

*Note:* Figures 12–15 were done by Elscint's Gyrex MRI Scanner or Excel 2400 CT Scanner.

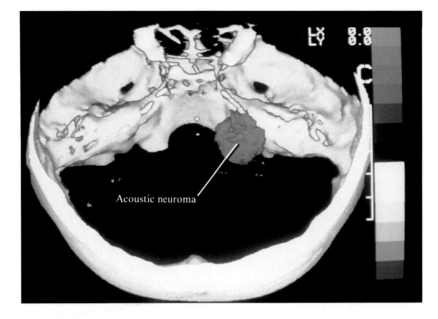

Figure 14.   Acoustic neuroma (green mass).

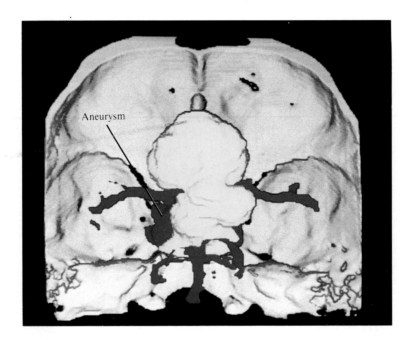

Figure 15.   Pituitary tumor (yellow mass) with aneurysm
(arrow) on left side of circle of Willis.

# Essentials of the Neurologic Examination

## HISTORY

As with all branches of medicine, the history of the illness is of primary importance to an accurate diagnosis of the neurologic disease. It should at the very least consist of the following four elements:

1. Chief complaint
   - Nature
   - Duration
   - Factors that worsen or lessen the complaint
2. Personal medical history with review of major systems
3. Detailed family history
4. Social and occupational history

## EXAMINATION

### General Physical Examination

Before the specific neurologic examination, the physician should also perform a general examination of other systems, including cardiovascular, respiratory, gastrointestinal, genitourinary, and skeletal, paying particular attention to possible problems suggested by the review of systems while the history was taken. For each system, this examination should involve:

- inspection (eg, deformities of limbs or head)
- palpation (eg, lumps and fontanelles)
- auscultation (eg, carotid bruit or heart murmur)
- percussion (eg, of sinuses)

The neurologic examination, as with other subspecialties, begins with inspection of the patient *as he or she enters the room*, with close attention being paid to any obvious disorders of movement, gait, speech, and so forth. The examination itself can be divided as follows.

### Mental Status and Higher Cerebral Functions

- Level of consciousness
- Orientation: time, space, self
- General behavior: appearance, mannerisms, level of activity
- Mood: depression, anxiety, fear, aggression
- Language: comprehension of spoken and written word, ability to read and write, ability to name objects by sight and feel, flow of speech
- Memory: recent and long term
- Judgment and insight
- Intellectual capacity
- Capacity for arithmetic calculation
- Thought content: obsessions, delusions, compulsions, hallucinations

### Cranial Nerves

- Olfactory (I): detection of the odor of, for example, coffee in each nostril
- Optic (II): visual acuity, for example, by Snellen chart or finger counting in severe cases; remember to do fundoscopy
- Oculomotor (III), trochlear (IV), and abducens (VI): ocular movements; size, shape, and reactivity of pupils to light and accommodation
- Trigeminal (V): sensation over face and corneal reflex; motor activity by chewing or biting
- Facial (VII): facial expression at rest and when smiling, raising eyebrows, and closing eyes; assess taste on anterior two thirds of tongue with sweet, sour, salt, and bitter test solutions
- Vestibulocochlear (VIII):
  1. Cochlear portion, for air and bone conduction by tuning fork tests or by audiogram
  2. Vestibular portion, by caloric test (normally, cool water produces nystagmus on the opposite side, and warm produces it on the same side)
  3. Remember to do otoscopy
- Glossopharyngeal (IX): gag reflex (should be done bilaterally); also taste on posterior third of tongue
- Vagus (X): phonation, ability to swallow; remember to inspect uvula
- Accessory (XI): rotation of head and shrugging of each shoulder against resistance

- Hypoglossal (XII): examine tongue at rest (for atrophy and fasciculations) and on protrusion from the mouth (for deviation)

**Motor Systems**

- Inspection of patient for:
  1. skin lesions
  2. atrophy of muscles (unilateral or bilateral)
  3. tremors, fasciculations, or other involuntary movements such as chorea, athetosis, or myoclonus
  4. posture and gate (have patient walk)
- Palpation and passive movement of muscles for:
  1. tone (increased or decreased)
  2. rigidity
  3. spasms
- Additional testing of motor function for speed and strength might include holding up the limbs against gravity and against resistance, buttoning and unbuttoning clothes (see also Cerebellar Function and Reflexes Routinely Tested, below)

**Cerebellar Function**

- Alternating movements of hands at increasing speed
- Finger-to-nose test: patient touches own nose and then examiner's finger at increasing speed
- Heel-to-shin test: patient touches own knee with opposite heel and rubs heel of hand down shin
- Romberg test

**Sensory Systems (Localization According to Dermatome or Cranial Nerve)**

- Pain, temperature, and touch over hands, trunk, and feet

- Vibration at ulnar process, maleoli, iliac crest, and spine
- Position sense
- Two-point discrimination
- Stereognosis and topognosis

**Reflexes Routinely Tested**

- Biceps
- Triceps
- Patellar (knee jerk)
- Achilles (ankle)
- Superficial abdominal
- Cremasteric
- Plantar (Babinski)

**USEFUL MNEMONIC**

When organizing in your mind the possible differential diagnoses associated with the presenting history and physical examination, think of the word *vitamins*. This will remind you that the neurologic diseases can be classified (as in Chapter 23) into the following etiologies:

**V**ascular

**I**nfectious

**T**raumatic

**A**utoimmune

**M**etabolic

**I**diopathic and degenerative

**N**eoplastic

**S**ubstance abuse and toxins

If you think of *vitamin C*, you will also include **C**ongenital.

# Self-Examination Drawing Plates

## INSTRUCTIONS

On the plates provided, write the *name of the structure* indicated by the pointer or *draw the specific pathway* requested. I suggest using pencil for easy correction. For answers, refer to the original, unaltered plates and figures in the text.

Write the names of the indicated gyri or sulci on this lateral view of the brain.

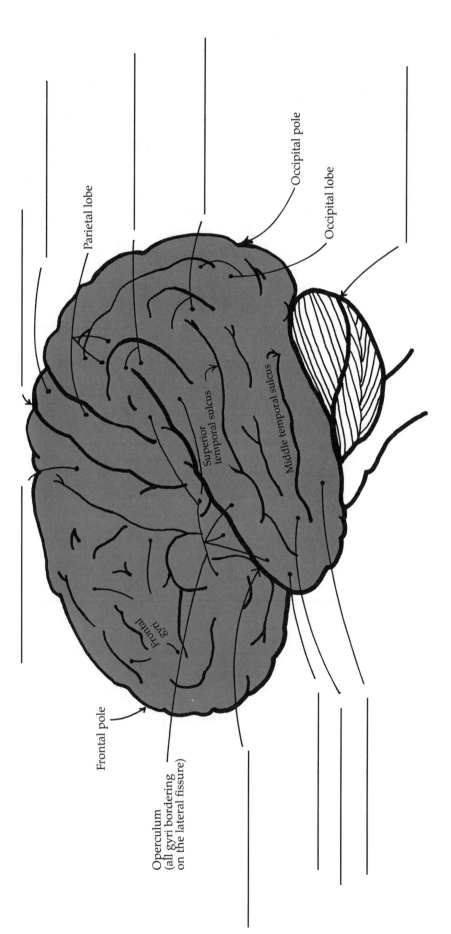

Parietal lobe

Occipital pole

Occipital lobe

Superior temporal sulcus

Middle temporal sulcus

Frontal gyri

Frontal pole

Operculum
(all gyri bordering
on the lateral fissure)

(Unaltered plate found on page 102.)

*Label the indicated structures on this midsagittal view of the brain.*

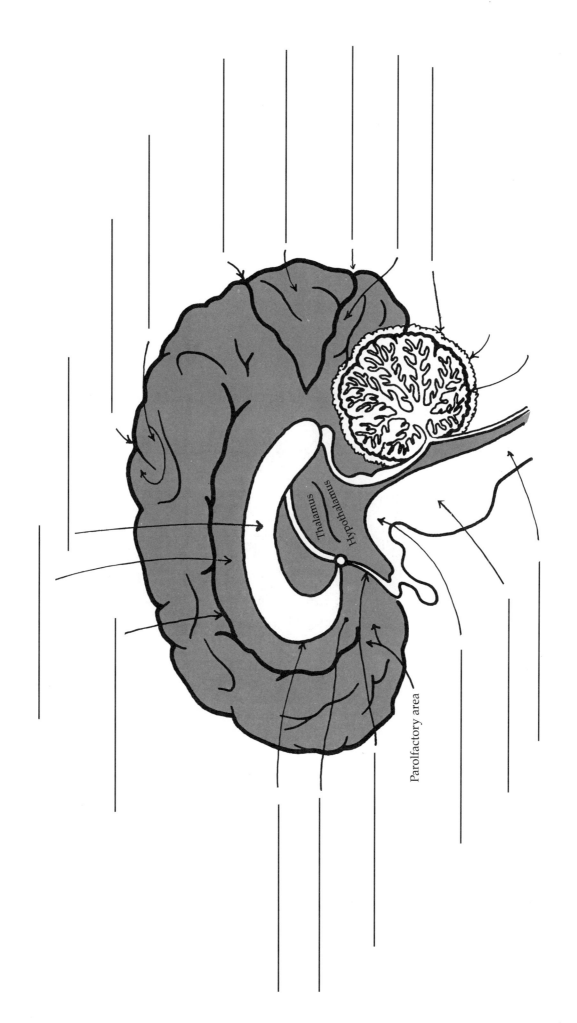

Thalamus

Hypothalamus

Parolfactory area

(Unaltered plate found on page 104.)

151

*Label the indicated arteries on this view of the base of the brain.*

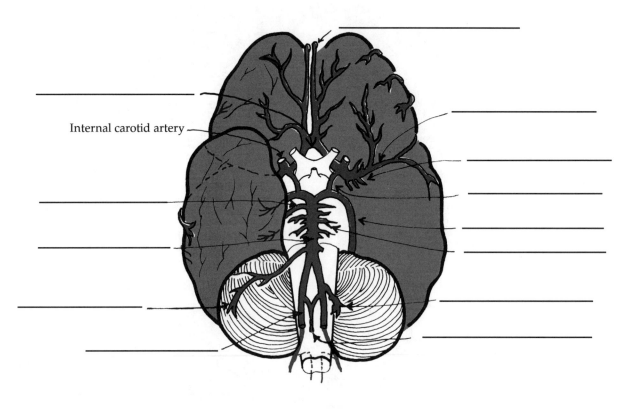

Internal carotid artery

*(Unaltered figure found on page 79.)*

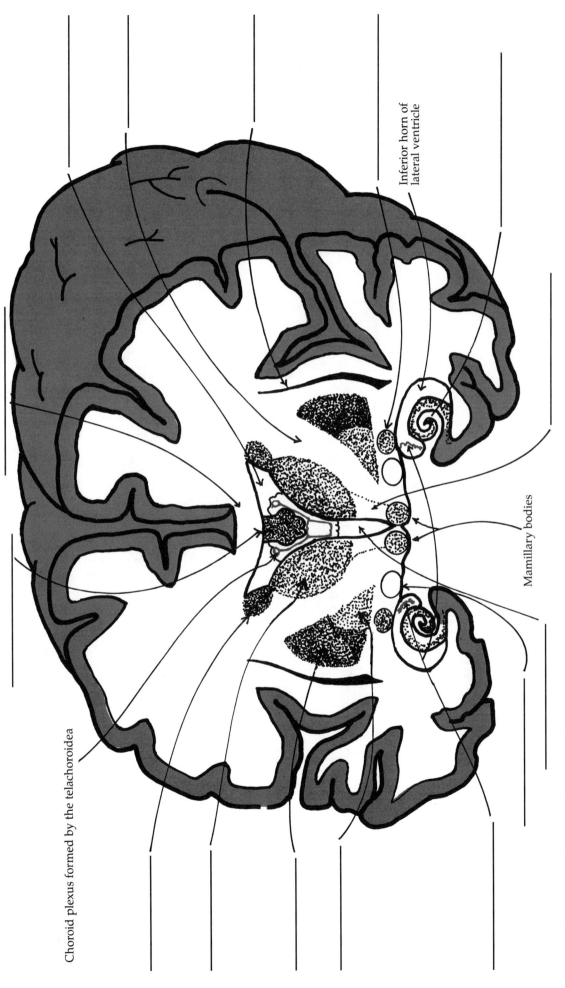
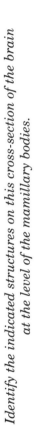

Identify the indicated structures on this cross-section of the brain at the level of the mamillary bodies.

Inferior horn of lateral ventricle

Mamillary bodies

Choroid plexus formed by the telachoroidea

(Unaltered plate found on page 107.)

153

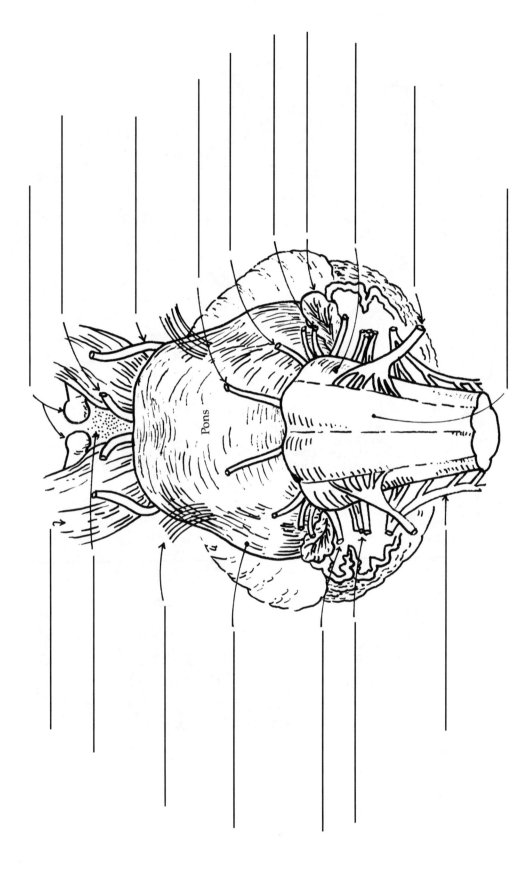

*Identify the indicated cranial nerves and structures on this ventral view of the brain stem.*

Pons

*(Unaltered plate found on page 108.)*

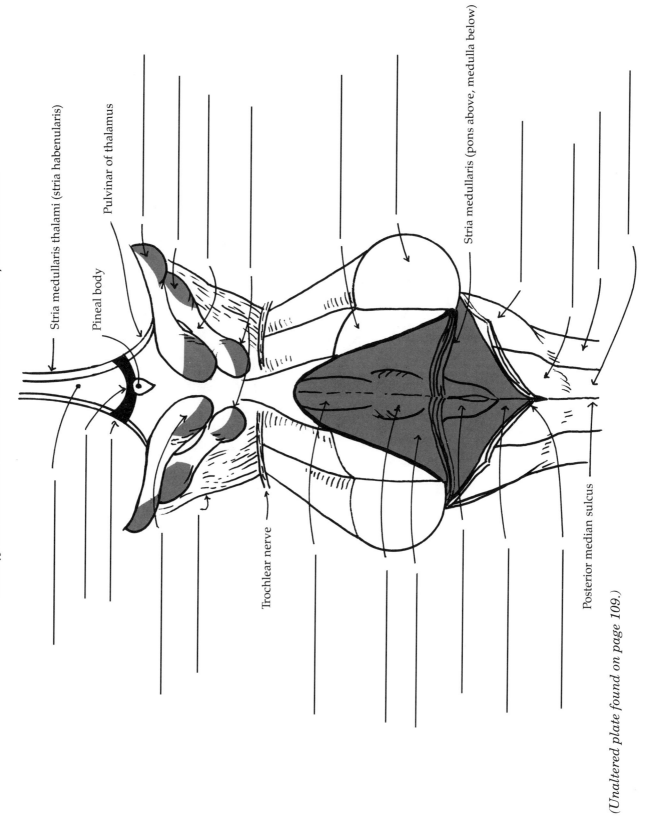

Identify the indicated structures on this dorsal view of the brain stem.

Stria medullaris thalami (stria habenularis)

Pulvinar of thalamus

Pineal body

Stria medullaris (pons above, medulla below)

Trochlear nerve

Posterior median sulcus

(Unaltered plate found on page 109.)

*Identify the indicated structures on this cross-section of the midbrain
at the level of the superior colliculus.*

Superior colliculus

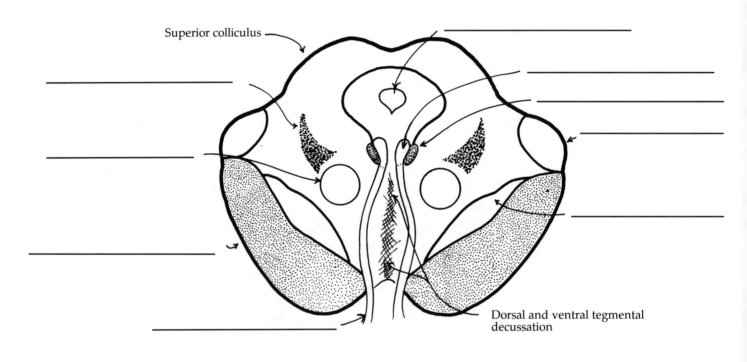

Dorsal and ventral tegmental
decussation

*(Unaltered plate found on page 110.)*

Identify the indicated structures on this cross-section of the pons
at the level of the facial colliculus.

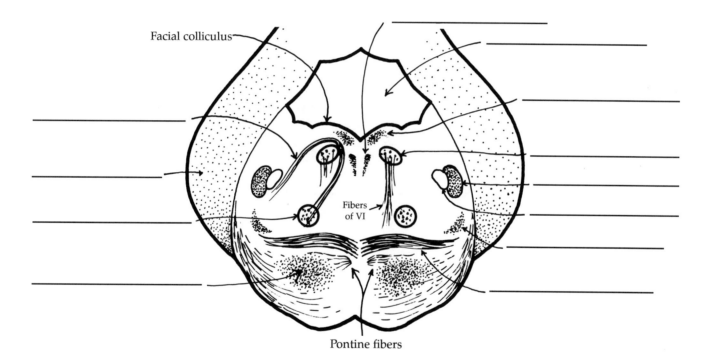

Facial colliculus

Fibers
of VI

Pontine fibers

(Unaltered plate found on page 111.)

Identify the indicated structures on this cross-section through the rostral medulla.

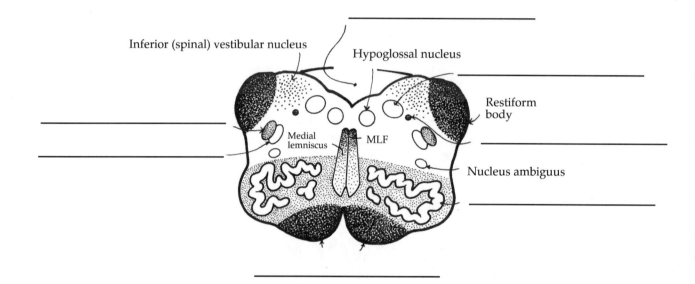

Inferior (spinal) vestibular nucleus

Hypoglossal nucleus

Restiform body

Medial lemniscus

MLF

Nucleus ambiguus

*(Unaltered plate found on page 112.)*

*Complete the pathway of pain and temperature to conscious level and label the indicated related structures.*

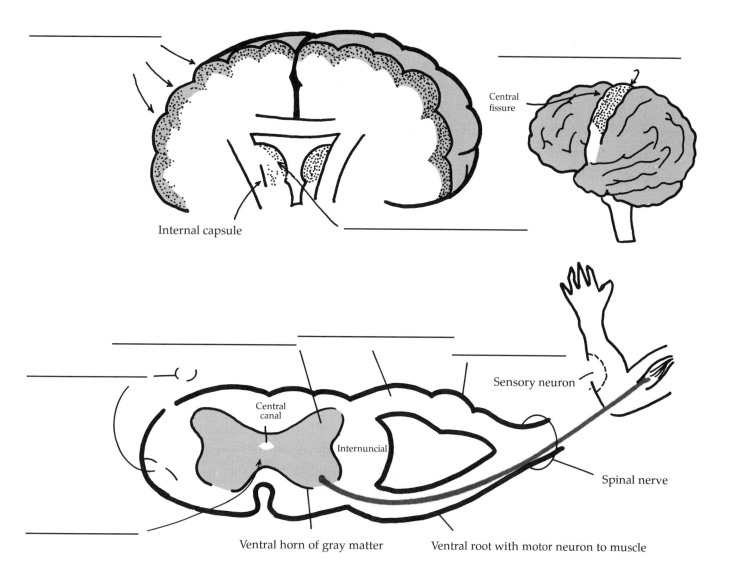

Central fissure

Internal capsule

Sensory neuron

Central canal

Internuncial

Spinal nerve

Ventral horn of gray matter

Ventral root with motor neuron to muscle

*(Unaltered figure found on page 11.)*

*Complete the pathway of fine touch to conscious level and label
the indicated related structures.*

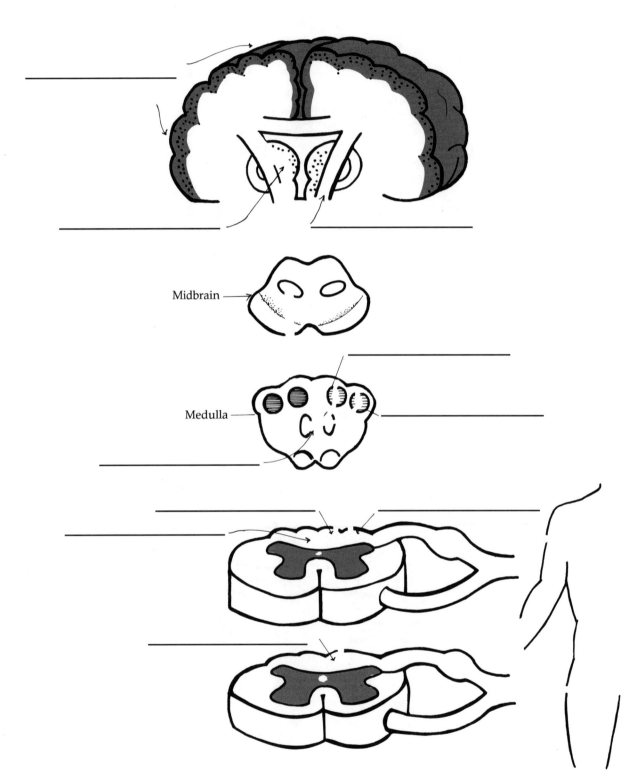

Midbrain —

Medulla —

*Label the indicated structures along the course of the pathway of pain*
*from the face to conscious level.*

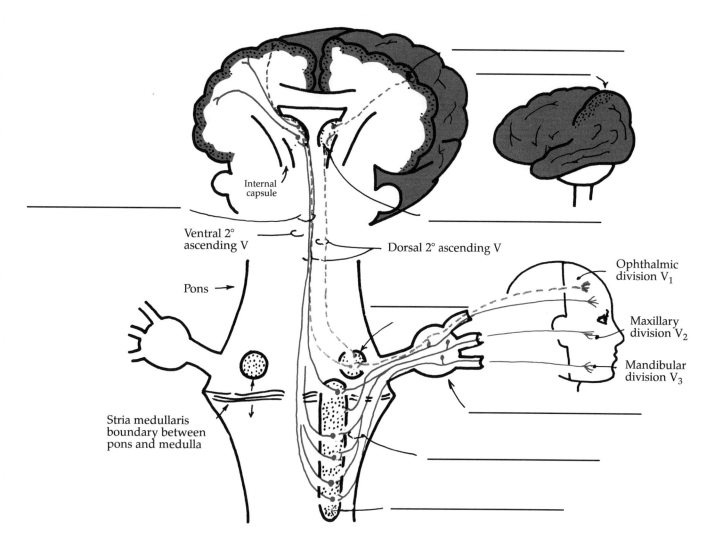

Internal capsule

Ventral 2° ascending V

Dorsal 2° ascending V

Pons →

Ophthalmic division V₁

Maxillary division V₂

Mandibular division V₃

Stria medullaris boundary between pons and medulla

*(Unaltered figure found on page 19.)*

*Complete the pathway of voluntary movement of the arm and leg
and label the indicated related structures.*

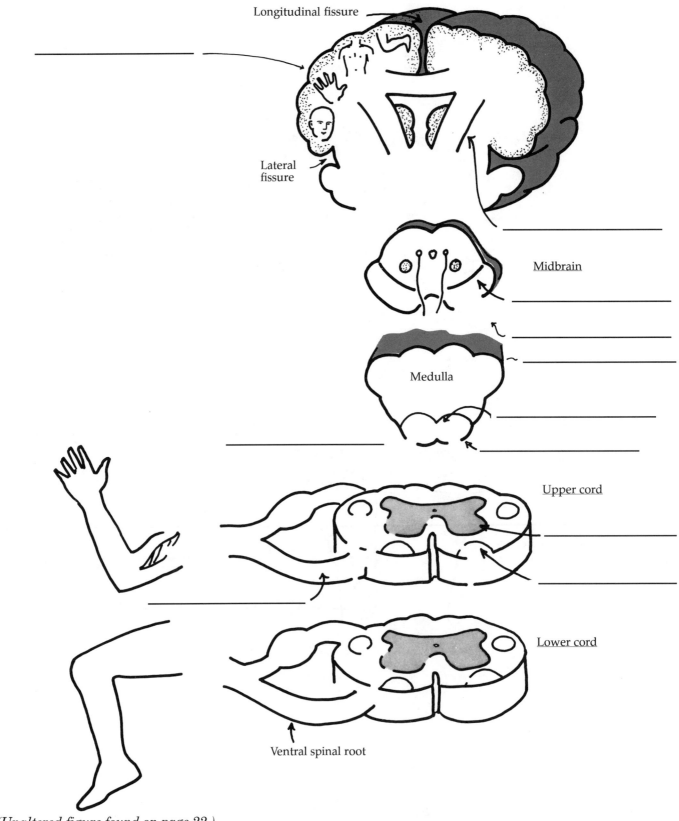

Longitudinal fissure

Lateral fissure

Midbrain

Medulla

Upper cord

Lower cord

Ventral spinal root

*(Unaltered figure found on page 22.)*

*Draw the two principal pathways for proprioceptive inputs to the cerebellum and label the indicated related structures.*

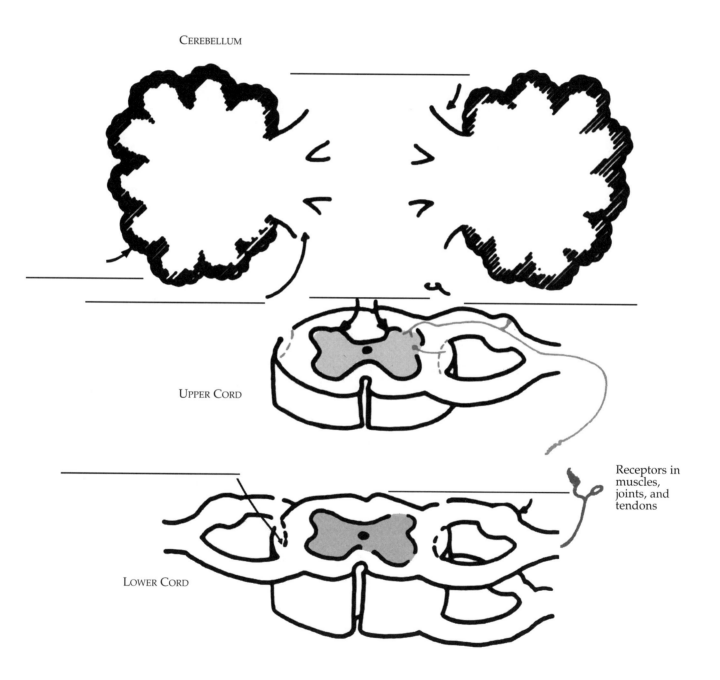

CEREBELLUM

UPPER CORD

LOWER CORD

Receptors in muscles, joints, and tendons

*(Unaltered figure found on page 37.)*

*Identify the indicated structures related to feedback pathways of the cerebellum.*

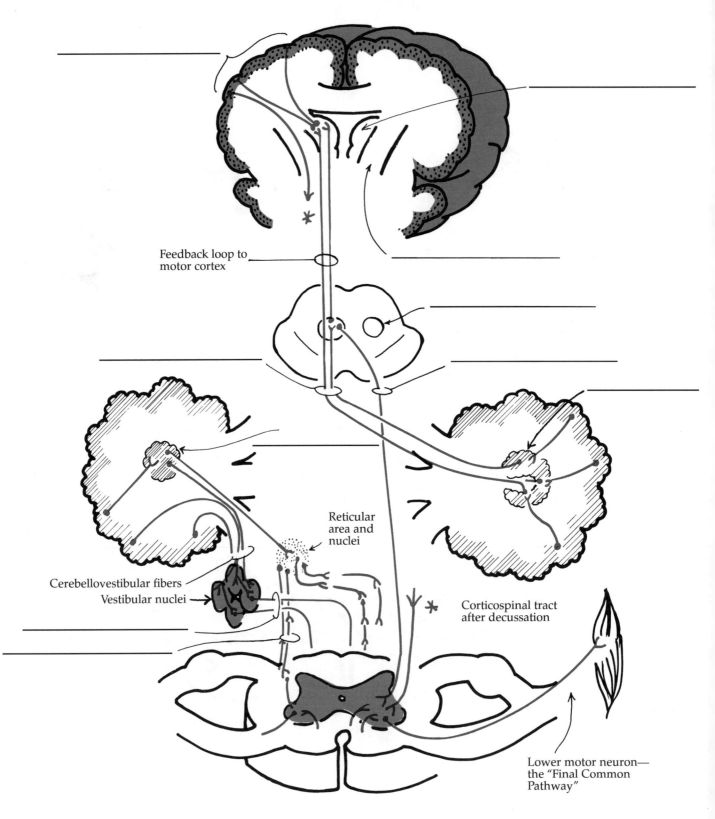

Feedback loop to
motor cortex

Reticular
area and
nuclei

Cerebellovestibular fibers
Vestibular nuclei

Corticospinal tract
after decussation

Lower motor neuron—
the "Final Common
Pathway"

*(Unaltered figure found on page 40.)*

164

*Complete the pathway of auditory inputs to conscious level and identify the indicated related structures.*

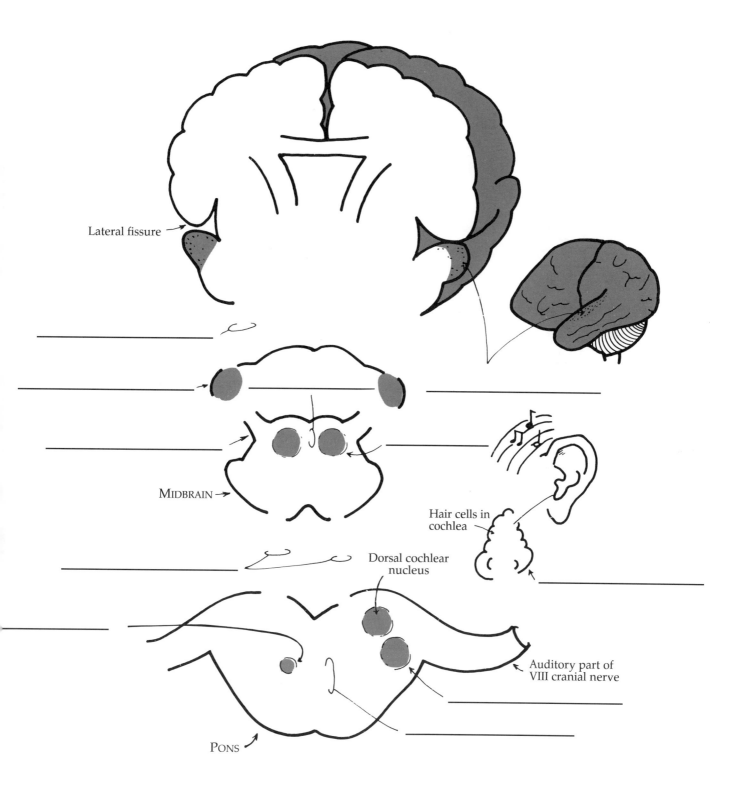

Lateral fissure

MIDBRAIN →

Dorsal cochlear nucleus

Hair cells in cochlea

Auditory part of VIII cranial nerve

PONS

*(Unaltered figure found on page 56.)*

*Draw the visual field defect obtained by lesions 1 through 6*
*and give the correct name for each defect.*

OPTIC PATHWAYS

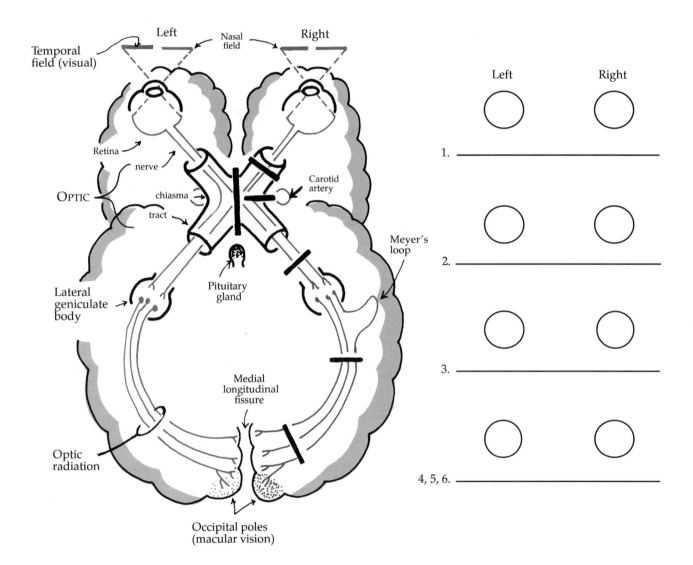

*(Unaltered figure found on page 59.)*

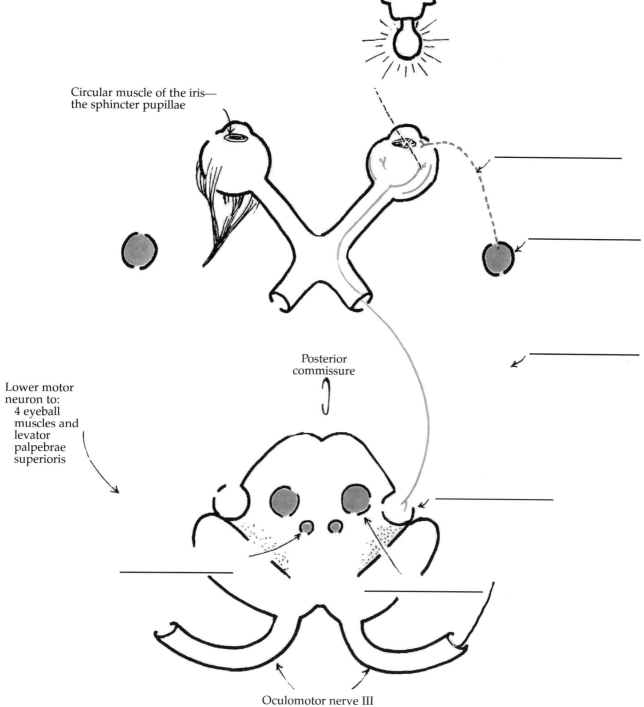

Circular muscle of the iris—
the sphincter pupillae

Posterior
commissure

Lower motor
neuron to:
  4 eyeball
  muscles and
  levator
  palpebrae
  superioris

Oculomotor nerve III

*(Unaltered figure found on page 60.)*

# Sample Examination Questions and Tips on Taking a Practical Laboratory Examination

1. Which of the following tracts or pathways is completely uncrossed in its entire course?
   a. Pain and temperature from the face
   b. Proprioception from the body
   c. Corticospinal
   d. Dorsal spinocerebellar
   e. Vestibular pathways

2. What condition results if the right optic nerve is cut?
   a. Left homonymous hemianopsia
   b. Bitemporal hemianopsia
   c. Right homonymous hemianopsia
   d. Binasal hemianopsia
   e. None of the above

3. Which of the following is not true concerning the hypothalamus?
   a. It is concerned with temperature regulation
   b. It has a hunger center
   c. It is concerned with equilibrium
   d. It influences pituitary secretions
   e. It has areas concerned with emotional reactions

4. Which of the following statements concerning the neuron is not true?
   a. It is very sensitive to oxygen deprivation
   b. If the axon is cut the cell body will always die
   c. Myelin is laid down by the sheath of Schwann in the peripheral nervous system
   d. Nissl bodies are found in the cytoplasm of the cell body
   e. Mature neurons don't undergo mitosis

5. Which of the following tracts doesn't synapse on the final common pathway?
   a. Rubrospinal tract
   b. Corticospinal tract
   c. Spinothalamic tract
   d. Vestibulospinal tract
   e. All of the above

6. Which of the following is not a sign of cerebellar injury?
   a. Uncoordinated movements
   b. Dizziness
   c. Athetosis
   d. Falling
   e. Intention tremor

In the following three questions, match the tract with the peduncle in which it runs:
7. Corticopontocerebellar tract     a. Superior cerebellar peduncle
8. Dentorubrothalamic tract     b. Middle cerebellar peduncle
9. Vestibulocerebellar tract     c. Inferior cerebellar peduncle

10. Obstruction of the left anterior cerebral artery past the anterior communicating artery is likely to cause defective movement or paralysis in the:
    a. Right lower limb
    b. Right upper limb
    c. Muscles of the face on the left side
    d. Muscles of the face on the right side
    e. Left lower limb

11. With respect to the subcortical motor areas (ie, basal ganglia, etc), all of the following statements are true except:
    a. Damage to them can result in pill-rolling tremor
    b. They aren't connected to the cerebral cortex
    c. They are part of the extrapyramidal system
    d. They are connected with the red nucleus
    e. They are connected with the thalamus

12. A patient exhibits bitemporal hemianopsia. In which of the following areas is the lesion most likely to be?
    a. Lateral geniculate body
    b. Midline of the optic chiasm
    c. Optic radiations
    d. Visual cortex
    e. Optic tract

13. Which of the following don't synapse in the thalamus?
    a. Pain and temperature from the face
    b. Fibers from the dentate nucleus
    c. Proprioception fibers from the body
    d. Auditory fibers
    e. Pressure and touch fibers from the face

14. A patient has an upper neuron paralysis that affects the arm. The lesion can be in any of the following areas except:
    a. Motor cortex
    b. Internal capsule
    c. Crus cerebri (basis pedunculi cerebri)
    d. Tegmentum of the midbrain
    e. Pyramid
    f. Lateral white column of the spinal cord

15. If the dorsal spinal root is cut in the sacral region, which of the following would show wallerian degeneration in the cervical area of the cord?
    a. Spinothalamic tract
    b. Fasciculus cuneatus
    c. Ventral spinocerebellar tract
    d. Lateral corticospinal tract
    e. Fasciculus gracilis

16. The cell bodies of the preganglionic parasympathetic fibers that innervate the descending colon are situated in the:
    a. Dorsal motor nucleus of the vagus
    b. Nucleus ambiguus
    c. Lateral gray column of the spinal cord in the thoracic segments T-10 to T-12
    d. Inferior mesenteric ganglion
    e. Lateral gray column of the spinal cord in the S-2 to S-4 sacral segments

17. A patient has total deafness in the left ear. In which of the following areas is the lesion most likely to be?
    a. Left superior temporal gyrus
    b. Right and left cochlear nuclei
    c. Left auditory nerve
    d. Left lateral lemniscus
    e. Right and left inferior colliculi

18. Examination reveals that a patient doesn't sweat in the area supplied by thoracic spinal nerves T-1 to T-2. A lesion in which area *won't* give rise to this condition?
    a. Sympathetic trunk
    b. Intermediate lateral gray column of the spinal cord

    c. Ventral roots of the spinal cord
    d. White rami communicantes
    e. Dorsal roots of spinal nerve
    f. Gray rami communicantes

In the following three questions, three common reflexes are listed. Match them with the correct cranial nerves that are involved in the reflex arc.

19. Corneal reflex          a. optic-facial
20. Horizontal              b. vestibular-facial
    nystagmus               c. glossopharyngeal-vagus
21. Gag reflex              d. vestibular-oculomotor and
                               abducens
                            e. trigeminal-facial
                            f. trigeminal-vagus

Answer the following questions by indicating the letter of the statement that correctly applies.
    a. If both statements are true and there is a causal relationship between the two
    b. If both statements are true but there is no causal relationship between the two
    c. If the first statement is true but the second is false
    d. If the first statement is false and the second is true
    e. If both statements are false

22. Most of the spinocerebellar fibers enter the cerebellum on the ipsilateral side, and therefore injury to the right inferior cerebellar peduncle results in a person falling to the right side.

23. Damage to the genu of the left internal capsule results in a paralysis of the entire right side of the face because the corticobulbar fibers are located in the genu of the internal capsule.

24. If the right thalamus is damaged, then the patient will lose all somatic sensations on the left side of the body and face because these fibers all eventually cross over to the opposite side from which they entered the cord and brain stem.

25. A positive Babinski sign is generally associated with a lesion in the:
    a. Lateral vestibulospinal tract
    b. Rubrospinal tract
    c. Corticospinal tract
    d. Dorsal white columns
    e. Tectospinal tract

26. The structure that separates the thalamus from the lentiform nucleus is the:
   a. Fornix
   b. Posterior limb of internal capsule
   c. Posterior commissure
   d. Anterior limb of internal capsule
   e. None of the above

27. PICA (the posterior inferior cerebellar artery) is usually a branch of the:
   a. Basilar artery
   b. Labyrinthine artery
   c. Vertebral artery
   d. Middle cerebral artery
   e. Posterior cerebral artery

28. Which of the following empties into the cavernous sinus?
   a. Vein of Galen
   b. Thalamostriate vein
   c. Straight sinus
   d. Middle superficial cerebral vein
   e. Superior cerebral vein

29. Match the cranial nerve with its action or pathologic sign:
   a. Swallowing reflex        1. Glossopharyngeal
   b. Dry eye (cornea)         2. Accessory
   c. Ptosis                   3. Abducens
   d. Medial strabismus        4. Oculomotor
   e. Difficulty in lifting    5. Facial
      the shoulder

30. The middle cerebral artery and its branches supply all the areas listed below except:
   a. Hearing area
   b. Broca's speech area
   c. Visual area
   d. Internal capsule
   e. Most of voluntary motor cortex

Answer questions 31 through 45 as follows:
   a. If 1, 2, and 3 are correct
   b. If 1 and 3 are correct
   c. If 2 and 4 are correct
   d. If 4 is correct
   e. If all are correct

31. Which subcortical area influences voluntary muscle activity?
   1. Caudate nucleus
   2. Putamen
   3. Pallidus
   4. Amygdala

32. Which area is involved with Parkinson's disease?
   1. Uncus
   2. Hypothalamus
   3. Precentral gyrus
   4. Substantia nigra

33. Which are parts of the voluntary motor pathway?
   1. Precentral gyrus
   2. Anterior limb of internal capsule
   3. Lower motor neuron
   4. Posterior white column

34. Which are parts of the extrapyramidal system?
   1. MLF
   2. Dentorubrothalamic tract
   3. Reticulospinal tract
   4. Rubrospinal tract

35. Which are parts of the mesencephalon?
   1. Substantia nigra
   2. Aqueduct of Sylvius
   3. Tectum
   4. Edinger-Westphal nucleus

36. Which of the following is (are) true of the microglia?
   1. They are derivatives of blood monocytes
   2. They may exist as ramified and nonramified populations
   3. They may release cytokines
   4. They have been shown to be involved with formation of myelin within the central nervous system

37. Which of the following is (are) likely to occur when a nerve is cut?
   1. The portion of the axon proximal to the cut degenerates in a process known as wallerian degeneration
   2. Growth of the proximal portion of the axon is facilitated by local proliferation of Schwann cells
   3. The cytoplasm shrinks, and the nucleus becomes eccentric
   4. Chromatolysis occurs with paling of the Nissl bodies

38. Which of the following is (are) true of the facial (VII) nerve?
   1. It innervates the orbicularis oculi and the posterior belly of the digastric

2. The cell bodies of all sensory fibers are situated within the geniculate ganglion
3. It transmits sensory impulses from taste buds in the hard palate
4. It innervates the tensor tympani and stapedius muscles of the middle ear

39. Which of the following is (are) true of the hippocampus?
   1. Pyramidal cells are connected to hypothalamic structures by way of fibers traveling in the fornix
   2. Lesions have been known to be associated with loss of recent memory
   3. Lesions have been known to be associated with seizure discharge
   4. Lesions have been known to be associated with Alzheimer's disease

40. Which of the following is (are) true concerning multiple sclerosis?
   1. Multiple sclerosis is a demyelinating disease that attacks primarily the very old
   2. Multiple sclerosis may be diagnosed by MRI and electrophoretic demonstration of oligoclonal immunoglobulin G bands from the pleural fluid
   3. Multiple sclerosis is associated with the presence of antibodies to acetylcholine receptors
   4. The pattern of myelin degeneration contributes to a multifocal clinical presentation

41. Which of the following structure–function relationships is (are) correct?
   1. Precentral gyrus–primary motor area
   2. Transverse temporal gyrus–primary auditory area
   3. Superior temporal gyrus–auditory association area
   4. Postcentral gyrus–primary sensory area

42. Which of the following cranial nerves has (have) voluntary motor fibers whose cell bodies are primarily in the nucleus ambiguus?
   1. Accessory (XI)
   2. Vagus (X)
   3. Glossopharyngeal (IX)
   4. Facial (VII)

43. Which of the following structure–function relationships is (are) correct?
   1. Hypothalamus–regulation of autonomic activity

2. Thalamus–integration, processing, and relay of sensory information to cortex
3. Subthalamus–extrapyramidal control
4. Inferior colliculus–relay of visual impulses

44. Which of the following is (are) true of the accommodation reflex?
   1. It involves relaxation of the ciliary muscle and flattening of the lens
   2. It involves convergence of both eyes
   3. It involves dilation of the pupils
   4. Its impulses reach the cortical level

45. Which of the following is (are) true of corticobulbar fibers of the pyramidal motor tracts?
   1. They are found in the anterior portion of the posterior limb of the internal capsule
   2. They are found in the medial portion of the middle third of the cerebral peduncles
   3. They supply crossed and uncrossed fibers to most voluntary motor nuclei of the brain stem
   4. They supply only uncrossed fibers to the hypoglossal nucleus

For questions 46 through 50, chose the *single*, best answer.

46. Which of the following groups of cranial nerves contains preganglionic parasympathetic fibers?
   a. II, III, VII, X
   b. III, VII, IX, X
   c. VII, IX, X, XI
   d. III, IX, X, XI

47. In which of the following parasympathetic terminal ganglia are found the cell bodies of postganglionic fibers that provide secretory motor innervation to the lacrimal gland?
   a. Submandibular ganglion
   b. Otic ganglion
   c. Pterygopalatine ganglion
   d. Ciliary ganglion

48. Which of the following is (are) *not* true regarding the pathway of pain and temperature from the face?
   a. Cell bodies of sensory fibers may be found in the trigeminal ganglion and geniculate ganglion
   b. Third-order neurons destined for the inferior aspect of the postcentral gyrus pass through the internal capsule

c. Central processes of the first neuron, regardless of the nerve of origin (V, VII, IX, or X), terminate in the spinal nucleus of the trigeminal nerve

d. Second-order neurons synapse primarily in the ventral posterolateral nucleus of the thalamus

49. Which of the following is (are) *not* true of the afferent connections to the cerebellum from spinal cord levels?
    a. The cell bodies of the first-order afferent neurons are located in the dorsal root ganglia of the spinal cord
    b. Proprioceptive fibers synapse in Clarke's nucleus of the spinal cord

c. Ascending fibers enter the posterior funiculus of the spinal cord

d. Ascending fibers enter the cerebellum primarily by way of the superior cerebellar peduncle

50. Which of the following is (are) *not* true of the glossopharyngeal nerve (IX)?
    a. It contains afferent fibers from the carotid sinus (baroreceptor)
    b. It innervates most intrinsic muscles of the pharynx
    c. It contains afferent fibers from the middle ear cavity
    d. It contains taste afferents as well as pain, temperature, and touch afferents from the posterior third of the tongue

ANSWERS

| | | | | | |
|---|---|---|---|---|---|
| 1. *d* | 10. *a* | 19. *e* | 28. *d* | 33. *b* | 42. *a* |
| 2. *e* | 11. *b* | 20. *d* | 29. *a–1* | 34. *e* | 43. *a* |
| 3. *c* | 12. *b* | 21. *c* | *b–5* | 35. *e* | 44. *c* |
| 4. *b* | 13. *d* | 22. *a* | *c–4* | 36. *a* | 45. *a* |
| 5. *c* | 14. *d* | 23. *d* | *d–3* | 37. *d* | 46. *b* |
| 6. *c* | 15. *e* | 24. *e* | *e–2* | 38. *a* | 47. *c* |
| 7. *b* | 16. *e* | 25. *c* | 30. *c* | 39. *e* | 48. *d* |
| 8. *a* | 17. *c* | 26. *b* | 31. *a* | 40. *d* | 49. *d* |
| 9. *c* | 18. *e* | 27. *c* | 32. *d* | 41. *e* | 50. *b* |

## TIPS ON HOW TO DO BETTER ON A NEURO LAB (PRACTICAL) EXAM

Here, based on 20 years of giving them (and also on having taken them as a medical student), are a few *Tips on How To Do Better on a Neuro Lab (Practical) Exam.*

1. *Look before you leap.* Spend most of the time getting oriented and identifying the object, and spend the last few seconds writing the answer. Dr. Liebman once gave a brain stem with a pin in the pyramid and many students came and thought "Brain stem—two bumps on the median dorsal surface" and wrote down the gracile tubercle. Their hastiness (a result of tension and excitement) caused them to assume that they were looking at the dorsal surface when it was really the ventral surface. Had they realized their error in orientation, I'm sure they would have written pyramid.

2. *Be as specific as possible.* For example, if in a midsagittal section of the brain a pin is sticking in the corpus callosum, don't just write down corpus callosum but also what part (ie, rostrum of or genu of or splenum of).

3. *If you don't know the name, then the first name that comes to mind is most often the correct one.* The increased pressure of an exam often causes our memory not to work so well—"our minds close up"—but deep down we generally know the answer, and it most often "pops up" or "creeps through."

4. *If you really don't know the name, give its function* (eg, if a pin is in the precentral gyrus of the frontal lobe and you don't remember this name, write down "cortical area for voluntary movement"). In a lecture, Dr. Liebman was once talking about the pineal body and in a side remark mentioned that the philosopher Descartes thought that it was the House of the Soul. In the practical exam, he put a pin in the pineal body and when a student, who forgot the name, wrote down the "House of the Soul" he gave him full credit (most neuroanatomists aren't full-time SOBs).

5. *Don't change your answer unless you're absolutely certain that it is wrong.*

## BASIC THINGS TO KNOW FOR A NEURO PRACTICAL

1. Know all the arteries shown on page 79 and all the superficial cerebral veins. Because of its clinical importance, I often like to pin the superior cerebral vein where it bridges the subdural space and enters the superior sagittal sinus.

2. Meninges

   • *Dura mater*: falx cerebri, tentorium, falx cerebelli, the superior and inferior sagittal sinuses, the straight sinus, the transverse sinus, and the confluence. Don't forget the important middle meningeal artery on the *outer* surface of the dura.
   • *Arachnoidea*: arachnoid granulations and bridging veins on the superior surface running in an anteroposterior direction along the midsagittal line.

3. On the skull you should know what nerves pass through the various foramina. Often a colored pipe cleaner is passed through a foramen, and the question is what nerve passes through, or it could be an artery or vein.

4. Know all the structures shown in Appendix II, plates I through VIII.

5. For the cerebellum you should be able to identify the three cerebellar peduncles: the inferior, coming in from the medulla; the middle, entering from the pons; and the superior, passing into the midbrain. Also know the flocculus, the nodule, the vermis, the tonsil, the superior and inferior medullary vela, the lingula, the lateral recess of the fourth ventricle, the first-degree and horizontal fissures, the choroid plexus, and, deep, the dentate nucleus.

6. On a cross-section of the midbrain you should be able to identify the tectum, the aqueduct of Sylvius, the tegmentum with its red nucleus, the substantia nigra, the crus cerebri, and the oculomotor nerve if it's present. On the lateral view of the midbrain, know the superior and inferior colliculi. Also know the lateral lemniscus entering the inferior colliculus and the thick brachium of the inferior colliculus, which passes to the medial geniculate body.

7. In the spinal cord, know the dentate ligament, filum terminale, dorsal and ventral roots of the spinal nerve, dorsal root ganglion, cervical enlargement, and cauda equina.

8. With the widespread and important use of CT and MRI, you should be able to identify *all* the structures in *all the normal* CTs and MRIs in this book.

9. Because some courses require one to know and identify structures in stained cross-sections of the brain stem and cord, plates IX through XV in Appendix II will help.

# Relax with "Did You Know?," "Odds and Ends," and "The Greatest Discoveries in Medicine"

## DID YOU KNOW?

...That to study medicine in England the first woman had to disguise herself as a man! "Dr James Barry kept the secret of her sex all her life and had a successful career in the British Army, where she was honored for distinguished service during the Battle of Waterloo. Only after her death in 1865 was her true sex and the fact that she had had a child revealed."[1] More about Dr Barry can be found in *Women in History: Thirty-Five Centuries of Feminine Achievement.*[2]

...That placing the cold water knob on the right side and the hot one on the left side of the water basin has a neuroanatomic basis! Most people (95%) are right-handed and instinctively reach out for and turn the knob on the right side. Therefore, to prevent inadvertent scalding, the right side controls the cold water. True, you left-handed people are being discriminated against, but you've always been treated with suspicion and disdain. The word *sinister* means "left-sided" in Latin, and honored guests are always seated on the right side of the host. Until recently, left-handed children were often forced to learn to write with the right hand, until it was discovered that this often produced great inner turmoil that was frequently expressed by stammering.

...That the philosophers Maimonides and William James and the authors Chekhov, John Keats, Somerset Maugham, and Sir Arthur Conan Doyle (the creator of Sherlock Holmes) were all physicians. Benjamin Rush, a signer of the Declaration of Independence, as well as Dr Guillotine, the inventor of the guillotine, were also renowned physicians.

...That for centuries the bodies of executed criminals were used for dissection. In Edinburgh in 1725 the body of Maggie Dickson "came back to life" shortly after she was hanged and before the medical students had a chance to get at it. She continued to live for many years afterward and was known as "Half-Hanged Maggie Dickson."

...That Oedipus had swollen feet! (That should have been his only problem.) Being told that his infant son would grow up and kill him, his father bound Oedipus' ankles and placed him on a mountainside to die. There, a wandering shepherd found him with his feet swollen by the tight rope. He adopted the unknown babe and named him Edepes after his most prominent feature (his swollen feet). *Ede-* in Greek means "swollen," from which is derived the word *edema*, and *pes* or *ped* means "foot," as in pedestrian, pedal, and pes hippocampus.

...That the red-and-white striped barber pole is a trademark of surgeons. In the Middle Ages, barbers, not physicians, did surgery, and to indicate their place of business to the general population (who couldn't read) they displayed their sign outside their shops: a pole with a red stripe symbolizing blood and a white one symbolizing bandages.

...That percussion, the technique of tapping the chest to diagnose conditions by the nature of the sound response, was discovered by Dr Auenbrugger. The idea came to him from having watched his father, a tavern keeper, tap on beer kegs to determine the extent to which they were full.

...That one of the codiscoverers of insulin didn't share the Nobel Prize because he was only a medical student! In June 1921, Dr Banting, a surgical resident, and George Best, a third-year medical student at McGill University, were reluctantly given a small, run-down laboratory in which to do their research by Dr McCloud, who then went away on his summer holiday. In 3 months at work, the two extracted and identified insulin from the pancreas. The Nobel Committee, however, awarded their prize to Banting and McCloud and overlooked Best because he was still only a medical student. Banting, however, showed his true worth and opinion by publicly sharing his half of the prize with Best.

...That the British are called "Limies" because for more than 200 years their sailors were required to drink lime juice to prevent scurvy, a disease caused by vitamin C deficiency.

…That the word *testify* and all its derivatives (eg, *testimony* and *testate*) come from the word *testicle*. In ancient Roman courts only men were allowed to give evidence. To prevent a woman from disguising herself as a man and giving evidence, all witnesses had to come before the judge to prove to him that they were male by lifting their togas and revealing their testicles. This isn't as strange as it sounds; in today's Olympic games women have to prove they are female by passing both a physical and a chromosomal examination. This testing is done because a few years ago one participating country managed to smuggle men disguised as women into the track and field events (especially discus, shot put, and javelin).

…That gauze was invented by the Arabs and named after the city where it was produced: Gaza.

…That Jenner got the idea for vaccination from a dairy maid, who told him "I can't get smallpox since I've already had cowpox" (the latter is a mild form of smallpox).

…That dice were for centuries carved from animal bones, and the crapshooter today still uses the expression "Roll them bones."

…That Paré, the great French surgeon, introduced ligatures. Until the 16th century, hemorrhage from sword or gunshot wounds was stopped by applying a hot poker or boiling oil to the wound. As late as 1870 antiseptic technique was unknown, and surgeons, while operating, kept the sutures in the buttonholes of their vests or jackets!

…That South American natives suture wounds by having ants bite on the approximated edges and then pinching off the body, leaving the gripping head attached!

…That pudendum is a Latin word meaning "shame," and an impudent person is one who is shameless.

…And speaking of shame, in China physicians once used small porcelain figures of the human body, and their female patients would point on them to the area that hurt them, thereby bypassing the need to be palpated or to use "coarse" words.

…And finally on the subject of shame, in parts of Europe in the 16th century, physicians, when doing a delivery, would place one end of a sheet around the woman's waist and tie the other end around their own neck and would deliver the child while "working blind."

…That for hundreds of years, bleeding a patient was a basic medical procedure, and to do it, leeches were often used. Today leeches are once again used in medicine to relieve venous congestion around sutured wounds, especially in plastic surgery. From the saliva of leeches comes one of the more recently used, and extremely potent, anticoagulants, Hirudin.

…That in ancient Egypt, gastritis and wound infections were treated by swallowing moldy bread for the first condition and applying it directly for the second. The mold on the bread is penicillin, and its name has the same Latin root as *pencil* and *penis* (ie, a small rod), because the mold has such a shape.

…That the bill for the first operation using general anesthesia still exists. It was made out by Dr Crawford Long of Georgia to one James Venable, and the total cost for the operation and ether anesthesia came out to $2.00! This was back in the 1840s.

…That *sarco-*, as in sarcoplasm, means "muscle," and you know it in the everyday word *sarcasm*, a remark that doesn't just get under the skin but goes deep and hurts.

…That Cosmos and Damian are the patron saints of surgery. They were Christian Arab physicians, and twin brothers, who were martyred in 303 AD. Many miraculous cures were attributed to them, the most famous being captured in a painting from the Middle Ages. One sees them by the bed of a white patient onto whom they have grafted the black leg of a dead Moor. The crowd looks on in amazement at this transplant, and an integrated one at that.

# ODDS AND ENDS

Henri de Mondeville was a renowned 14th century physician. Perhaps part of his fame was due to his method of supporting his patients: "Keep up your patient's spirit by music . . . or by giving him forged letters describing the death of his enemy."

Quarantine comes from the Italian word *quarantina*, meaning "forty," the number of days for which a suspected person was isolated.

Rhazes, the great Persian physician (841–926), in choosing a site for a hospital, hung fresh meat in different parts of the city and selected that place where the meat had spoiled the least.

The symbol for male, ♂, is the arrow of Mars, the god of war, whereas the one for female, ♀, represents the handmirror of Venus.

We complain about overspecialization in medicine, but listen to this: "The practice of medicine is so divided that each physician is a healer of one disease and no more, some of the eye, some of the teeth, and some of the belly." This was written 2500 years ago by the Greek historian Herodotus, who visited Egypt and described the situation there. One physician had the glorious title "Shepherd of the Anus." Imagine what Jay leno or a gag writer could do with this.

Today in Russia there are more female than male physicians. In the United States women make up 30% to 35% of those entering medical schools, but this percentage was not always so high. Twenty years ago only 8% to 10% of medical students were women. The first medical school in America was founded in Philadelphia in 1765, but it wasn't until 1850 that the first medical school for women was opened: the Women's Medical College of Pennsylvania in Philadelphia.

The symbol Rx on prescriptions comes from ancient Egypt. Originally it was shaped R and represented the eye of Horus, the god of protection and recovery.

The ancient Egyptian treatment for baldness consisted of spreading onto the scalp a mixture of the fat of the lion, the hippo, the deer, and the crocodile; one medical historian commented that the Egyptian pharmacy schools must have had hunting as part of their curriculum! We know so much about ancient Egyptian medicine via two papyri, the Smith and the Ebers, which are named after their discoverers and date back 3600 years.

Sterile wax is used in neurosurgical operations to staunch bleeding from the skull bones.

Migraine is a corruption of the French words *hemicrain*, meaning "half the head." Over a period of time the first two letters *he* were dropped, leaving the word *micrain* or as it is now spelled, *migraine*.

Bed-side teaching of students was popular in ancient Rome, but the writer Martial poked fun at it in this verse:

> I called you Dr Symmachus for a
> slight indisposition.
> You brought your hundred students
> as befits a real clinician.
> With hands all chilled by winter's blasts,
> they practiced their palpatation.
> The fever that I didn't have
> is now a conflagration.

In the Middle Ages, most surgery was done by barbers (never by physicians), but it was also done by bathhouse keepers, pig gelders, and executioners! (In the last case, one could say that practice made perfect.)

Physicians now complain about malpractice suits, but as the old saying goes, things could be worse. For example, the Code of Hammurabi, dating back to 1900 BC, states "If a doctor shall open an abscess with a bronze knife and shall kill the patient, his hands shall be cut off."

*Teton* is a French word for the breast, and the explorers who discovered the range of sharp mountain peaks around Jackson Hole in Wyoming showed their French background by calling them the Grand Tetons.

One recent article in a prestigious medical journal had 23 named coauthors, as well as numerous coinvestigators, and was umpteen pages long. In contrast, Pasteur needed less than a page to report on his work on anthrax vaccination, and Herring needed two pages to describe his work on the carotid sinus reflex. Also, the following Nobel Prize works were reported in two pages or fewer: Von Behring and Kitasato's work on diphtheria immunization; Stanly's work on virus crystallization; Enders, Wellers, and Robbins' breakthrough discoveries on the cultivation of the polio virus, which paved the way for the Sabin and Salk vaccines; Joliot and Curie's work on the transmutation of one element to another; and Watson and Crick's discovery of DNA. As Shakespeare said, "Brevity is the soul of wit."

The shortage of bodies for medical school dissection in the 19th century gave rise to men who would rob a fresh grave and sell the body. Because the grave would be open and empty the next day, they were known as "resurrectionists"!

In Edinburgh medical school, the cadaver shortage became acute in 1827 but was soon relieved by William Hare and his wife. They ran a cheap boarding house for old, solitary, down-and-out lodgers and, when they died, sold the unclaimed bodies to Dr Knox, the head of the anatomy department. As so often happens, however, Hare and his wife got greedy and enlisted the help of one William Burke, who helped them send their lodgers to an "early dissection" by suffocating them with a pillow (thereby leaving no marks of violence on the bodies). The three were caught, tried, and hanged; Dr Knox, though innocent, had to leave Edinburgh in disgrace. During the trial, the following little ditty was bandied about by the enthralled public:

Burke's the butcher, Hare's the thief,
Knox is the man who buys the beef.

# THE GREATEST DISCOVERIES IN MEDICINE

Most of us like lists, so here's one with some of the greatest discoveries in modern medicine, many of which resulted in a Nobel Prize.

## GENERAL ANESTHESIA

In 1842, Dr Crawford Long, a country general practitioner in Georgia, first started using ether as a general anesthetic in his practice, but he didn't publish his work until 1849. Meanwhile, working independently in New England, Drs Morton and Wells and C.T. Jackson, a pharmacist, also discovered ether's anesthetic properties in 1846. Later that year it was used for the first time at Massachusetts General Hospital, and from there its use spread rapidly throughout the world.

## GERMS AS THE CAUSE OF DISEASE

From 1860 to 1870, Louis Pasteur, a French biochemist, discovered and laid down the facts that form the basis of bacteriology and microbiology ("the germ theory"). In addition, he discovered the vaccine against rabies as well as the process of heating such substances as milk to kill microorganisms (pasteurization).

## ANTISEPTIC TECHNIQUE

Before 1876, physicians would operate in their street clothes with the surgical sutures kept in the buttonholes of their jackets or vests and pulled out as needed! Then, in that year, Lord Lister of England proposed and used in his operations sterile, antiseptic techniques. As a result, his mortality rates dropped from 45% to 15%, which is very good considering the fact that there were no antibiotics, and that they didn't know about fluid replacement and acid–base balance.

## X-RAYS

In November 1895, Dr William Roentgen, a German physicist, discovered X-rays. Within a year of announcing his findings, more than 1000 papers on this new diagnostic technique were published throughout the world. One English newspaper even ran an ad for special underwear that guaranteed to "keep the private parts private" during an X-ray examination.

## DISCOVERY OF BLOOD GROUPS

Blood transfusions from sheep to humans and from human to human were tried by Robert Boyle and others as early as 1667 but were banned when some of the patients died after the procedure. It wasn't until 1903 that Karl Landsteiner of the Rockefeller Institute discovered the four major blood groups, which explained compatibility and incompatibility and thus permitted safe transfusions. In 1940, Landsteiner, working with Dr Wiener, discovered the Rh factor.

## DISCOVERY OF INSULIN

In 10 weeks of research during the summer of 1921, Dr Banting, a second-year surgical resident who had never done any research, and Charles Best, a third-year medical student, discovered insulin and later used it successfully for the first time on a dying diabetic patient. Dr Banting won the Nobel Prize, but the Nobel Committee refused to give it to Best because he was only a student. Initially they worked in a run-down laboratory and used 10 dogs for their work.

## THE ISOLATION OF AND THE ROLE PLAYED BY NEUROTRANSMITTERS

During the 1920s, Sir Henry Dale in England and Otto Loewi in Germany did a series of simple yet brilliant experiments in which they discovered acetylcholine and epinephrine and demonstrated their function as neurotransmitters.

## ANTIBIOTICS

In 1927, Alexander Fleming, an English researcher, accidentally left open a Petri dish of *Staphylococcus* organisms that he was culturing. Returning several days later, he noticed that the colonies of cocci were being destroyed by a mold, and this led him to investigate the mold, *Penicillium notatum*. He didn't follow up on the therapeutic implications of this finding, however, and it was not until 1940 that Chain and Florey at Oxford did so and published their findings in a three-page report in *The Lancet*. Finally in 1948, Waxman discovered the broad-spectrum antibiotic streptomycin.

## DNA

The work of Watson and Crick on DNA in the early 1950s opened the door to the age of molecular biology, modern genetics, and all their offshoots. Their paper is less than a page long and is a model of clear thought that presents in simple, easy-to-understand English one of the greatest discoveries of the 20th century. It exemplifies perfectly Einstein's dictum "that theory is best which explains the most with the least."

## COMPUTED TOMOGRAPHY AND MAGNETIC RESONANCE IMAGING

As mentioned previously, the physicists Godfrey Hounsfield and the neuroradiologist James Ambrose discovered computed tomography, and the physicists Bloch and Purcell performed the theoretical work that led to the use of magnetic resonance imaging.

## THE DISCOVERY OF THE UNIQUENESS OF FINGERPRINTS AND THEIR USE IN IDENTIFICATION

In the 1870s, William Herchel, a British administrator in India, and Dr Henry Fauds, a Scottish physician living in Japan, realized, independent of each other, that the inked fingerprints that the natives affixed to documents were different from individual to individual and that the print of each finger was different. In 1880 they published their findings and said that it was a good method for identification, but their work was ignored for 8 years. Then, Darwin's cousin, Sir Francis Galton, came on their work, expanded it, and wrote a book in 1882 entitled *Fingerprints*, but the big problem still remained: how to classify efficiently the vast number of prints. This was solved at the turn of the century by the work of Juan Vucetich of the Buenos Aires police department and Edward Henry, the Inspector General of Bengal in India.

## THE CAUSE AND TRANSMISSION OF MALARIA

Malaria has been a worldwide scourge throughout history. It was prevalent in ancient Greece and Rome; in Elizabethan England it existed and was called marsh fever. The brilliant "detective work" of several different investigators finally coalesced to give the true picture of the disease. First Alphonse Laveran in 1880 saw and described the microorganism (*Plasmodium falciparum*) in the red blood cells of humans. Then Sir Patrick Manson showed that the mosquito was the insect vector between humans in the transmission of the filarial disease elephantiasis, but despite his discovery, how malaria was transmitted remained a mystery. Sir Harold Ross, working under the influence of

Manson, then demonstrated the malarial microorganism in the stomach of the mosquito. Finally, and in a Hollywood-like finish, Sir Patrick Manson took infected mosquitoes and allowed them to bite his son, who developed malaria, whereas three co-workers didn't develop it because they lived in a mosquito-proof hut situated in a region dense with the insects.

## DEVELOPMENT OF MODERN CHEMOTHERAPY AND THE ANTIGEN–ANTIBODY REACTION

Paul Ehrlich (1854–1915), along with Pasteur, was one of the towering figures in the history of medical science; the term *genius* almost seems to be an understatement. Working in Vienna, he developed, on a rational, scientific basis, modern chemotherapy (the "magic bullet" theory, that a substance, when injected into the patient, wouldn't harm his or her cells but would seek out and destroy the invading pathogenic organism). He then went on to discover salvarsan (606), the first drug to help cure syphilis, which had been ravaging Europe and America for 400 years (much in the manner that acquired immunodeficiency syndrome (AIDS) is today). Ehrlich went on to discover and explain the antigen–antibody reaction, discovered complement, introduced the concept of minimal lethal dose, and finally developed and explained the basis and techniques of staining tissues. Not surprising, he was awarded the Nobel Prize in medicine.

## ROLE OF WHITE BLOOD CELLS IN BODY DEFENSES

Elie Metchnikoff (1845–1916), a biologist by training and a pupil of Pasteur, was probably Russia's greatest medical scientist and spent many years investigating the role of the white blood cells. His work culminated in the discovery of their role as phagocytes in the inflammatory process.

## ELECTROCARDIOGRAPHY AND CARDIAC CATHETERIZATION

In the early 1920s, William Einthoven, a physiologist at the University of Leyden in Holland, developed the sensitive electrocardiography machine, which helped transform cardiology into a modern science. Einthoven was a Nobel laureate in 1927 for his pioneering and far-reaching work.

In 1929, a young German intern named Werner Forseman inserted a sterile urethral catheter into his cubital vein, threaded it into his heart, and then walked up several flights of stairs to the radiology department. There he injected a contrast medium into the catheter and then X-rayed himself, thus performing the first human cardiac catheterization plus X-ray. (The first angiogram on a living person was performed by Heuser in 1919, who injected potassium iodide into the veins of the hand to visualize the forearm veins.) Forseman's superior, the then-renowned Professor Sauerbruch, derided this work, saying "Such tricks aren't worthy of a respectable German hospital but are appropriate in a circus!" and soon afterward fired him.[3] Unfortunately, Professor Sauerbruch wasn't alive in 1956 when Werner Forseman picked up a Nobel Prize for his "little circus trick."

In case you're wondering why it took so long for him to receive the prize, a great deal of pressure, politics, and the like is involved in the awarding of these prizes, so much so that it makes big city politicians appear to be "babes in the woods" by comparison. Consider the fact that Tolstoy (the author of one of the world's greatest novels, *War and Peace*) never won the prize for literature, although he died several years after it was started, and neither did James Joyce.

## DEVELOPMENT OF NEUROSURGERY

General anesthesia was first used publicly in 1846 and enabled the fast and vast growth of general surgery. The complexity of the brain and the high operative mortality rates, however, deterred surgeons, and the procedure was rarely done until Harvey Cushing of Philadelphia (1869–1939) came into the field at the beginning of this century and became the greatest neurosurgeon in the world. He "dared to go where angels feared to tread" and, single-handedly, developed the field in terms of technique,* the study and classification of brain tumors, and, perhaps most important, the training of hundreds of excellent and ambitious residents. They, in their time, refined and improved techniques and, in turn, trained another generation of neurosurgeons. Therefore, one can easily say that all neurosurgery ultimately traces back to the work of this great man.

---

*He lowered his operative mortality rates to 8% in an era before antibiotics.

## DEVELOPMENT OF OPEN-HEART SURGERY AND REVASCULARIZATION PROCEDURES

The heart had been looked upon with awe in the medical profession, and surgery on it was done with great reluctance and hesitation. The post–World War II development of the heart–lung machine gave surgeons greater operative freedom, and this was seized upon by Dr Huffnagle of Georgetown University, who went in for the first time and implanted artificial valves in the aorta. His daring work paved the way for many new cardiac operations and developments.

Among the great advances in medicine that have been responsible for the prolongation of life, and the improvement of its quality, are two procedures used in patients with severe atherosclerotic coronary artery disease: *coronary artery bypass grafting* (CABG) and *percutaneous transluminal coronary angioplasty* (PTCA).

The first CABG is reported to have been done by R.G. Favaloro in Argentina in 1964. This now widely used procedure involves the harvesting of the saphenous vein from the leg of the patient and interposing it between the aorta and a site or sites on the coronary artery(ies) distal to the critical obstruction. This procedure therefore bypasses the occlusion and restores blood flow to the supplied myocardium. More recently, to this procedure has been added the use of the left internal thoracic artery (also referred to as the left internal mammary artery); the distal end of this artery is detached from its substernal position and is anastamosed, most commonly, to the left anterior descending coronary artery distal to the site of stenosis.

In 1963, C.T. Dotter, in an attempt to perform an abdominal angiogram in a patient with suspected renal artery stenosis, inadvertently recanalized an occluded iliac artery. This was recognized by him as an accident of great therapeutic importance, and in 1964 he reported the first intentional, successful PTCA performed on the left popliteal artery of an 82-year-old patient with gangrene who refused amputation. It was not until 1977 that Gruentzig and Myler performed the first human coronary angioplasty intraoperatively. The first PTCA in an awake patient was done by Gruentzig 2 weeks later, in Zurich, in a 37-year-old patient with an isolated proximal left anterior descending coronary artery stenosis. One-month and 10-year follow-up angiograms showed no restenosis. This great achievement ushered in the current, extremely active, era of interventional cardiology, the goal of which is to provide maximum persistent revascularization with minimum suffering and risk without having to subject the patient to the highly invasive open-chest procedures.

## ORGAN TRANSPLANTATION

The major problem in organ transplantation was, and remains (but to a lesser degree), rejection by the host of the "foreign" organ. With the development of immunosuppressive drugs, a second problem arose, namely the suppression of the recipient's immune system, whereby he or she became more vulnerable to infections. The first transplants were of the corneas, and because they don't have a blood supply the recipient didn't develop antibodies to them, and the success rate was and is very high. Next came kidney transplants, which were first done in 1954. Today the success rate is 80% to 90% when the kidney is donated by a close relative whose tissue is similar. In 1969, Christian Barnard did the first successful heart transplant, and the entire field has skyrocketed.

## "THE PILL"

The development of the birth control pill by Drs Pincus, Chang, Rock, and Garcia, and its introduction to the public in the early 1960s, not only represented a medical turning point but also had, and have, great sociologic and economic ramifications. Dr Pincus also did work on artificial parthenogenesis ("fatherless animals") by taking ova from rabbits; putting them in a saline solution, which caused fertilization; and then reimplanting them in the rabbit uterus, where they developed to term. The newspapers got hold of this story and played it up a bit ("Virgin Birth," etc). Dr Pincus once showed to Mike's father a letter from a concerned woman who wondered whether she would get pregnant by swimming in the ocean!

## GENETIC ENGINEERING

After Watson and Crick's work on DNA, the world of molecular biology "exploded," and among the major developments were the discovery by Dr Dan Nathan of restriction enzymes, which are able selectively to split DNA; the method of putting a DNA fragment into another species (recombination), which was done by Stanly Cohn and David Berg; and finally the work of Fred Sanger, a double Nobel Prize winner, who among other things plotted out the base sequence on DNA molecules.

## IN VITRO FERTILIZATION ("TEST TUBE BABIES")

The late Dr Alan Steptoe was the first person to remove a human ovum, fertilize it in vitro, and then reintroduce the egg into the womb, where it developed successfully to term. This technique has brought much happiness to childless couples, but it also opened a Pandora's box of legal, ethical, and religious questions that must be dealt with by groups composed of physicians, lawyers, and religious leaders.

### REFERENCES

1. Taylor A. The female doctor's dilemma. *Illus Lond News.* December 1983;271:45.
2. Raven S, Weir A. *Women in History: Thirty-Five Centuries of Feminine Achievement.* London: Weidenfeld & Nicholson; 1981.
3. Mueller RL, Sanborn TA. The history of interventional cardiology: Cardiac catheterization, angioplasty, and related interventions. *Am Heart J.* 1995;129:146–172.

# Index

Page numbers in *italics* denote figures.

idiopathic and degenerative, 90–91
infectious, 85–87
magnetic resonance images of, *144–147*
metabolic, 89–90
neoplastic, 92
substance abuse and toxins, 92–93
traumatic, 87
vascular, 84–85
Neurosurgery, 183
Neurotransmitters, 1, 43, 181
Nicotine, 100
Nissl granules, 1, *2*
Nitric oxide, 1
Nodes of Ranvier, 1, *2*
Norepinephrine, 1, 43, 45
Nucleolus, 1, *2*
Nucleus, nuclei
    ambiguus, 25, *47*, 52, *52*, 53, *112*, *160*
    amygdaloid, 62, *63*, 64, *145*
    caudate, *8*, 28, *29*, 31, *106*, *107*, *135*, *143*
    central, 65
    Clarke's, *37*
    cochlear, 55, *56*, *111*, *167*
    cuneatus, *16*, *112*
    dentate, 7, 39, *40*, *166*
    Edinger-Westphal, 43, *44*, 48, *48*, *60*, 61
    emboliform, 7, 39
    facial, *44*
    fastigial, 7, *33*, 35, 39, *40*, *66*
    globose, 7, 39
    gracilis, *16*, *112*
    hypoglossal, *112*, *160*
    inferior, 65
    of inferior colliculus, 55, *56*, *110*
    lenticular, 31
    lentiform, 28, *29*, *107*, *135*, *143*, *145*
    medial, *69*, 70
    mesencephalic, 18, *19*
    of neuron, 1, *2*
    oculomotor, *44*, *48*, *60*, *110*
    paraventricular, *69*, 70
    of Perla, 61
    preoptic, *69*
    pretectal, 58, *60*, 61
    red, 7, 28, *29*, 39, *40*, *110*, *143*
    reticular, *40*, 65, *69*, 70, *166*
    salivatory, 43, *44*, 45, *50*, *52*
    solitarius, *47*, 49, *50*, 51–53, *52*, *112*
    of spinal tract V, 18, *111*, *112*
    subcortical, 28–31, *29*

subthalamic, 28, *29*, 65, *66*, 72
superior olivary, 55, *56*
supraoptic, *69*, 70, *71*
tegmental, 65, *66*
thalamic, 62, 65
trochlear, *110*
ventral posterolateral, 10, *11*, 13, *14*, 15, *16*, 18
vestibular, 32, *33*, *34*, *38*, 39, *111*, *112*, *160*, *166*
Nystagmus, 35, 39

# O

Obex, *109*
Oculogyric attack, 45
Olfactory system, 62–64, *63*, 70, 72
Oligodendrocytoma, 92
Oligodendroglia, 1, 3, 99
Olive, *108*, *112*
Olivopontocerebellar atrophy, 3
Open-heart surgery, 183–184
Operculum, 7, *102*, *152*
Orbit, *136*
Organ transplantation, 184
Osmoregulation, 68–70
Ossicles, *136*
Otosclerosis, 55

# P

Pain, 10–12, 97
    diagnostic tests for, 12
    pathways for, 10, *11*, 45, *161*
        for face and adjacent regions, 18, *19*, *163*
    phantom limb, 12
    referred, 12
Paleocerebellum, 7
Paleocortex, 72
Paleostriatum, 31
Pallidotomy, 30
Papilledema, 83
Paralysis, 21, 72
    agitans, 28, 91
    in botulism, 85
    flaccid, 23
    lower motor neuron, 23, 27
    spastic, 23
    upper motor neuron, 23–24, 27
Paraplegia, 24
Parasympathetic nervous system, 41, 43–45
Parasympathomimetics, 45
Parkinsonism, drug-induced, 30

Parkinson's disease, 28–30, 91
Pasteurization, 181
Pathways
    auditory, 55–57, *56*, *167*
    cerebellar feedback, 39, *40*, *166*
    olfactory, 62–64, *63*
    for pain and temperature, 10–12, *11*
    for pressure and crude touch, 13, *14*
    for proprioception, fine touch, and vibratory sense, 15–17, *16*
    sensory, from face and related areas, 18–20, *19*
    spinocerebellar, 36
    of vestibular system, 32–35, *33–34*
    visual, 58–61, *59–60*
    for voluntary muscle activity, 21–24, *22*
    to voluntary muscles of head, 25–27, *26*
Peduncle(s), 99
    cerebellar, 7, *8*, *33*, 36, *37*, *103*, *108*, *109*
    cerebral, 7, *8*, *103*, *109*, *110*
Percutaneous transluminal coronary angioplasty, 183–184
Perineurium, *2*
Peripheral nervous system, 5
Personality, 5, 72
Phenylketonuria, 89
Physical examination, 149
Physostigmine, 88
Pia mater, 76, *77*, 99
Pinealomas, 92
Plant toxins, 93
Plate
    cribriform, *113*
    orbital, *113*
Plexus, choroid, 81, *107*, *135*, *155*
Plexus, nerve, 54
    cervical, 121
    sacral, 124
    tympanic, *52*
Poikilothermic, 68
Poisoning, 92–93
Pole(s)
    frontal, 5, *6*, *8*, *73*, *102*, *152*
    occipital, *6*, *8*, *59*, 72, *73*, *102*, *152*, *168*
    temporal, *8*
Poliomyelitis, 23, 86
Polyneuritis, acute, 89
Polyuria, 70
Pons, *6*, 7, *8*, *19*, *26*, *33*, *44*, *47*, *50*, *56*, *66*, 99, *104*, *105*, *111*, *135*, *142*, *145*, *159*

# Notes

# Notes

# Notes

# Notes